MAIN COURSE SALADS

Creative Salads That Satisfy

DONNA RODNITZKY

AVERY PUBLISHING GROUP

Garden City Park • New York

Cover Design: Phaedra Mastrocola
Cover Photograph: SuperStock, Inc.
Interior Color Photographs: Victor Giordano
Photo Food Stylist: BC Giordano
Text Illustrator: John Wincek
Typesetter: Gary A. Rosenberg
In-House Editor: Joanne Abrams

Avery Publishing Group, Inc.
120 Old Broadway
Garden City Park, New York 11040
1-800-548-5757
www.averypublishing.com

Library of Congress Cataloging-in-Publication Data
Rodnitzky, Donna.
    Main course salads: creative salads that satisfy / Donna
Rodnitzky.
      p. cm.
    ISBN 0–89529–928–3
    1. Salads. 2. Entrées (Cookery) I. Title.
TX740.R543 1999
641.8′3—dc21   99-15219
                                                                CIP

Printed in the United States of America

10 9 8 7 6 5 4 3 2 1

Contents

Acknowledgments

I would like to thank publisher Rudy Shur, editors Marie Caratozzolo and Joanne Abrams, and the exceptional staff of Avery Publishing Group for their constant support and professionalism in guiding this book to publication.

I would also like to thank several friends who shared their special recipes with me. They include Jo Gail Wenzel, Sonia Ettinger, Kathy Moyers, Patti Yamada, Ginny Butzer, Kitch Sommers, and Carolyn Huff.

Most of all, I would like to dedicate this book to my husband, Bob, my companion for over thirty years, who has supported and guided me in all of my endeavors; and my children, David, Adam, and Laura, whose achievements and passion for living will always be an inspiration to me.

Preface

Main course salads are one of the most appealing dining trends of our times. They have become *haute cuisine* for health-conscious individuals seeking novel and nutritious ways to enrich their diet without adding extra fat or calories. Many of us who enjoy a salad before or after a meal have discovered that this garden bounty can be elevated to main course status by simply complementing it with a well-chosen portion of fruit, cheese, poultry, meat, seafood, pasta, rice, or beans. As a fringe benefit, these salads are ideal fare for a busy lifestyle, since most of the ingredients can be prepared ahead of time and quickly assembled just before serving.

Main Course Salads is the ultimate resource for delicious and healthy dining. Whether preparing a nutritious meal for your family or an elegant dinner for your most discerning guests, this book will provide you with a host of tempting dishes that are both delicious and easy to make.

In creating the recipes for this cookbook, my goal was to devise dishes that are easy to prepare, have visual and taste appeal, and keep fat and calories to a healthy level. Most important, I wanted each salad to be satisfying enough to stand by itself as a main dish. Once I had selected my criteria, the next important step was to prepare each recipe—and then to improve upon it. Every recipe in

this book went through this process, and some required as many as five incarnations before I perfected the ease of preparation or reduced the fat and calorie contents. In some cases, despite a number of trials, the finished product was less than satisfying. These recipes were simply abandoned.

Let me share with you the techniques I developed for meeting my goals for creating the ideal main course salad. Anybody with a busy lifestyle knows how important it is to speed preparation time. Fortunately, the main ingredient in most salads—the greens—are inherently easy to prepare because they need only be rinsed and torn into bite-sized pieces. Even better, many greens, from spinach to romaine to mixed baby greens, are now available prewashed and packaged. For a number of other salad components, I have often given you the option of using ingredients such as commercial marinades and jarred roasted peppers—great products that are easy to find and even easier to use. The result is a selection of dishes that are not only satisfying, but relatively fuss-free to make.

How did I make my salads as healthy as they are delicious? Most of my recipes have a great starting point in this regard, as they begin with salad greens, which are naturally high in nutrients and free of fat. The challenge was to keep the additional ingredients as healthful as the greens—and this is where some ingenuity was required. I soon learned that I could reduce the amount of oil needed in most salad dressings by substituting fat-free chicken broth, puréed cooked potatoes, or corn syrup. I also learned that salads could be made more substantial and inviting by adding lean, well-seasoned poultry, meat, seafood, and meat substitutes, as well as liberal amounts of pasta and fruit. For each recipe, I determined the proper balance of greens and more substantial ingredients such as meats so there is just enough of the latter to lend the salad a stick-to-the-ribs level of satisfaction, but not so much that calorie and fat counts skyrocket out of control. Just as important, I experimented with a variety of readily available condiments, herbs, and spices to create an infinite number of unique and impressive flavors. This means that, though healthy, these salads are anything but bland and boring.

As far as visual appeal is concerned, the naturally vivid colors and varied shapes of leafy greens and other fruits and vegetables have allowed me to achieve a degree of artistry possible with very few other entrées. For ease of preparation, you can often simply toss the ingredients together, and still enjoy a beautiful mingling of shapes, colors, and textures. For many recipes, though, I have detailed a more artistic way of combining the ingredients for a striking presentation. You'll find these instructions under the "Serving Suggestion" headings.

A few additional words are in order regarding salad dressings. Because a well-chosen dressing can make a good salad delectable, while a poor choice can be the undoing of even a great dish, I have devoted an entire chapter to dressings. By referring to this chapter, you can select the dressing that appeals to you most or find the suggested dressing for the salad you have chosen to prepare. For most salads, I tested a variety of different dressings, and suggested several—both homemade and commercial—that proved to be most appealing. Usually, I marked my personal preference with a star (★). For a few salads, I concluded that a single dressing was far superior to other alternatives, and recommended that choice only.

It is my hope that with *Main Course Salads* as your inspiration and guide, you will discover how easy it is to make a salad that not only is mouth-watering and satisfying, but can also take its place in a healthy lifestyle. The key is to incorporate healthy, delectable foods that complement one another in color, texture, and taste, and then unleash your creative spirit to fashion an impressive presentation. Soon, like an artist reaching for colors on a palate, or a sculptor carefully combining shapes, you, too, will create tantalizing salad masterpieces—dishes that will be enjoyed and appreciated by friends and family alike.

Introduction

Salads have been an essential component of good meals for centuries. The ancient Romans, for example, enjoyed *herba salata,* or "salted greens." The Colosseum crowd dressed their simple greens with only oil, vinegar, and a few available herbs. Today, though, salads have evolved into a spectacular cornucopia of tastes and colors. Many novel salad greens and vegetables once considered seasonal or exotic are now readily available year-round at your local supermarket. As a result, the modern salad brims with a surprising variety of greens adorned with an array of both traditional and exotic vegetables harvested all over the world. And in our kitchens, these sophisticated creations can be raised to even greater gourmet heights by the addition of a savory vinaigrette or an imaginative sauce, all topped with an artful garnish. But the most exciting development in the evolution of salads is that they no longer need to be relegated to second-class citizenship, appearing only at the beginning or end of a meal. The addition of fruit, cheese, poultry, meat, seafood, pasta, or rice to your favorite salad can elevate your dish to main course status.

But as tempting as a cheese-, meat-, or poultry-topped salad may be—and as beautifully as it can take its place as a one-dish meal—it should be recognized that many ingredients can contribute more fat than is considered acceptable in an otherwise healthful diet. Fortunately, this dilemma doesn't have to prevent salads from taking center stage at the dinner table. The recipes in this book will guide you in choosing your ingredients wisely and in combining them in new yet simple ways. The result is a galaxy of salads that are both satisfying and healthy.

Although most of us have become more health conscious in recent years, a busy lifestyle can make it difficult to find the time to prepare the most healthful foods for our daily menus. The main course salads presented in this book solve this dilemma, too. Because most of the vegetables, vinaigrettes, garnishes, and other key ingredients can be prepared several hours ahead of time, or even kept fresh overnight, these salads are the ultimate way to assemble a nutritionally balanced meal at the last minute. Moreover, with the widespread availability of a variety of freshly prepared meats, poultry, and seafood that have already been delicately seasoned or marinated—as well as the easy accessibility of beautifully cut fruits, vegetables, and cheeses in most markets—making a main course salad could not be simpler or more deliciously rewarding. Best of all, with the addition of an appealing garnish or one of the exotic dressings found in this book, your main course salad can become a memorable dining experience, both in taste and appearance. As you sample these recipes, you will experience the international cuisines of the Orient, Italy, Spain, India, Mexico, the Pacific Rim, and the Middle East. You will discover how delightfully piquant and zesty a salad can become with the addition of flavorful condiments like sriracha hot chili sauce or kecap manis. Be prepared for a new level of excitement about whole meal salads among your family and friends.

Main Course Salads begins by providing you with all of the information you need to select and prepare the essential ingredients of a delicious and satisfying salad. In Chapter 1, you will become acquainted with the many available salad greens, oils, and vinegars, as well as a range of other ingredients, and will learn how they can be easily incorporated into a sumptuous dish. The simple kitchen tools that are most useful for preparing salads are also discussed here. If you are prompted to ask, "Why choose a main course salad instead of a juicy porterhouse steak for dinner?" the answer will be found in this chapter. You will discover the role that main course salads can play in limiting your caloric intake and your dietary fat—as well as why these nutritional goals are vital to maintaining good health. Plus, I will divulge the secrets of adding unbelievably rich flavor to salads, and share my techniques for combining colors and shapes to create a dazzling visual display.

Each of the subsequent four chapters concentrates on a specific type of ingredient that you can choose to elevate your salad to main course status. Thus, in Chapter 2, you will learn delicious, healthful, and innovative ways to incorporate poultry into a salad. In case you think that turkey can be enjoyed only on Thanksgiving along with stuffing and candied yams, you will be delighted to discover that an entrée such as Santa Fe Turkey Salad is

just as appealing—and has a fraction of the calories and almost no fat. As for chicken, a forkful of Spicy Chicken, Mandarin Orange, and Mango Salad will make you forget that you were ever tempted by a plate of deep-fried wings.

You may be surprised to find that healthy salads can be made with beef, pork, or lamb, but in Chapter 3, you will see that by choosing the leanest cuts of meat and using healthy amounts, your salad can be both satisfying and nutritionally sound. So treat yourself to delightfully spicy Beef Fajita Salad, a dish with true south-of-the-border flavor. Or, for a stick-to-your-ribs—but not to your waistline—meal, try Roast Beef and Potato Salad.

Are you a seafood lover? If so, you will be delighted by the more than thirty-five tantalizing recipes presented in Chapter 4—recipes that feature the bounty of the ocean in simple yet simply delicious salads. If you favor the mysterious tastes of the islands, you will adore Caribbean Shrimp and Mango Salad. Are your tastes closer to home? Indulge yourself with a mouth-watering meal of Southwestern Rubbed Salmon Salad.

More and more people now enjoy vegetarian meals, either as an occasional break from meat, poultry, and fish, or as an everyday lifestyle. If you are looking for tempting vegetarian fare, Chapter 5 is the one for you. California Spinach, Alfalfa Sprouts, and Tofu Salad is one tempting vegetarian offering. Other possibilities include hearty Greek Pasta Salad, colorful Fruit Salad With Strawberry Sorbet, and tart Vegetarian Teriyaki Citrus Delight.

The final chapter of this book is devoted to the crowning touch of any salad—the salad dressing. Here you will find a wonderful array of dressings, from tangy Lemon and Dill Vinaigrette, to sweet Pear Dressing, to spicy Caribbean Dressing. The salad recipes themselves each include recommendations for dressings that I feel complement that salad. I've even marked my number-one choices with a star (★). But don't be afraid to personalize your salad by choosing any of the other flavorful dressings that appeal to you. And, of course, keep in mind that your local supermarket offers a wonderful selection of dressings, many of which can be successfully paired with the salads in this book.

If ease of preparation, luscious flavors, and tempting presentations suit your fancy, this book is sure to turn you into a main course salad lover. So put away the roasting pan and reach for the salad tongs. Whether your lifestyle is hectic or relaxed—and whether you favor meat-and-potatoes fare or a light medley of pasta and veggies—*Main Course Salads* is sure to become a source of inspiration that you will turn to time and time again.

1

Main Course Salad Basics

Fresh and appealing. Hearty and satisfying. Crisp and light. All of these phrases can be used to describe a main course salad. And when the salad is as good for you as it is tempting, other words are equally descriptive—words like healthful and low-fat. Just why is it important for a salad to be both delicious and low in fat and calories? This chapter will briefly examine the importance of a low-fat, low-calorie, high-nutrient diet. It will then acquaint you with the various healthful and flavorful ingredients used throughout this book, as well as some basic kitchen equipment that can make all of your salad-making adventures faster and easier. Finally, it will provide some suggestions for presenting your salads as artfully and attractively as possible, as well as some tips that can help insure salad-making success.

THE NUTRITIOUS MAIN COURSE SALAD

If you have ever searched for that magical technique that will allow you to shed unwanted pounds, you have probably discovered that the only proven way to accomplish this goal is to reduce your fat and calorie intake, eat a balanced diet that is high in nutrients, and exercise regularly. Although exercise sugges-

tions are beyond the scope of this book, the following chapters will introduce you to a wide variety of ways to meet your dietary goals. Almost all of the recipes in *Main Course Salads* are very low in fat and calories—although I have included a few of my favorite salad recipes that are somewhat higher in fat, for those few occasions when a special indulgence is appropriate. Plus, hearty helpings of nutrient-rich vegetables, salad greens, grains, and other ingredients optimize nutritional value. Let's take a look at the importance of each of these criteria for a healthy meal.

A Bounty of Nutrients

Although it's important to keep fat and calories under control, this strategy alone does not make a dish healthy. Consider fat-free cookies, for example. Low in fat—containing no fat, actually—these treats are nevertheless far from being nutritional powerhouses. Why? Made from refined flour, refined sugar, and other nutrient-poor ingredients, the cookies provide little or none of the vitamins, minerals, and fiber needed for good health.

The dishes found in *Main Course Salads* are different. These salads start with plenty of fresh vegetables and fruits, whole grains, and other foods that supply a wealth of vitamins, minerals, and fiber. Lean meats and meat substitutes, legumes, and low- and no-fat dairy products then provide protein, calcium, and other essential nutrients while keeping fat and cholesterol to a minimum. The result? Dishes that are not just low in fat, but also high in nutrients and wonderfully high in flavor.

A Limit on Fat

By now, most people know that a high-fat diet is to be avoided. Yet many people still don't have a clear idea of why a large amount of dietary fat is so harmful. Although whole books can be—and have been—written on the dangers of fat, really just two concepts are important to keep in mind. The first is the relationship between fat and calories. The second is the relationship between fat and a number of serious illnesses.

It doesn't surprise most people to learn that fat is fattening. In fact, each gram of fat contains more than *twice* the number of calories found in a comparable amount of carbohydrate or protein. More important, dietary fat quickly converts into body fat. While carbohydrate and protein also turn into fat when eaten in excess, the conversion process itself burns up some calories. Consequently, individuals who eat a diet rich in fat are more likely to experience weight gain than are those whose diet is high in carbohydrate and protein.

Because of the fat-calorie connection, fat is a major culprit in cases of obesity, a problem that has reached epidemic proportions in the United States. And this excess weight can exacerbate other conditions, such as arthritis. But dietary fat is guilty of more than just this. High-fat diets have been associated with atherosclerosis, the most common type of cardiovascular disease; with high blood pressure; with diabetes; and even with cancer.

It's important to keep in mind, though, that fat is not always a villain. Certain types of fat are actually good for you, and play a vital role in the maintenance of healthy cells and the production of hormone-like substances that are essential to normal body functions. Other fats, however, have been associated with the problems discussed above. The inset on page 8 will acquaint you with the different forms of dietary fat, and let you know which should be avoided and which are an important part of a healthful diet.

Budgeting Your Fat

You now know that fat should be limited in a healthy diet, but that it should *not* be eliminated. Exactly how low should you go? The American Heart Association recommends that no more than 30 percent of your daily caloric intake be derived from fat, and some health experts believe that a 20- to 25-percent limit constitutes a still healthier diet. Because people's calorie needs depend on factors such as age, body frame, weight, gender, and daily exercise, these needs can vary greatly. Your family physician or a nutritionist can help you devise a diet that is right for you. However, the following table gives a rough idea of your daily calorie needs, and also provides two maximum daily fat-gram budgets—one based on 20 percent of calorie intake, and one based on 25 percent of calorie intake. If you now weigh more or less than you would like to, go by your goal weight.

ABOUT THE INGREDIENTS

The salads in this book are as varied and satisfying as they are healthy because they make use of such a wide range of ingredients, from crisp greens to lean poultry to whole grains to savory vinegars. This section was designed to acquaint you with these foods—some of which may be new to you—and to guide you in choosing the best ingredients possible for your main course salads.

RECOMMENDED DAILY CALORIE AND FAT INTAKES

Weight (Pounds)	Recommended Daily Calorie Intake (13–15 Calories per Pound)	Daily Fat Gram Intake (20% of Calorie Intake)	Daily Fat Gram Intake (25% of Calorie Intake)
100	1,300–1,500	29–33	36–42
110	1,430–1,650	32–37	40–46
120	1,560–1,800	34–40	43–50
130	1,690–1,950	38–43	47–54
140	1,820–2,100	40–46	51–58
150	1,950–2,250	43–50	54–62
160	2,080–2,400	46–53	58–67
170	2,210–2,550	49–57	61–71
180	2,340–2,700	52–60	65–75
190	2,470–2,850	55–63	69–79
200	2,600–3,000	58–66	72–83

Salad Greens

Greens are the foundation of most salads. These leafy vegetables are usually green, but occasionally are white or red. As such, they add not only texture and flavor to salads, but a variety of colors, as well.

Not too long ago, the term salad green was synonymous with iceberg lettuce. In fact, as most of us were growing up, iceberg lettuce was practically the only salad green available—and in some uninspired kitchens, it still is! But today, there is no reason to remain that conservative. With the garden treasures available at most supermarkets, you can choose from an amazing array of exotic tasting and visually interesting greens for your next salad masterpiece. In addition to such staples as spinach and loose-leaf lettuce, you may want to consider sorrel, mesclun, bok choy, or even an edible flower for a special culinary adventure. Whatever greens you choose, just make sure that they are as fresh as possible, with both a just-plucked appearance and a fresh aroma. (For more information on choosing greens, as well as preparing and storing them, see the inset on page 11.)

Before you navigate the aisles of your favorite produce department or farmer's market, use the following information to become familiar with some of the most widely available salad greens.

Arugula. This soft-textured Italian green consists of small leaves that are dark green in color. Arugula lends a sharp, peppery taste to salads, and should therefore be used sparingly to avoid overpowering the taste of other ingredients. Choose arugula with leaves that are free of any dark or yellow spots, and, preferably, that still have the roots attached to preserve the flavor. Wash the leaves thoroughly to remove any sand, dry with care, and serve right away. When arugula is unavailable, use

Knowing Your Fats

As you choose healthful foods for use in your main course salads, it's important to keep in mind that although dietary fat as a whole should be limited, some fat is necessary for good health. Just as important, not all fats are the same. It is therefore very important to know your fats so that you can select them wisely for all your cooking needs.

Generally speaking, dietary fats fall into three major categories: saturated, monounsaturated, and polyunsaturated. Most foods that are high in fat contain all three types. However, many foods are much higher in one type than in another. That is why a food may be described as being "saturated" or "monounsaturated."

Saturated Fats

Saturated fats are abundant in tropical oils such as coconut oil, palm kernel oil, and palm oil. They are also found in animal foods—meat, lard, poultry, and dairy products such as butter.

Most people are familiar with the danger of foods high in saturated fats. A diet rich in these fats can lead to a variety of serious conditions, including cardiovascular disease, diabetes, and some forms of cancer. As a result, saturated fats should be limited as much as possible.

Polyunsaturated Fats

Most polyunsaturated fats fall into one of two categories: omega-6 fats and omega-3 fats. Both of these fats are called essential fatty acids because they are needed for good health, but must be obtained from the diet.

Omega-6 fatty acids are found in vegetable oils such as corn oil, sunflower oil, safflower oil, cottonseed oil, sesame oil, and walnut oil, as well as in products made from these oils, such as mayonnaise and salad dressings. These fats are also found in sesame seeds, sesame butter, walnuts, soybeans, and soybean products such as tofu and tempeh. Although omega-6 fats are essential for certain body functions, such as blood clotting, an excess of these fats favors the development of blood clots, high blood pressure, cancerous tumors, and inflammatory disorders such as arthritis.

---

watercress instead, as it has a similar peppery taste.

Baby Greens. Also known as *mesclun* (French), *misticanza* (Italian), and *spring greens*, mixed baby greens—a mixture of salad leaves and herbs—provide a wonderful array of vivid colors, contrasting textures, and exotic flavors. Originally, these interesting salad ingredients could be obtained only from the wild in Europe. Now, garden-fresh mixed baby greens can be purchased by the pound or in cellophane bags.

Belgian Endive. This form of chicory resembles a cigar in shape since its white leaves are tightly coiled into a cylinder. The Belgian endive has a subtle bitter flavor. Avoid endives with green leaves, though, because they tend to be excessively bitter. The relatively sharp taste of the endive complements sweet and tangy dressings.

Bok Choy. Also called Chinese cabbage, bok choy has wide white stems and ribs, and dark green leaves. The name derives from the Chinese term *Pakchoi*, which means "white veg-

Omega-3 fats are most abundant in salt-water fish such as albacore tuna, salmon, anchovies, and sardines, and in flaxseeds and flaxseed products. Lake whitefish, sweet smelt, trout, bass, carp, and other freshwater fish contain slightly lower amounts of these fats. Unlike omega-6 fats, omega-3 fatty acids help lower blood pressure, reduce blood triglycerides, inhibit tumor formation, and protect against inflammatory diseases.

Unfortunately, because most people eat too little fish and too much vegetable oil, most consume too few omega-3 fats and too many omega-6 fats. A more healthful balance of fats can be achieved by limiting foods like vegetable oils and mayonnaise, and including healthy amounts of omega-3-rich fish.

Monounsaturated Fats

Monounsaturated fats are found in olive, canola, and macadamia oils, as well as in avocados, olives, hazelnuts, almonds, and almond butter. Scientists believe that monounsaturated fats, unlike saturated fats and some polyunsaturated fats, probably do not harm cardiovascular health, and may even benefit it.

However, it is important to remember that the calorie count is equally high for all types of fat, whether monounsaturated, polyunsaturated, or saturated.

Hydrogenated Fats

One other type of fat deserves your attention—hydrogenated fat. This type of fat is formed when liquid vegetable oils are chemically altered by high heat and the addition of hydrogen, a process that transforms the oil into solid margarines and shortenings. Unfortunately, this process also creates undesirable by-products known as trans-fatty acids or trans fats—substances that act much like saturated fats to raise blood cholesterol levels.

While the subject of fats is a complex one, the selection of healthful foods need not be difficult. Most important, limit your dietary fat as much as possible to avoid the problems caused by specific fats and by high-calorie foods in general. Then choose foods highest in omega-3 fatty acids and monounsaturated oils. This, coupled with a balanced diet and regular exercise, is the surest prescription for good health.

---

etable." Look for the smaller heads of bok choy, because they are the tastiest. Chard can be substituted for bok choy when necessary.

Butterhead Lettuce. These greens are also called *hearting lettuce* because their inner leaves are packed tightly together. Farther from the center, the leaves gradually become larger and softer. Both the inner and outer leaves are excellent additions to a salad, but the innermost leaves are the most tender and sweet. There are two varieties of butterhead: Boston (butter) lettuce and Bibb (Kentucky limestone) lettuce. Because of its soft texture and mild flavor, butterhead lettuce is best complemented by lighter dressings. Choose heads that are crisp and have a white base, and leaves that are bright green on the outer edge.

Chicory. This term is applied to a family of greens that includes Belgian endive, curly endive, escarole, and radicchio. See the separate listings.

Curly Endive. Also known by its French name, *frisée*, curly endive is in the chicory family. It has a distinctively bitter flavor and a characteristic frilly or curly leaf from which it gets its name. Choose leaves that are crisp, and be sure to wash them thoroughly to remove any sand.

Edible Flowers. Flowers add color and interest to salads. They not only are decorative, but add a noticeable piquancy to salads, as well. Among the most widely available edible flowers are calendula flowers, rose petals, violets, carnations, chrysanthemums, and nasturtium flowers or leaves. These flowers are available in packages—prewashed and free from harmful chemicals—in the produce section of many supermarkets. Dried edible flowers are available in some gourmet stores. Avoid fresh flowers from the florist, because they may be sprayed with chemicals.

Escarole. Similar to curly endive, this member of the chicory family is less bitter in taste. When choosing escarole, look for heads with loose, broad leaves and a discernible heart. Combine this green with sweeter greens to balance the flavors.

Iceberg Lettuce. This well-known lettuce has a tight, dense head with crisp leaves. Because it is 90 percent water, iceberg can be refrigerated for long periods of time without spoiling. Although this lettuce does not have a prominent flavor, it is often a valuable addition to salads because its crisp and rigid texture prevents the leaves from wilting under heavy dressings such as Thousand Island.

Lamb's Lettuce. Also known by its French name, *mâche*, lamb's lettuce derives its name from its dark green leaves, which are similar in size and shape to a lamb's tongue. When choosing lamb's lettuce, look for leaves that are soft, but not limp. Because the mild taste of lamb's lettuce is similar to that of spinach,

it can be substituted for spinach in salads —especially when a more exotic touch is desired.

Loose-Leaf Lettuce. This lettuce, which includes greens such as red leaf and oak leaf, neither forms heads like its iceberg cousins, nor forms hearts like butterhead lettuce. Instead, its leaves are large, curly, and frilly. Usually light green in color—although some varieties are shaded with red—loose-leaf lettuce is particularly useful as a garnish in large salad bowls or on platters.

Radicchio. This lettuce has been cultivated on the Italian peninsula for centuries. Verona radicchio, the popular variety found in the United States, has a deep red, round head with white veins. Although it is often included with other lettuce leaves for its contrasting color, its crunchy leaves also impart an interesting bitter flavor to salads.

Romaine (Cos) Lettuce. Named for the Greek island of Cos, where it originated, this lettuce has long, coarse green outer leaves. However, the whiter leaves in the center are the tastiest and crispiest.

Sorrel. Actually an herb, sorrel will impart a tart lemon flavor to your salads. French sorrel leaves are wide at the base and are less tart in taste, while the garden sorrel grown in the United States has narrow, swordlike leaves and is more flavorful. For the best flavor, choose sorrel with young leaves.

Spinach. With deep green arrow-shaped leaves, a rich color, and a strong but nonbitter taste, spinach is among the most versatile of salad ingredients. Because spinach is said to have been the favorite food of the sixteenth-century French monarch Catherine De Medici of Florence, French recipes containing this marvelous vegetable are described as being *à* *la Florentine.* Look for baby spinach or spinach with especially crisp, dark green leaves. Because it is a low-lying plant that collects sand and soil particles while growing, it is very important that spinach leaves be carefully washed before you prepare your salad.

Watercress. This versatile salad green has a peppery taste, making it delicious in salads or as a garnish. Choose watercress with dark green leaves, and be certain that the plant has an abundance of leaves rather than stems.

Oils and Vinegars

When creating a low-fat salad, it is very important to reduce the amount of oil used, or, if possible, to eliminate the oil entirely. Yet some oil is often desirable or necessary, and a salad cookbook would not be complete without a

Preparing and Storing Salad Greens

Because most salads have a base of greens, the quality of your greens and the care with which they are prepared can have a great effect on the appearance, texture, and taste of the finished dish.

When shopping for greens, always choose those with fresh, crisp leaves and a garden-fresh smell. Avoid greens that are spotted with brown marks and those with oversized or wilted leaves.

Although many salad greens can be found prewashed in bags, you may sometimes be unable to find the desired greens in packages, or you may simply prefer to use loose produce. If so, once you have chosen your greens, you will have to wash and dry them. A simple method is to first gently tear the leaves into generous bite-sized pieces or to tear large leaves along the central rib. Just don't make the pieces too small, or they will lose their crunch. Small leaves also typically result in a salad that is less attractive.

Next, immerse the leaves in a pot or sink filled with cold water and swish the leaves around with your hands to remove any grit. Another excellent way to wash greens is to rinse the leaves under cold running water. When working with more tightly packed greens *like iceberg lettuce, try removing the core and running very cold water into the hollow, allowing the leaves to fall apart. Finally, keep in mind that many salad spinners are designed to wash the greens as well as dry them.*

After the leaves have been washed, the next step is to dry them. This is also a great time to discard any leaves that are brown or wilted. As you scoop up the leaves with your hands, gently shake them to remove as much water as possible. Another drying method—one for the athletically inclined—is to place the washed leaves in a pillowcase, tightly close the neck, and swing the bag in a circle outdoors. A variation on this theme, and one that I like best, is to place the tightly closed pillowcase in the washing machine and turn on the "spin" cycle. I sometimes run this cycle twice. Naturally, a salad spinner is especially made to turn moist lettuce into dry greens.

After your greens are dry, place them in a salad crisper or wrap them loosely in a paper or cloth towel. Roll up the towel and place it in a plastic bag, poking several holes in the bag so that any excess moisture is able to escape. Then refrigerate the greens until you are ready to use them. Greens that have been properly dried can remain crisp for four to five days.

discussion of the most common oils used to enhance a salad. Please note that not all of the oils discussed below are used in the dressings in this book, as I have usually limited myself to those oils that are most readily available and most affordable. However, you may wish to experiment with some of the other oils mentioned, using them to vary the taste of your dressings according to your mood and your preferences.

The other half of this culinary duo, vinegar, is also available in a wide variety of flavors, qualities, and origins. Your choices of vinegar and oil can often make the difference between an ordinary salad and an impressive culinary feast. As is true of fine wines and chocolates, the highest-quality oils and vinegars usually have the best flavor.

Oils

Canola Oil. Although you would never guess it from the name, canola oil is actually made from the seeds of the rape plant. Its rapid rise in popularity is largely due to its healthful profile, which includes a very low saturated fat content, a higher monounsaturated fat content than any oil except for olive oil, and the presence of health-promoting omega-3 fatty acids. Although canola oil is blander than high-quality olive oil, it nevertheless makes an excellent salad dressing ingredient—especially when a more neutral-tasting oil is desired.

Hazelnut Oil. The best hazelnut oils are imported from France. These oils make a delicious vinaigrette when combined with champagne vinegar and used to dress spinach or seafood. Once a bottle of hazelnut oil has been opened, be sure to store it in the refrigerator, as it can quickly become rancid at room temperature.

Olive Oil. Olive oil is the most commonly used and versatile salad oil. Although the dis-

tinguishing terms associated with olive oil—"extra virgin," "fine virgin," and "pure," for instance—can be confusing, an understanding of these terms will help you pick the best oil for each of your culinary needs.

The terms used on olive oil labels actually describe the method of extracting the oil from the olives, and the amount of acidity found in the final product. The traditional method of making olive oil is to crush the olives between two very large stone wheels. This oil is extracted without the use of heat or chemical solvents, and is therefore termed "cold pressed." Oil that comes from the first pressing can bear the term "virgin" on its label. The percentage of acidity in cold-pressed olive oil determines its relative quality.

Extra virgin olive oil, the aromatic product of the first pressing of the highest-quality olives, has 1 percent or less acid. The finest extra virgin oils have considerably less than 1 percent. *Superfine virgin olive oil* has less than 1.5 percent acid; *fine virgin*, less than 3 percent; and *virgin*, no more than 4 percent.

Italian extra virgin olive oil is made from a combination of green and black ripe olives. This oil is greener in color than other oils, and has a discernible fruity flavor. French olive oil, frequently made from black olives, is golden in color and has a pleasingly buttery flavor. There is also a variety of olive oils made in Greece and Spain, as well as a variety produced in the United States.

Olive oil bearing the label "pure" is usually made from a second pressing, and is often extracted with chemical solvents and heat. Oils of this quality have a less pleasant taste, and should be reserved for cooking only. For the best results in salads, choose only extra virgin olive oils.

Peanut Oil. Peanut oil is made in the United States, as well as in France and China. Because the oil made in the States has been highly refined, it does not have the distinctive peanut flavor characteristic of the French and Chinese products. Good peanut oils are available in gourmet specialty shops and health foods stores. Once opened, peanut oil should be refrigerated if kept longer than a month.

Sesame Oil. Sesame oil is available in two varieties. The first kind, which is pressed from raw white sesame seeds, is pale yellow in color and has a very mild flavor. The variety I prefer is Oriental sesame oil, which is pressed from roasted sesame seeds. Rich orange in color, this oil imparts a very strong, nutty flavor to salads. Only a small amount of Oriental sesame oil is needed to richly flavor salads and other foods. It is nicely complemented by rice vinegar, as well as by fresh lemon or lime juice. To keep your sesame oil from turning rancid, be sure to refrigerate the bottle once it has been opened.

Walnut Oil. This strong-flavored oil is frequently used in France. Imported cold-pressed walnut oil has the best flavor. Walnut oil combines well with sherry vinegar, and is especially good on chicory and other bitter greens. Once a bottle of walnut oil has been opened, it should be refrigerated.

Vinegars

Apple Cider Vinegar. Made from fermented apples, good-quality apple cider vinegars are full-bodied and have a wonderful apple aroma, with just a hint of a fruity taste. This vinegar combines well with cole slaw and other cabbage salads, and is also delicious on warm potato salad.

Balsamic Vinegar (*Aceto Balsamico*). This aromatic vinegar is made from the unfermented juice of the white Trebbiano grape, and aged in fragrant wooden casks for 6 to 120 years. The longer balsamic vinegar ages, the more mellow—and the more expensive—it

becomes. This product is produced in the Modena region of Italy.

Champagne Vinegar. Made from grapes originating in the Champagne region of France, champagne vinegar is similar to wine vinegar, but has a lighter taste.

Raspberry Vinegar. Raspberry vinegar is made by combining fresh raspberries with distilled or white wine vinegar. Because of its characteristic fruity flavor, it is an excellent choice for pork and chicken salads, as well as composed fruit salads.

Red Wine Vinegar. A full-bodied product, red wine vinegar is a good choice for salads featuring bolder-tasting greens, as well as those made with beef, pork, and lamb.

Rice Vinegar. A delicately flavored Asian product made from rice wine, this vinegar has less acidity than apple cider vinegar. It is a wonderful addition to most Oriental salads, and tastefully complements seafood salads, as well.

Sherry Vinegar. Made from Spanish sherry, this vinegar is rich and full-bodied with a nutty flavor. It goes well with duck, game, and fruit salads.

White Wine Vinegar. In keeping with its white-wine origin, this vinegar has a more delicate flavor than red wine vinegar, and nicely accents chicken and seafood salads. The highest quality—and often most expensive—white wine vinegars have the best flavor.

Poultry

The addition of chicken or turkey can quickly transform an otherwise uninspired bowl of greens into a main course salad. When prepared without the addition of cooking oils and with skin removed, poultry receives high marks for being low in fat and calories. And when cooked properly, whether sautéed, poached, baked, broiled, or grilled, even low-fat poultry can remain highly flavorful, juicy, and tender. Keep in mind that turkey and chicken are interchangeable in most recipes.

Chicken

At most markets, chicken can be purchased whole, split, quartered, or cut up. When following a low-fat diet, though, the best choice is a chicken breast that has been boned and skinned, with all visible fat removed.

There are a number of ways to determine if a chicken breast is done. You can pierce the meat with a sharp knife or fork to see if the juices run clear; you can cut into the center of the meat to be sure that no pink remains; or you can use a meat thermometer to make certain that the center registers 170°F.

Turkey

Although your market is sure to offer a wide selection of turkey parts, when making low-fat main course salads, you'll want to choose turkey breast tenderloins. This cut is both easy to prepare and very flavorful. Better yet, the next time you serve turkey at a holiday dinner, freeze the leftover breast meat by dividing it into twelve-ounce portions and placing each individual portion in a freezer bag. Write the date and contents on the bag—frozen turkey stays fresh for up to three months—and you will have a head start the next time you decide to make a turkey salad.

When cooking turkey, you can test for doneness just as if you were cooking chicken. You can pierce the meat with a sharp knife or fork to see if the juices run clear; cut into the center of the meat to be sure that no pink remains; or use a meat thermometer to make certain that the center registers 170°F.

A host of turkey-based processed alternatives are also available, including turkey bacon, sausage, and ham. These products make pleasing additions to a salad, and are much lower in fat than their traditional pork and beef counterparts. It is important to realize, however, that the sodium content of processed meats is often high, so that these products should be avoided if you are following a low-sodium diet.

Beef

Beef is naturally higher in fat and calories than poultry, but the good news is that it is being bred much leaner today. By choosing leaner cuts, it is possible to add beef to a salad and convert it into main course fare *without* adding an unacceptable amount of calories or fat.

Flank steak is an excellent example of a lean cut that is easy to prepare and incorporate into a salad. A useful rule of thumb to follow when looking for other lean cuts of beef is to choose those with the words "loin" or "round" in the name, such as beef eye round, top round, round tip, top sirloin, sirloin top loin, and tenderloin. To be certain that the fat and calorie content is in the healthful range, each individual serving should be no larger than three ounces, or the equivalent in size to a deck of cards.

The United States Department of Agriculture (USDA) recognizes eight grades of beef. In general, the higher and more expensive grades, such as Prime and Choice, have more fat due to a greater amount of marbling—streaks or flecks of fat that make the meat more juicy and tender. Select meats have the least degree of marbling, and therefore the least fat. Do keep in mind, though, that amounts of fat can vary even within a grade, so once you've decided on your cut, be sure to choose the product that is bright red to deep red in color, and has the least amount of marbling.

Since leaner cuts of beef tend to be less tender and tasty, they benefit most from being marinated for several hours in a liquid or paste mixture. Better yet, choose from among a variety of very savory ready-made lean roast beefs. Available at your local deli, these products are perfect whenever beef is called for in a main course salad recipe—especially when you're short on time.

When preparing beef yourself, test for doneness by inserting a meat thermometer in the thickest part of meat. A temperature of 120°F to 135°F indicates that the meat is rare; 135°F to 140°F indicates that it is medium rare; 140°F to 150°F suggests medium; and 155°F to 165°F suggests well done. Ordinarily, it is best to avoid well-done beef since it tends to be less tender and flavorful.

Any leftover beef can be divided into twelve-ounce portions and placed in individual freezer bags. Write the date and contents on the bag before freezing—beef can be frozen for two to three months—and your next beef salad will be fuss-free.

Pork

Like beef, pork is being bred leaner today, making it a healthy alternative to other meats. A good rule of thumb when shopping for leaner cuts of pork is to look for the word "loin" in the name—tenderloin, sirloin chops, loin chops, and loin roast, for instance. Also look for a pale pink color, which indicates that the pork came from a younger animal. Another good choice is 95-percent lean ham.

I like to cook pork until a meat thermometer registers 155°F. At this temperature the meat is safely cooked, but still tender and juicy.

Like beef, pork can be divided into portions, sealed in freezer bags, and kept in the freezer for two to three months.

Lamb

One of the most naturally flavorful meats, lamb comes from sheep that are less than two years old. When making salads, I like to use a leg of lamb that has been butterflied. Your butcher can butterfly the leg by cutting it down the center, almost all the way through, and removing the bone. The meat is then fanned open and laid flat, resembling a butterfly.

When cooking lamb, test for doneness by inserting a meat thermometer in the thickest part of the meat. If the thermometer registers 145°F to 150°F, the lamb is medium-rare; if it registers 160°F, it is medium. Like beef, lamb becomes less tender and has a less intense flavor when it is cooked beyond medium doneness.

Like other meats, cooked lamb can be divided into twelve-ounce portions and placed in individual labeled freezer bags. Store the lamb in the freezer for two to three months.

Fish

Fish is one of your healthiest salad ingredient options. It is renowned for being low in fat and cholesterol, yet high in critical vitamins, minerals, and omega-3 fatty acids.

When buying whole fish, choose those that are firm to the touch, and have firm, glossy scales and bright clear eyes. Fillets and steaks should have a moist, glossy sheen and a translucent appearance. The edges should be clean and even. All fish should have a sea smell rather than a fish odor.

When preparing fish, avoid overcooking it. To check for doneness, insert a fork into the thickest part of the fish and determine if the flesh is flaky and no longer translucent. If using a meat thermometer, the fish should have an internal temperature of 140°F.

Grains

Whole grains are an excellent source of fiber and other important nutrients, including vitamin E, magnesium, chromium, zinc, and potassium, to name just a few. As an added bonus, grains are low in fat and calories.

The addition of grains is an ideal way to convert a vegetable salad into a hearty yet delicious and nutritious low-fat meal. A salad can be enhanced by a variety of grains, including pearl barley; buckwheat groats; bulghur wheat; couscous; hominy grits; millet; rolled oats; polenta (cornmeal); quinoa; brown rice; short-, medium-, and long-grain white rice; wild rice; and wheat berries.

I have chosen to discuss only a few grains and grain products here—ones that I feel are exceptionally delicious in salads. Using this list as a starting point, I hope you will explore the produce, grain, and pasta sections of your local supermarket and experiment with many other options.

Barley. In its raw form, barley consists of a kernel enclosed by two layers of hull. When barley is processed into pearl barley, both layers of hull are removed and its inner kernel is polished. Pearl barley has a distinctively nutty flavor. It takes forty-five to fifty minutes to cook regular pearl barley. A quick-cooking variety, available in most supermarkets, can be prepared in ten to twelve minutes.

Bulghur Wheat. Bulghur is cracked wheat made from wheat berries. The berries are steamed, crushed, and then dried or dehydrated. When cooked, bulghur has a nutty flavor and is somewhat crunchy.

Couscous. Made from whole or refined flour, couscous is actually a pasta that has been shaped into small grains. Couscous originated in North Africa, and has remained a staple there and in the Middle East, where it is consumed as a cereal or as an alternative to rice, potatoes, or pasta.

Orzo. Orzo is an oval-shaped pasta resembling a grain of rice. It is available in health foods stores and in the pasta section of most supermarkets.

Quinoa. Pronounced *keen'-wa*, quinoa is a South American wheat-free grain that is an excellent source of protein, minerals, and other nutrients. In fact, quinoa is higher in protein than any other grain. Often used as a substitute for rice or couscous, quinoa makes a delicious salad ingredient.

Rice. One of mankind's most essential foods, rice is the dietary staple of over half the world's population. In some countries, this grain is the main, if not the only, source of protein. While unadorned rice is often served as an accompaniment to a meal, rice is also delicious when combined with other foods and included in a salad.

Brown rice is the whole, unpolished rice grain. Because it retains the outer layer of bran, it is brown in color, and contains vitamin E, protein, fiber, and other nutrients. Brown rice has a nutty flavor and is chewier in consistency than the white variety, making it an excellent salad ingredient.

White rice is dehulled and refined—meaning that the bran and germ have been removed. During this process, the grain loses most of its vitamin E and some of its protein, making it less nutritious than brown rice. White rice can be purchased in long-, medium-, and short-grain forms. In most salads, long-grain rice works best because the grains separate when cooked, allowing the rice to intermingle with the other salad ingredients. In some salads, however, a short-grain rice such as arborio is a good choice.

Wild rice is a North American aquatic grass, not a rice. Because its small black seeds are the same size and shape as rice, the early European explorers of the Americas named it "wild rice." Most wild rice is cultivated in Minnesota, Wisconsin, and Michigan, with some now being grown in California, as well. Like white rice, wild rice is available in long-grain, medium-grain, and short-grain forms. Although long-grain is the most expensive, the medium-grain variety is best for use in salads.

Legumes

Legumes include lentils, chickpeas (garbanzo beans), split peas, and dried beans such as kidney beans, lima beans, black beans, pinto beans, fava beans, soybeans, and Great Northern beans. Rich in protein and fiber, and low in fat, these foods typically constitute the lion's share of a healthy vegetarian diet. Accordingly, in some recipes calling for meat or poultry, legumes can be substituted as a tasty alternative.

Other Ingredients

A variety of other ingredients—from fresh fruits and vegetables to herbs and spices—can add a range of intriguing flavors and textures to your salads. Here are some additional favorite main course salad ingredients.

Asian Hot Sauce. Also called *Sriracha hot chili sauce,* this is a smooth red sauce made from serrano chilies. Although Asian hot sauce is milder and thicker than other hot sauces, you can easily substitute your favorite hot pepper sauce for this ingredient in any of the recipes in this book.

Avocados. Also known as *alligator pears,* avocados are native to Central America. Although these fruits are high in fat and calories, the fat is monounsaturated and comes packaged with a bounty of nutrients. So although avocados should be eaten only in moderation, they do have a place in a healthy diet. Choose ripe avocados that are slightly soft with a skin that is green and smooth or dark purple and pebbly.

Bean Thread Vermicelli. Also called *cellophane noodles* or simply *bean threads,* this pasta is made from mung bean flour. These very thin noodles are delicious both in salads and soups.

Capers. The unopened flower buds of the Mediterranean caper bush, capers are typically pickled in vinegar, and therefore should be rinsed before using. Used as a garnish or condiment, capers add piquancy to any dish. They are found in gourmet shops and in the olive section of most supermarkets.

Cilantro. Also known as *Chinese parsley* or *fresh coriander,* cilantro is one of the most popular herbs in the world. The term *coriander* usually refers to the entire plant, which includes the seeds, stems, roots, flowers, and leaves, all of which are edible. More precisely, *cilantro* refers only to the leaves and the stem of the coriander plant. Although cilantro has a very unique combination of flavors, some people describe it as having a soapy taste. Scientists have concluded that this aversion to cilantro is either genetic or the result of an unfamiliar palate for the herb. When buying cilantro, look for bunches that have an aromatic fragrance, as well as undamaged flat leaves that are crisp and green. Fresh cilantro is found in the produce section of many supermarkets.

Feta Cheese. This soft, white cheese is imported from Greece, the Balkans, or the Middle East. Made from goat's or sheep's milk, it is cured in salt brine. The final product is crumbly and has a slightly sour, salty taste. It is a staple in Greek salads.

Ginger. A rhizome or root that originated in India, ginger is now cultivated in the Orient and the West Indies, as well. The whole ginger root is light brown and knotty on the outside, and golden and juicy on the inside. Its flavor is both sweet and spicy. Ginger is found in Asian food stores and in the produce section of many supermarkets. Always peel ginger before adding it to your dish.

Hearts of Palm. These ivory-colored buds are found at the top of certain palm trees grown in

Secrets of Creating Healthful and Delicious Salads

There are several useful guidelines that I have discovered for creating salads that are healthful and lower in fat, yet satisfying and appealing. Use these tips to create your own main course salads or to modify mine. You won't be disappointed.

❏ *Whichever components of a salad you choose, be sure to use only the freshest ingredients, including those that are commercially prepared.*

❏ *In most cases, tear greens with your hands rather than cutting them, as cutting them with a knife may impart a bitter taste and cause the edges to brown. Tear large leaves along the central rib to create the most attractive salad. However, when using compact greens such as Belgian endive, feel free to use a knife. Other greens with small leaves, such as watercress, baby spinach, and arugula, should have their stems removed with a knife.*

❏ *Add tomatoes just before you are ready to serve your salad. Otherwise their juices will seep out, causing other vegetables to wilt and salad dressings to thin.*

❏ *Become aware of the wide variety of low-fat ingredients now available, including turkey bacon and low- and no-fat cheeses, croutons, mayonnaise, yogurt, and sour cream. Many cannot be distinguished from their full-fat counterparts when combined with the right greens, herbs, and spices.*

❏ *Oil—one of the most important yet fat-laden salad ingredients—can be reduced significantly, if not totally eliminated, when making your main course salads. When most of the oil in a vinaigrette is replaced with a puréed boiled potato, fat-free chicken broth, or corn syrup, the flavor and the consistency of the dressing are usually not appreciably changed. In most instances, the vinaigrette maintains its ability to cling to salad ingredients and retains its zestful flavor.*

Florida and the Caribbean. Available in cans, hearts of palm can be found in the gourmet or canned vegetable section of most supermarkets.

Jicama. Pronounced *hik'-a-ma*, this root vegetable, which resembles a turnip, is covered with a thin light brown skin. The inside, which is crisp and has a mild flavor similar to that of an apple, makes a wonderful addition to salads.

Kalamata Olives. These glossy black, almond-shaped Greek olives are cured in red wine vinegar, giving them a salty-sweet taste. Rich and meaty, kalamata olives are frequently used in salads. Although, like all olives, Kalamatas are high in fat, you need use only a few to add zest to your salads. Kalamata olives can be purchased by the pound at most specialty food stores or delis, and can be found in jars in the gourmet or olive section of your supermarket.

Kecap Manis. An Indonesian condiment, this sweet soy sauce is made with palm sugar, making it denser than ordinary soy sauce. Kecap manis can be found in Asian food stores. If you are unable to find this ingredient, feel free to substitute your favorite soy sauce.

Pepperoncini. Harvested and pickled before they ripen, these small green peppers add

Experiment to find which proportions of ingredients you like best.

❏ *Use salad dressings sparingly. All that is needed to complement a salad is enough vinaigrette to make the greens glisten.*

❏ *Although most dressings can be made in advance, they should not be added to the salad until just before serving unless the recipe specifies otherwise.*

❏ *Be aware that you can further reduce the fat content of almost any salad by changing the proportions of ingredients. For example, when a recipe calls for twelve ounces of poultry, the fat content can be reduced by using only six to eight ounces of poultry and adding more vegetables, grains, or fruit.*

❏ *Use your hands, salad tongs, or two large spoons to toss a salad. This will prevent delicate leaves from getting bruised.*

❏ *Always serve salads made with rice, pasta, or other grains at room temperature.*

❏ *When a salad is made in advance or when leftover salad must be stored, keep it in a covered container to prevent wilting and drying.*

❏ *Feel free to experiment on your own to modify the recipes in this book. This will allow you to tailor them to suit your own tastes or, if desired, to reduce preparation time. For example, I prefer to make my own vinaigrettes, but there are many excellent commercial vinaigrettes that are readily available and easily substituted. Just be certain to choose one that is relatively low in fat. If your diet permits, try adding a teaspoon or more of olive oil to the commercial fat-free vinaigrettes you're using. Even a small amount of a flavorful olive oil will enhance the dressing. Be aware that substitutions of key ingredients are also often possible. In recipes that use chicken as the main ingredient, try replacing the chicken with turkey or pork. In many other salad recipes, different varieties of seafood and poultry can be interchanged. And, of course, the substitution of an unusual garden green or the use of an edible flower garnish often produces a surprisingly delightful result.*

both crunch and a wonderfully spicy flavor to salads. Look for pepperoncini in the olive or pickle section of your supermarket.

Pine Nuts. Also called *pignoli nuts* or *pinon nuts,* pine nuts are small edible seeds found in the cones of the Mediterranean stone pine tree. Toasted pine nuts—which are more flavorful than the raw nuts—enhance salads by providing texture and a nutty flavor. Although pine nuts are very high in fat, when used in moderation, they can add interest to a variety of salads without compromising nutrition. Pine nuts can be found in health foods stores and in the gourmet section of many supermarkets.

Portabella Mushrooms. These cultivated mushrooms have open caps that are dark brown and lightly speckled. Meaty and satisfying, these behemoths measure from four to ten inches across. When roasted or grilled, a single Portabella mushroom can be large enough for a sandwich. Slivered, Portabellas make a flavorful addition to any salad. They are found in the produce section of supermarkets.

Shallots. Like onions and garlic, the shallot is a bulbous member of the lily family. Shallots are milder in taste than onions and less pungent than garlic. Similar in size to a clove of garlic, a shallot can be identified by its brown papery skin and an elongated bulb that is tapered on one end. Look for shallots that are small, plump, and firm. Avoid any that are dried out, as they tend to have little flavor. Shallots are found in the produce section of most supermarkets.

Shiitake Mushrooms. Sometimes called *golden oak, Black Forest,* or *Chinese mushrooms,* shiitake are tan to dark brown in color with a white veil on their underside between the cap and stem. Only the cap of the mushroom is eaten, and shiitake mushrooms are never eaten raw. But when lightly sautéed, they add texture, color, and an interesting smoky flavor to salads. Dried shiitake mushrooms are an acceptable option to fresh, especially when the fresh variety is in short supply. Both can be found in the produce section of most supermarkets.

Star Fruit. Also called a *carambola,* this juicy fruit has a sweet flavor resembling that of grapes or apples, as well as a citrusy tang. With a waxy yellow-orange edible skin, the star fruit is so called because it has five distinct ridges. Thus, when it is sliced, it produces a star-shaped outline. When choosing star fruit, look for ridges that are just beginning to darken.

Sweet Ginger Sesame Hibachi Grill Sauce. This mildly sweet Asian-style ginger sauce is delicious when brushed onto poultry or beef before grilling or broiling. As a bonus, this sauce is both fat-free and low in calories. You will find this product in the Oriental section of most supermarkets. If it is not available, substitute your favorite low-sodium teriyaki marinade.

Teriyaki Marinades and Sauces. These products give you a quick and easy way to add flavor to a variety of dishes. Do be aware, though, that many of these products are quite high in sodium. Fortunately, several brands have almost half the sodium of most teriyaki marinades and sauces. Look for Kikoman Lite, Rice Road, S & W, World Harbors, and Maple Grove Farms of Vermont.

Tofu. Also called *bean curd,* this high-protein soybean food is eaten throughout Asia. Although tofu has a very bland taste, it readily absorbs other flavors. This versatility allows tofu to be used in soups, salads, and baking, and as a substitute for meat. Tofu comes in a variety of consistencies. When making salads, though, you'll want to use low-fat extra-firm tofu, which is firm enough for slicing and cubing, and low enough in fat to be part of a healthy diet. Look for tofu in Asian food stores and in the produce section of supermarkets.

EQUIPMENT

An extensive array of equipment is not required to become a successful saladmeister. But you will find the following items useful in achieving the best results quickly and with a minimum of effort.

Blenders

A blender consists of a glass food container that is fitted with a blade at the bottom. It sits on a base with a control panel that allows the blades to whirl at different speeds so that they can liquefy, purée, chop, or whip virtually any food that is reasonably soft. The blender is a great tool when making salad dressings.

Food Processors

This versatile appliance chops, purées, blends, emulsifies, minces, shreds, grates, whips, and slices. It comes in several sizes, each consisting of a motor base, work bowl, and a pusher assembly. It is similar in principle to a blender, except that it has a more powerful motor and an array of blades and discs that extend into the food container, allowing the appliance to cut and slice foods into discrete pieces. This is an invaluable kitchen aid whenever you want to quickly shred, slice, or otherwise process salad ingredients. It can also be used to make salad dressings.

Juicers

Juicers come in a variety of sizes and shapes, and in both manual and electric models. A juicer is the ultimate way to prepare fresh-squeezed lemon, lime, grapefruit, orange, and tangerine juice for use in salad dressings. Although cans, bottles, and cartons of juice are available, I prefer the flavor of the freshly squeezed variety. To extract the maximum amount of juice from lemons or limes, first place them in the microwave, one at a time, and cook on high for ten seconds.

Meat Thermometers

A meat thermometer is the most reliable way to determine when meat is properly cooked. The instrument reads the food's internal temperature, which is the best indication of doneness. To insure an accurate reading, insert the tip of the thermometer into the deepest part of the meat without touching the bone. There are many kinds of thermometers available, but the best is the instant-read variety. Once inserted into the meat, a digital reading is displayed within seconds. I use the Taylor Digital Pocket Thermometer 9840. It is reasonably priced and very accurate.

Nonstick Cookware

Nonstick cookware is an invaluable tool for preparing food without the addition of fats and oils. The cooking surface is covered with a special coating, so that once you follow the easy directions for "seasoning" this nonstick layer, you can fry, sauté, or stir-fry with little or no fat. Skillets, griddles, Dutch ovens, saucepans, and indoor grill pans are widely available with a nonstick surface, and the range of costs makes them affordable for almost any budget.

Oil Misters

Although vegetable and olive oil cooking sprays can be purchased in all supermarkets, it is more economical to buy your own refillable canister designed specifically for this purpose. All that is necessary is to fill it with the oil of your choice, attach the special non-aerosol cap, and pump to pressurize the contents. When ready to use, simply depress the nozzle and spray the oil onto foods or cookware.

It is important to remember that there is a limit to how long you should spray the oil. For example, spraying your vegetables for approximately fifteen seconds is equivalent to using one tablespoon of oil—14 grams of fat, in other words. To limit the length of the spray, hold the canister twelve to fifteen inches above the pan or food and use a quick circular action. Try to keep the total amount of spraying time to less than two seconds. When you use nonstick cookware, a quick spray, if any at all, is all that is needed to keep food from sticking to the pan.

Salad Spinners

A salad spinner is a convenient way to dry greens. To use the spinner, you simply place wet greens in an inner perforated container. A device such as a crank allows you to rotate the container rapidly, forcing the water into an outer container, which acts as a receptacle. Some salad spinners combine both washing and drying functions. Greens are placed in a drain basket fitted with a lid that has holes on top. When the spinner is set under cold running water, the soil on the greens is washed away. Then, with a few turns of the crank, the leaves are spun dry.

Common Cooking Terms

The process of creating a salad can involve a wide array of cooking methods and techniques. Most of these steps are very simple, but a few require some additional culinary expertise. Happily for the busy chef, many meats, poultry, greens, or dressings can be purchased with much of the required preparation already completed. Your meat or poultry can be boned or butterflied by the butcher at your local supermarket or purchased already cooked. Many cheeses are available in grated form. And most greens can be purchased prewashed and ready for the salad bowl.

Despite the abundance of time-saving alternatives at your market, some salad recipes include steps that you may prefer to carry out yourself. The list below defines a few of the terms you will find in the instructions provided throughout this cookbook.

Boil. To heat liquid until bubbles appear on the surface and begin to vaporize.

Bone. To remove the bones from poultry and meats.

Broil. To cook food under direct heat provided either by a hot flame or by a heating element.

Butterfly. To split poultry or meat down the center—cutting almost all the way through— and remove the bone. The poultry or meat is then fanned opened and laid flat, or "butterflied."

Caramelize. To cook a vegetable at a high temperature so that its sugar breaks down and the vegetable turns brown in color, with an intensely rich flavor.

Chop. To cut food into very fine pieces.

Cube. To cut food into $1/4$- to $1/2$-inch cubes.

Dice. To cut food into $1/8$- to $1/4$-inch cubes.

Grate. To shred food or reduce it into fine particles using a hand grater or food processor.

Grill. To cook food quickly over high heat on either an indoor or an outdoor grill.

Julienne. To cut vegetables, meat, or cheese into matchlike strips.

Mince. To cut food into cubes of $1/8$ inch or less.

Purée. To reduce food to a thick saucelike consistency, usually by using either a blender or a food processor.

Sauté. To cook food quickly in an open pan.

Shred. To cut food into slivers.

Simmer. To cook food just below the boiling point.

Stir-Fry. To cook food quickly over high heat while constantly stirring or tossing.

Steamers

A steamer is an excellent way to cook vegetables and still preserve all of their flavor, color, and vital nutrients. The food is placed in a basket or folding colander that sits in a larger covered pot. Boiling water is then placed in the bottom of the pot so that the steam from the liquid can cook the food.

CREATING ARTFUL SALAD PRESENTATIONS

A busy lifestyle often allows barely enough time to buy dinner ingredients, assemble them, and hope that the resulting dish will be acceptably nutritious and palatable. With time at a premium, the visual appeal of a dinner creation can become the lowest priority. One of the amazing features of a main course salad, however, is that because its ingredients vary in color, shape, and texture, it is a majestic visual presentation waiting to happen. The possible ways of creating an artful salad presentation are endless. Below, I discuss just a few of the techniques I have discovered. But with this book as your inspiration, I am certain you will develop many artistic touches of your own.

One of my favorite techniques is to dress greens lightly with a vinaigrette and make a nest of them in the center of a dinner plate. Next, fan slices of meat, fish, or poultry on one or both sides of the nest, and arrange vegetables, cheese, or other salad components to fill in the open spaces.

For another appealing presentation, first place a bed of undressed greens on a dinner plate. Then arrange slices of meat, poultry, or fish slightly overlapping one another over the salad. Distribute julienned vegetables over the top, and tuck asparagus spears or hearts of palm underneath so that they radiate out from under the salad. Finally, drizzle some of the dressing over each serving.

An easy technique can be used to create a dramatic presentation of any salad—even one that's been quickly tossed together. Simply place strips of baked tortillas (page 35) or cylinders of tightly rolled red leaf lettuce in the center of the salad so that they point upward, adding height and interest to your presentation. Tomato roses (page 179) and scallion flowers (page 42) are other means of "dressing up" a salad.

Using simple techniques like these, you will be able to keep your family and guests in awe of not only your ability to create a flavorful salad, but your culinary artistry, too. And you will be delighted to discover that with just a bit of imagination—and very little effort—you, too, can become a Rembrandt of the radicchio.

ABOUT THE NUTRITIONAL ANALYSIS

The nutritional facts that accompany each recipe in this book were calculated by using the nutritional analysis program Master Cook Deluxe (Sierra On-Line, Inc., Bellevue, Washington). Because you often have the choice of using one of several dressings, with a few exceptions, the analysis of each salad reflects a single serving of the salad alone. Each salad dressing recipe is accompanied by a separate analysis that, again, reflects the nutrients found in a single serving. When an option is provided for an alternative ingredient, the nutritional analysis always reflects the primary ingredient rather than the alternative. However, in most cases, the alternative has a nutritional profile similar to that of the primary ingredient.

As you can see, salads have grown up over the years. They are now more interesting, more varied, and more satisfying than ever before. Yet, they are relatively quick and easy to prepare. Best of all, main course salads have very few rivals as a healthful dinner entrée. Armed with the information included in this chapter and the exciting recipes found throughout this book, your future sojourns into the kitchen are sure to become simpler, more enjoyable, and deliciously rewarding. I wish you the best of health!

Savory Chicken
and Turkey Salads

Everyone loves chicken and turkey. Our love affair with these foods is evident both at weekday meals and at holiday events, when foods like roasted turkey are often an important part of the festivities. This chapter will show that there is yet another way to delight in these two favorites without the fuss—or the excess dietary fat—that so often accompanies standard poultry dishes. In the following pages, over forty salad recipes blend low-fat cuts of chicken and turkey with ingredients as varied as juicy mangos, crisp water chestnuts, creamy blue cheese, and hot Cajun spices. The result is a cornucopia of dishes that beautifully demonstrate the unique pleasures of main course salads.

Chicken and Asparagus Salad

If you need an excuse to prepare this appealing salad, it is the perfect light lunch to serve on St. Patrick's Day. The whiteness of the chicken breast against the green asparagus and lettuce will put you in a festive Emerald Isle mood. To enhance the green and white motif, you could add or substitute hearts of palm, broccoli, green beans, cauliflower, or even some light pasta. Serve with slices of kiwi fruit, honeydew melon, and pears.

1 boneless, skinless chicken breast (12 ounces)

½ cup commercial fat-free zesty vinaigrette

24 fresh asparagus spears (1 pound), tough ends removed, or 1 can (15 ounces) asparagus spears, drained

6 cups loose-leaf lettuce

2 scallions, thinly sliced

Suggested Dressings

★ 1 recipe Honey Dijon Vinaigrette (page 223)

1 recipe Lemon and Dill Vinaigrette (page 224)

½ cup commercial fat-free or low-fat honey Dijon vinaigrette

½ cup commercial fat-free lemon Dijon dressing

NUTRITIONAL FACTS
(per serving, salad only)
Calories: 314
Carbohydrates: 47.8 g
Cholesterol: 52 mg
Fat: 2.8 g
Calories From Fat: 7.8%
Protein: 26.2 g
Sodium: 407 mg

1. Rinse the chicken, and pat it dry with paper towels.

2. Place the chicken and vinaigrette in a resealable plastic bag. Seal the bag, turn to coat, and refrigerate for several hours or overnight, turning the chicken at least once.

3. Line a baking sheet with 1-inch sides with aluminum foil. Remove the chicken from the marinade, discarding the marinade, and transfer the chicken to the baking sheet.

4. Place the chicken under a preheated broiler, 4 inches from the heat source, and broil for 4 to 5 minutes on each side, or until golden brown on the outside and no longer pink on the inside. Allow the chicken to cool for 10 minutes before cutting into thin slices. Set aside.

5. Cut the asparagus into 2-inch lengths. If using fresh asparagus, cook in a steamer for 2 to 3 minutes, or just until fork tender. Drain well, and allow to come to room temperature.

6. To serve, combine the chicken, asparagus, lettuce, and scallions in a salad bowl. Add the vinaigrette, and toss gently to coat. Serve immediately.

YIELD: **4** SERVINGS

Carolyn's Chicken and Wild Rice Salad

The smoky flavors of grilled chicken and red peppers intermingling with wild rice, onion, celery, and raisins is marvelous in this savory salad. I like to serve it on a wreath of spinach leaves, garnished with diced or thin strips of roasted red pepper.

Suggested Dressings

★ 1 recipe Tarragon Vinaigrette (page 240)

1 recipe Spicy Vinaigrette (page 236)

½ cup commercial fat-free or low-fat honey Dijon vinaigrette

Time-Saving Tip
❑ Substitute ½ cup of commercial sweet roasted bell peppers for the home-made roasted peppers.

NUTRITIONAL FACTS
(per serving, salad only)

Calories: 314
Carbohydrates: 47.8 g
Cholesterol: 52 mg
Fat: 2.8 g
Calories From Fat: 7.8%
Protein: 26.2 g
Sodium: 407 mg

1 boneless, skinless chicken breast (12 ounces)
¼ cup low-sodium teriyaki marinade
2 red bell peppers
1 cup wild rice
½ cup minced red onion
½ cup diced celery
½ cup dark raisins
½ cup toasted slivered almonds (page 69) (optional)

1. Rinse the chicken, and pat it dry with paper towels.

2. Combine the chicken and teriyaki marinade in a resealable plastic bag. Seal the bag, turn to coat, and refrigerate for several hours or overnight, turning the chicken at least once.

3. To roast the peppers, place the peppers on a baking sheet that has been lined with aluminum foil. Broil under a preheated broiler, turning the peppers as the skins blacken, for 20 to 25 minutes, or until the skins are charred all over. Once roasted, place in a plastic bag, seal, and allow to steam for 15 minutes. When the peppers are cool enough to handle, peel away the skin and remove the tops and seeds. (Do not rinse the peppers.) Cut the peppers into cubes, and set aside.

4. While the peppers are roasting, cook the rice according to package directions, omitting butter or margarine. Allow the rice to come to room temperature.

5. Remove the chicken from the marinade, discarding the marinade. Place the chicken over moderately hot coals on a grill coated with cooking spray. Cover the grill and cook, turning the chicken every 3 minutes, for 6 to 9 minutes, or until golden brown on the outside and no longer pink on the inside. Alternatively, place the chicken under a preheated broiler, 4 inches from the heat source, and broil for 4 to 5 minutes on each side. Allow the chicken to cool for 10 minutes before cutting into cubes.

6. Combine the chicken, roasted peppers, wild rice, onion, celery, and raisins in a salad bowl. Add the vinaigrette, and toss gently to coat. Cover and refrigerate for several hours or overnight.

7. Remove the salad from the refrigerator 1 hour before serving. Add the almonds, if desired, and blend well. Serve immediately.

Caesar Salad With Cajun Chicken

Spicy Cajun-style chicken adds a real bite to this much adored salad. Serve with slices of cantaloupe and French bread.

1 boneless, skinless chicken breast (12 ounces)
Olive oil cooking spray
3 tablespoons fresh lemon juice
1½ teaspoons Cajun spices
1 head romaine lettuce, torn into generous bite-sized pieces (about 6 cups)
1½ cups commercial fat-free Caesar-flavored croutons
3 Roma tomatoes, cut into wedges
1 yellow bell pepper, cut into julienne strips
½ cup grated fat-free Parmesan cheese

Suggested Dressings

★ 1 recipe Caesar Dressing (page 216)

½ cup commercial fat-free or low-fat Caesar dressing

Time-Saving Tip
❏ Substitute 12 ounces of sliced cooked turkey breast for the broiled chicken.

NUTRITIONAL FACTS (per serving, salad only)
Calories: 179
Carbohydrates: 13.7 g
Cholesterol: 64 mg
Fat: 2.8 g
Calories From Fat: 13.5%
Protein: 26.1 g
Sodium: 248 mg

1. Rinse the chicken, and pat it dry with paper towels. Lightly coat the chicken with the cooking spray.

2. Place the chicken and lemon juice in a resealable plastic bag, and turn to coat.

3. Spread the Cajun spices on a plate, and turn the chicken in the spices to coat.

4. Line a baking sheet with 1-inch sides with aluminum foil. Transfer the chicken to the baking sheet, and place under a preheated broiler, 4 inches from the heat source. Broil for 4 to 5 minutes on each side, or until golden brown on the outside and no longer pink on the inside. Allow the chicken to cool for 10 minutes before cutting into thin slices.

5. To serve, combine the chicken, romaine lettuce, croutons, tomatoes, yellow pepper, and Parmesan cheese in a salad bowl. Add the dressing, and toss gently to coat. Serve immediately.

Chicken and Orzo Salad

YIELD: **4 SERVINGS**

Bursting with the wonderful flavor of curry, this chicken and orzo salad can be served on a bed of greens or topped with an assortment of condiments such as sliced bananas, raisins, coconut, or toasted slivered almonds.

Suggested Dressing

★ 1 recipe Curry Vinaigrette (page 220)

8 ounces orzo pasta*
1 boneless, skinless chicken breast (12 ounces)
2 teaspoons tandoori paste,** or ½ teaspoon curry powder
1 cup green seedless grapes, stemmed and halved
½ cup diced red bell pepper
½ cup golden raisins
3 scallions, thinly sliced

NUTRITIONAL FACTS
(per serving, salad only)
Calories: 470
Carbohydrates: 82.9 g
Cholesterol: 52 mg
Fat: 3.7 g
Calories From Fat: 6.9%
Protein: 29.6 g
Sodium: 71 mg

* Orzo can be found in the pasta or rice section of most supermarkets.

**A blend of ground Indian spices, tandoori paste is available in Asian and Indian food stores, or in the ethnic section of most supermarkets.

1. Cook the orzo according to package directions. Drain well, and set aside.

2. Rinse the chicken, and pat it dry with paper towels.

3. Line a baking sheet with 1-inch sides with aluminum foil. Transfer the chicken to the baking sheet. If using tandoori paste, brush both sides of the chicken with the paste. If using curry powder, first lightly coat the chicken with olive oil cooking spray. Then sprinkle a scant 1/4 teaspoon of curry powder on each side of the chicken.

4. Place the chicken under a preheated broiler, 4 inches from the heat source, and broil for 4 to 5 minutes on each side, or until golden brown on the outside and no longer pink on the inside. Allow the chicken to cool for 10 minutes before cutting into cubes.

5. Combine the orzo, chicken, grapes, red pepper, raisins, and scallions in a salad bowl. Add the vinaigrette, and toss gently to coat. Cover and refrigerate for several hours or overnight.

6. Remove the salad from the refrigerator 1 hour before serving. Blend gently, and serve.

Chicken and Pear Salad

With its vivid green and pale yellow ingredients, this salad will remind you of spring. The flavors of the chicken, pears, green beans, and yellow pepper deliciously intermingle with one another. Serve with fresh low-fat pineapple muffins.

1 boneless, skinless chicken breast (12 ounces)
Olive oil cooking spray
¼ teaspoon freshly ground pepper
⅛ teaspoon salt
12 ounces green beans, trimmed
6 cups mixed baby greens
4 pears, cored and thinly sliced
1 large yellow bell pepper, cut into julienne strips
3 scallions, thinly sliced

1. Rinse the chicken, and pat it dry with paper towels.

2. Line a baking sheet with 1-inch sides with aluminum foil. Transfer the chicken to the baking sheet. Lightly coat both sides of the chicken with the cooking spray, and season with pepper and salt.

3. Place the chicken under a preheated broiler, 4 inches from the heat source, and broil for 4 to 5 minutes on each side, or until golden brown on the outside and no longer pink on the inside. Allow the chicken to cool for 10 minutes before cutting into thin slices. Set aside.

4. Cook the green beans in a steamer for 7 minutes, or just until fork tender. Drain well, and allow to come to room temperature.

5. To serve, combine the chicken, green beans, mixed baby greens, pears, yellow pepper, and scallions in a salad bowl. Add the vinaigrette, and toss gently to coat. Serve immediately.

Suggested Dressings

★ 1 recipe Honey Dijon Vinaigrette (page 223)

1 recipe Tarragon Vinaigrette (page 238)

½ cup commercial fat-free or low-fat honey Dijon vinaigrette

½ cup commercial fat-free or low-fat poppy seed dressing

Serving Suggestion

For a more artistic presentation, first divide the mixed baby greens among 4 dinner plates, piling the greens in the center of each plate. Fan the chicken slices over the top, and alternately tuck sections of sliced pears, yellow pepper, and green beans under the chicken. Finally, drizzle the vinaigrette over each salad, and garnish with the scallions.

NUTRITIONAL FACTS
(per serving, salad only)
Calories: 285
Carbohydrates: 44.9 g
Cholesterol: 52 mg
Fat: 3.4 g
Calories From Fat: 10.1%
Protein: 23.8 g
Sodium: 139 mg

YIELD: **4 SERVINGS**

Chicken and Tangerine Salad

This light-tasting, easy-to-make salad boasts broiled chicken, tangerines, and asparagus. For a double dose of tangerines, dress the salad with Tangerine Vinaigrette.

1 boneless, skinless chicken breast (12 ounces)
Olive oil cooking spray
1/4 teaspoon freshly ground pepper
1/8 teaspoon salt
24 fresh asparagus spears (1 pound), tough ends removed, or 1 can (15 ounces) asparagus spears, drained
3 cups escarole, torn into generous bite-sized pieces
3 cups red leaf lettuce, torn into generous bite-sized pieces
4 seedless tangerines, peeled and segmented
1 orange bell pepper, cut into julienne strips
3 scallions, thinly sliced

Suggested Dressings

★ 1 recipe Tangerine Vinaigrette (page 237)

1 recipe Citrus Vinaigrette (page 219)

1/2 cup commercial fat-free or low-fat poppy seed dressing

1/2 cup commercial fat-free honey French dressing

Serving Suggestion

For a more artistic presentation, make a bed of the escarole and lettuce on each of 4 dinner plates. Fan the chicken slices, slightly overlapping the greens. Center whole asparagus spears under the chicken, and arrange tangerine segments on one side of the asparagus and orange pepper slices on the other. Drizzle with the dressing, and garnish with the scallions.

1. Rinse the chicken, and pat it dry with paper towels.

2. Line a baking sheet with 1-inch sides with aluminum foil. Transfer the chicken to the baking sheet. Lightly coat both sides of the chicken with the cooking spray, and season with pepper and salt.

3. Place the chicken under a preheated broiler, 4 inches from the heat source, and broil for 4 to 5 minutes on each side, or until golden brown on the outside and no longer pink on the inside. Allow the chicken to cool for 10 minutes before cutting into thin slices.

4. Cut the asparagus in half. If using fresh asparagus, cook in a steamer for 2 to 3 minutes, or just until fork tender. Drain well, and allow to come to room temperature.

5. Combine the chicken, asparagus, escarole, lettuce, tangerines, orange pepper, and scallions in a salad bowl. Add the dressing, and toss gently to coat. Serve immediately.

NUTRITIONAL FACTS
(per serving, salad only)

Calories: 181
Carbohydrates: 18.6 g
Cholesterol: 52 mg
Fat: 2.8 g
Calories From Fat: 13.1%
Protein: 22.9 g
Sodium: 158 mg

The Treasure of Tangerines

Tangerines are wonderful eaten as a snack, but they are equally delectable when used to create a marmalade, a juice, or a citrus vinaigrette. And tangerines are available most of the year—from the end of fall through most of the spring. Here are the varieties you are most likely to find at your local market:

Clementines. *Glossy-skinned Clementines are juicier and more flavorful than other tangerines, and are almost seedless. You will find them from the end of November through April.*

Dancy Tangerines. *These tangerines have a reddish-orange skin that peels easily, and a flesh that is deep orange in color. Wonderfully sweet, Dancy tangerines are available in December and January.*

Honey Tangerines. *Uniquely rich in flavor, honey tangerines are slightly flat in appearance with a thin glossy skin. They can be found from January through April.*

Satsuma Tangerines. *With a mildly sweet flavor and a nearly seedless flesh, these juicy tangerines are available from mid-October through December.*

Chicken Fajita Salad

YIELD: **4** SERVINGS

This incredibly delicious salad is topped with creamy sour cream and flavorful salsa. Serve with squares of grilled polenta.

Suggested Dressings

★ 1 recipe Roasted Red Pepper Dressing (page 233)

1 recipe Tomato Vinaigrette (page 240)

½ cup commercial fat-free or low-fat sun-dried tomato dressing

Serving Suggestion

For a more artistic presentation, allow the romaine lettuce leaves to remain whole, and arrange the leaves in a spoke design on each of the individual plates. Overlap slices of chicken and red onion on the lettuce, and top with the dressing. Garnish each salad with a dollop of sour cream, some salsa, and a few olive slices. For the ultimate garnish, top each salad with a few baked tortilla strips (page 35).

NUTRITIONAL FACTS
(per serving, salad only)

Calories: 151
Carbohydrates: 11.1 g
Cholesterol: 53 mg
Fat: 2.9 g
Calories From Fat: 16.6%
Protein: 22.2 g
Sodium: 415 mg

Marinade

¼ cup fresh lime juice
½ teaspoon freshly ground pepper
¼ teaspoon salt

1 boneless, skinless chicken breast (12 ounces)
1 head romaine lettuce, torn into generous bite-sized pieces (about 6 cups)
1 cup thin red onion rings
¼ cup fat-free sour cream
½ cup low-sodium salsa
½ cup sliced black olives (optional)

1. Rinse the chicken, and pat it dry with paper towels.

2. To make the marinade, combine all of the marinade ingredients in a resealable plastic bag, and shake to blend. Add the chicken and turn to coat. Seal the bag, and refrigerate for several hours or overnight, turning the chicken at least once.

3. Remove the chicken from the marinade, discarding the marinade. Place the chicken over moderately hot coals on a grill coated with cooking spray. Cover the grill and cook, turning the chicken every 3 minutes, for 6 to 9 minutes, or until golden brown on the outside and no longer pink on the inside. Alternatively, place the chicken in a preheated grill pan or nonstick skillet over medium heat, and cook for 5 to 7 minutes on each side. Allow the chicken to cool for 10 minutes before cutting into thin slices.

4. Combine the chicken, lettuce, and onion rings in a salad bowl. Add the dressing, and toss gently to coat.

5. To serve, divide the salad among 4 dinner plates. Garnish each serving with a dollop of sour cream, 2 tablespoons of salsa, and, if desired, a few olive slices. Serve immediately.

Making Baked Tortilla Strips

To add height and whimsical interest to a salad, garnish it with baked tortilla strips that point upward from the center of the salad. Simply cut and remove the sides of a corn tortilla to form a square, and cut the square into ¼-inch strips. Then pour ½ to 1 teaspoon of olive oil in a resealable plastic bag, add the tortilla strips, and turn to coat. Transfer the tortilla strips to a baking sheet, and sprinkle with ⅛ teaspoon salt, if desired. Bake in a preheated 450°F oven for 3 to 5 minutes, or until golden brown. Allow the tortilla strips to cool before using.

Oriental Chicken Salad

A teriyaki marinade imbues the chicken with a marvelous spicy flavor that is intensified by grilling. But even when the chicken is cooked under a broiler, it is a delight. Serve with slices of melon.

1 boneless, skinless chicken breast (12 ounces)
1 tablespoon plus 1 teaspoon commercial low-sodium teriyaki marinade
4 cups mixed baby greens
3 scallions, thinly sliced
3 carrots, peeled and cut into julienne strips
⅓ cup toasted slivered almonds (page 69)

1. Rinse the chicken, and pat it dry with paper towels.

2. Brush both sides of the chicken with the teriyaki marinade, and place the chicken over moderately hot coals on a grill coated with cooking spray. Cover the grill and cook, turning the chicken every 3 minutes, for 6 to 9 minutes, or until the chicken is golden brown on the outside and no longer pink on the inside. Alternatively, place the chicken under a preheated broiler, 4 inches from the heat source, and broil for 4 to 5 minutes on each side. Allow the chicken to cool for 10 minutes before cutting into thin slices.

3. Combine the chicken, mixed baby greens, scallions, carrots, and almonds in a salad bowl. Add the dressing, and toss gently to coat. Serve immediately.

YIELD: 4 SERVINGS

Suggested Dressings

★ 1 recipe Oriental Chicken Salad Vinaigrette (page 229)

1 recipe Orange Vinaigrette (page 228)

½ cup commercial fat-free or low-fat poppy seed dressing

**NUTRITIONAL FACTS
(per serving, salad only)**

Calories: 140
Carbohydrates: 8.6 g
Cholesterol: 38 mg
Fat: 2.4 g
Calories From Fat: 15.7%
Protein: 20.9 g
Sodium: 152 mg

YIELD: **4** SERVINGS

Chicken, Green Bean, and Red Pepper Salad

This chicken salad is a must for tarragon lovers. The chicken derives its wonderful flavor from the tarragon and lemon marinade, and later can be dressed with a tarragon vinaigrette. Serve with French bread.

Suggested Dressings

★ 1 recipe Tarragon Vinaigrette (page 238)

1 recipe Caper Vinaigrette (page 217)

½ cup commercial fat-free or low-fat lemon Dijon dressing

Serving Suggestion

For a more artistic presentation, first divide the salad greens among 4 dinner plates. Fan the chicken slices over the top, and tuck sections of green beans and red pepper under the chicken. Randomly distribute the red onion rings over the top. Finally, drizzle each serving with dressing. Garnish with a tomato rose (page 179), if desired.

NUTRITIONAL FACTS
(per serving, salad only)

Calories: 172
Carbohydrates: 16.2 g
Cholesterol: 52 mg
Fat: 2.7 g
Calories From Fat: 13.5%
Protein: 22.9 g
Sodium: 176 mg

Tarragon and Lemon Marinade
¼ cup fresh lemon juice
1 clove garlic, finely chopped
¼ teaspoon dried tarragon
¼ teaspoon salt
¼ teaspoon freshly ground pepper
⅛ teaspoon dried thyme

1 boneless, skinless chicken breast (12 ounces)
12 ounces green beans, trimmed
2 cups chicory, torn into bite-sized pieces
4 cups Bibb lettuce, torn into generous bite-sized pieces
1 cup thin red onion rings
1 large red bell pepper, cut into julienne strips

1. Rinse the chicken, and pat it dry with paper towels.

2. Combine all of the marinade ingredients in a plastic bag, and shake to blend. Add the chicken, seal the bag, and refrigerate for several hours or overnight, turning the chicken at least once.

3. Line a baking sheet with 1-inch sides with aluminum foil. Remove the chicken from the marinade, discarding the marinade, and transfer the chicken to the baking sheet.

4. Place the chicken under a preheated broiler, 4 inches from the heat source, and broil for 4 to 5 minutes on each side, or until golden brown on the outside and no longer pink on the inside. Allow the chicken to cool for 10 minutes before cutting into thin slices. Set aside.

5. Cook the green beans in a steamer for 7 minutes, or just until fork tender. Drain well, and allow to come to room temperature.

6. Combine the chicken, green beans, chicory, lettuce, onion, and red pepper in a salad bowl. Add the dressing, toss gently, and serve.

Chicken Pasta Salad

*This simple but tasty salad is delicious served on
a bed of thinly sliced cantaloupe wedges.*

8 ounces bow-tie pasta

1 boneless, skinless chicken breast (10 ounces)

1-inch slice fresh ginger, peeled

4 ounces fresh snow peas, strings removed

2 scallions, thinly sliced

1 red bell pepper, cut into julienne strips

1 can (8 ounces) sliced water chestnuts, drained

2 cantaloupes, halved, peeled, and cut into thin wedges

3 tablespoons toasted slivered almonds (page 69) (optional)

5 cups broccoli florets, steamed (optional)

1. Cook the pasta according to package directions. Drain well, rinse with cool water, and drain again. Set aside.

2. Rinse the chicken. Place enough water to cover the chicken in a medium-sized saucepan, and bring to a simmer over medium-high heat. Add the chicken and ginger, and simmer uncovered for 10 to 12 minutes, or until the chicken is no longer pink inside. Remove the saucepan from the heat, cover, and allow the chicken to come to room temperature.

3. While the chicken is cooling, place enough water to cover the snow peas in a medium-sized saucepan, and bring to a boil over high heat. Add the snow peas, and boil uncovered for 1 minute. Drain, rinse with cool water, and drain again. Set aside.

4. Transfer the cooled chicken to a strainer and drain well, discarding the ginger. Cut the chicken into cubes.

5. Combine pasta, chicken, snow peas, scallions, red pepper, and water chestnuts in a salad bowl. Add the dressing, and blend gently to coat. Cover and refrigerate for several hours or overnight.

6. Remove the salad from the refrigerator 1 hour before serving, and blend gently. Make a circle of cantaloupe wedges on each of 4 dinner plates. Spoon the chicken salad in the center of the cantaloupe wedges, and, if desired, garnish with the almonds. For an added touch of color, arrange the broccoli florets around the chicken salad with their stems tucked under the salad.

YIELD: 4 SERVINGS

Suggested Dressings

★ 1 recipe Soy Sauce Dressing (page 235)

1 recipe Oriental Dresssing (page 229)

Time-Saving Tip
❑ Substitute 10 ounces of cubed cooked turkey breast for the chicken.

**NUTRITIONAL FACTS
(per serving, salad only)**

Calories: 450
Carbohydrates: 65.2 g
Cholesterol: 43 mg
Fat: 3.4 g
Calories From Fat: 9.1%
Protein: 20.5 g
Sodium: 887 mg

Chicken Salad With Asparagus and Blue Cheese

I suggest using Maytag blue cheese in this recipe—not only because it is made in my home state of Iowa, but because it is a richly flavored cheese that has deservedly won numerous awards. Blue cheese is delicious when combined with grilled or broiled chicken, red onion, and asparagus, and cloaked with a balsamic or red wine vinaigrette. Serve with crusty bread.

Suggested Dressings

★ 1 recipe Balsamic Vinaigrette (page 215)

1 recipe Red Wine Vinaigrette (page 232)

½ cup commercial fat-free or low-fat balsamic vinaigrette

½ cup commercial fat-free or low-fat red wine vinaigrette

Serving Suggestion

For a more artistic presentation, first prepare the chicken salad as described above. Then use 4 cups of arugula to make a wreath on each of 4 dinner plates. Thinly slice 2 medium tomatoes, and arrange the slices in a circle on each plate, overlapping the arugula. Mound the chicken salad in the center of each wreath, and drizzle each serving with vinaigrette.

Time-Saving Tip

❏ Substitute ¼ cup of your favorite commercial citrus marinade for the Lemon and Herb Marinade.

Lemon and Herb Marinade

¼ cup fresh lemon juice
4 cloves garlic, finely chopped
½ teaspoon dried rosemary
½ teaspoon freshly ground pepper
¼ teaspoon dried basil
⅛ teaspoon crushed red pepper

1 boneless, skinless chicken breast (12 ounces)
24 fresh asparagus spears (1 pound), tough ends removed, or 1 can (15 ounces) asparagus spears, drained
12 sun-dried tomatoes (packaged without oil)
6 cups red leaf lettuce, torn into bite-sized pieces
1 yellow bell pepper, cut into julienne strips
1 cup julienne strips red onion
1 ounce Maytag blue cheese or other blue cheese, crumbled

1. Rinse the chicken, and pat it dry with paper towels.

2. To make marinade, combine all of the marinade ingredients in a resealable plastic bag, and shake to blend. Add the chicken and turn to coat. Seal the bag, and refrigerate for several hours or overnight, turning the chicken at least once.

3. Remove the chicken from the marinade, discarding the marinade. Place the chicken over moderately hot coals on a grill coated with cooking spray. Cover the grill and cook, turning the chicken every 3 minutes, for 6 to 9 minutes, or until the chicken is golden brown on the outside and no longer pink on the inside. Alternatively, place the chicken under a preheated broiler, 4 inches from the heat source, and broil for 4 to 5 minutes on each side. Allow the chicken to cool for 10 minutes before cutting into thin slices. Set aside.

4. Cut the asparagus into 2-inch lengths. If using fresh asparagus, cook in a steamer for 2 to 3 minutes, or just until fork tender. Drain well, and allow to come to room temperature.

5. Place the sun-dried tomatoes in a small heat-proof bowl, and add enough boiling water to cover. Allow to sit for 5 to 15 minutes, or until the tomatoes are soft. Drain well, and cut into thin slices.

6. To serve, combine the chicken, asparagus, tomatoes, lettuce, yellow pepper, onion, and blue cheese in a salad bowl. Add the vinaigrette, and toss gently to coat. Serve immediately.

NUTRITIONAL FACTS
(per serving, salad only)

Calories: 172
Carbohydrates: 16.2 g
Cholesterol: 52 mg
Fat: 2.7 g
Calories From Fat: 13.5%
Protein: 22.9 g
Sodium: 176 mg

Making Dried Tomatoes

Although sun-dried tomatoes are now widely available in supermarkets and specialty shops, you can easily make dried tomatoes at home and use them in any recipe that calls for the commercial product. This is an especially good idea when your summer garden provides you with more tomatoes than you can easily use in salads, sandwiches, and sauces.

Simply cut $1\frac{1}{4}$ to $2\frac{1}{2}$ pounds of Roma tomatoes in half. Place the tomatoes cut side up on a baking sheet, and sprinkle with $\frac{1}{4}$ to $\frac{1}{2}$ teaspoon salt. Bake in a preheated 190°F oven for 6 to 10 hours, or until the tomatoes are dried. Allow the tomatoes to cool before storing in an airtight container. Your homemade dried tomatoes will keep for up to three months.

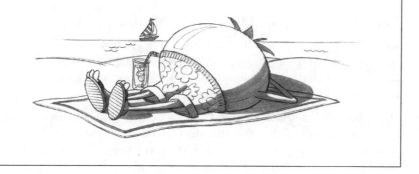

YIELD: **4** SERVINGS

Chicken, Black Bean, and Corn Salad

This salad is as versatile as it is delicious. The bean and corn salad alone makes an excellent vegetarian meal if you choose to omit the marinated chicken. Although the avocado lends some fat to the dish, this delicious fruit is nutrient-packed. And, if you prefer, the avocado can be omitted without seriously compromising the taste of the salad. Serve with squares of cornbread.

Suggested Dressings

★ 1 recipe Lime Vinaigrette (page 226)

1 recipe Southwestern Vinaigrette (page 235)

½ cup commercial fat-free or low-fat cilantro lime vinaigrette

Time-Saving Tip
❏ Substitute ½ cup of your favorite commercial Southwestern marinade for the homemade marinade.

NUTRITIONAL FACTS
(per serving, salad only)
Calories: 305
Carbohydrates: 34.2 g
Cholesterol: 52 mg
Fat: 8.5 g
Calories From Fat: 24.2%
Protein: 25.6 g
Sodium: 59 mg

Marinade

½ cup unsweetened pineapple juice

2 ½ tablespoons apple cider vinegar

1 tablespoon honey

¼ teaspoon ground coriander

¼ teaspoon chili powder

¼ teaspoon ground cumin

1 boneless, skinless chicken breast (12 ounces)

1 cup cooked or canned black beans, rinsed and drained

1 cup canned whole kernel corn, drained

1 avocado, peeled, pitted, and diced (reserve the pit)

1 can (2 ounces) chopped green chilies, drained

2 Roma tomatoes, seeded and diced

24 romaine lettuce leaves

½ cup fat-free sour cream

½ cup low-sodium salsa

4 red loose-leaf lettuce leaves rolled into tight cylinders (optional)

1. Rinse the chicken, and pat it dry with paper towels.

2. To make the marinade, combine all of the marinade ingredients in a resealable plastic bag, and shake to blend. Add the chicken and turn to coat. Seal the bag, and refrigerate for several hours or overnight, turning the chicken at least once.

3. Combine the black beans, corn, avocado, and chilies in a medium-sized bowl. Add just enough vinaigrette to coat. Place the reserved avocado pit in the salad to prevent the avocado from turning brown. Cover and refrigerate until ready to serve.

Top: Mexican Chicken Salad
(page 50)

Center: Teriyaki Turkey Salad
With Papaya (page 74)

Bottom: Chicken and
Tangerine Salad (page 32)

Top Left: Chinese Chicken Salad (page 43)

Top Right: Turkey, Fruit, and Rice Salad (page 63)

Bottom: Chicken Fajita Salad (page 34)

4. Remove the chicken from the marinade, discarding the marinade. Place the chicken over moderately hot coals on a grill coated with cooking spray, and cook, turning the chicken every 3 minutes, for 6 to 9 minutes, or until golden brown on the outside and no longer pink on the inside. Alternatively, place the chicken under a preheated broiler, 4 inches from the heat source, and broil for 4 to 5 minutes on each side. Allow the chicken to cool for 10 minutes before cutting into thin slices.

5. Remove the black bean and corn salad from the refrigerator, and discard the avocado pit. Add the tomatoes and blend gently.

6. To serve, arrange the leaves of romaine lettuce in a spoke design on each of 4 dinner plates. Spoon a serving of black bean and corn salad in the center of the lettuce, and slightly flatten the mound. Fan slices of chicken on top of the salad, and drizzle with the remaining vinaigrette. Garnish each serving with dollops of sour cream and salsa. For an added touch, stand a red leaf lettuce cylinder upright in the salad, if desired. Serve immediately.

Seeding a Tomato

To remove seeds from a tomato, first slice off the top and bottom of the tomato. Then turn the tomato so that one end is placed over a dish, and gently squeeze. The seeds should easily drop into the dish.

Making Scallion Flowers

Scallion flowers add color and a decorative touch to any salad, and are especially nice on Asian-style dishes. To make scallion flowers, discard the root ends of 4 scallions, and cut the remainder into 2-inch lengths. Insert the point of a needle ½-inch from the end of one of the segments, and carefully pull it up through the end of the scallion piece. (Note that this can also be done with a sharp paring knife.) Rotate the scallion slightly and repeat this process. Continue rotating the scallion and making cuts until the end of the scallion piece resembles a brush. Repeat the same procedure at the other end of the segment. Place the scallions in a bowl filled with ice water for 5 minutes, or until the scallions curl. Drain well, and use to garnish a variety of dishes.

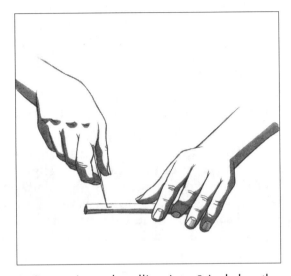

1. Cut a trimmed scallion into 2-inch lengths. Insert the point of a needle ½ inch from the end of each segment, and pull it up through the end of the scallion piece.

2. Rotate the scallion and repeat the process until the end of the scallion looks like a brush. Repeat this procedure at the other end of the segment.

3. Place the scallion segments in a bowl filled with ice water and set aside for 5 minutes, or until the ends of the scallions curl.

Chinese Chicken Salad

A zesty vinaigrette intensifies the exotic flavors of this marvelous composition of spicy Oriental chicken, vegetables, and pasta. Serve with orange wedges.

1 boneless, skinless chicken breast (12 ounces)
2 tablespoons Sweet Ginger Sesame Hibachi Grill Sauce* or other low-sodium teriyaki marinade
8 ounces rotini pasta or fresh Chinese noodles
4 ounces fresh snow peas, strings removed
1 red bell pepper, diced
1 can (8 ounces) sliced water chestnuts, drained
3 scallions, thinly sliced
2 large carrots, peeled and cut into julienne strips
3 tablespoons toasted sesame seeds (page 69)
4 scallion flowers (page 42) (optional)

* Sweet Ginger Sesame Hibachi Grill Sauce can be found in the Oriental or barbecue sauce section of most supermarkets.

1. Rinse the chicken, and pat it dry with paper towels.

2. Line a baking sheet with 1-inch sides with aluminum foil. Transfer the chicken to the baking sheet, and brush both sides with the grill sauce or marinade.

3. Place the chicken under a preheated broiler, 4 inches from the heat source, and broil for 4 to 5 minutes on each side, or until golden brown on the outside and no longer pink on the inside. Allow the chicken to cool for 10 minutes before cutting into cubes.

4. Cook the pasta according to package directions. Drain, rinse with cool water, and drain again. Set aside.

5. Place enough water to cover the snow peas in a medium-sized saucepan, and bring to a boil over high heat. Add the snow peas, and boil uncovered for 1 minute. Drain and rinse with cold water. Cut the snow peas in half on the diagonal, and set aside.

6. To serve, combine the chicken, pasta, snow peas, red pepper, water chestnuts, scallions, carrots, sesame seeds, and vinaigrette in a salad bowl, and toss gently. Serve immediately, or refrigerate for several hours, removing the salad from the refrigerator 1 hour before serving. Garnish each serving with a scallion flower, if desired.

YIELD: 4 SERVINGS

Suggested Dressings

★ 1 recipe Orange Vinaigrette (page 228)

1 recipe Spicy Vinaigrette (page 236)

½ cup commercial fat-free or low-fat Oriental vinaigrette

NUTRITIONAL FACTS
(per serving, salad only)

Calories: 348
Carbohydrates: 54.9 g
Cholesterol: 52 mg
Fat: 2.4 g
Calories From Fat: 15.7%
Protein: 26.5 g
Sodium: 276 mg

Cobb Chicken Salad

Suggested Dressings

★ 1 recipe Cobb Salad Dressing (page 220)

1 recipe Maytag Blue Cheese and Balsamic Vinaigrette (page 227)

½ cup commercial fat-free or low-fat blue cheese dressing

½ cup commercial fat-free or low-fat peppercorn ranch dressing

Time-Saving Tip

❑ When you're short on time, omit the marinade. Instead, lightly coat the chicken breast with an olive oil cooking spray, and season with ¼ teaspoon of freshly ground pepper and ⅛ teaspoon of salt before broiling.

NUTRITIONAL FACTS
(per serving, salad only)

Calories: 324
Carbohydrates: 27.6 g
Cholesterol: 73 mg
Fat: 12.2 g
Calories From Fat: 37.5%
Protein: 30.3 g
Sodium: 512 mg

Cobb salad was made famous by Bob Cobb's Brown Derby restaurant in Los Angeles, California. This salad is ideal fare when having friends over for a casual dinner. Start the meal with mugs of chilled gazpacho, and serve with a basket of pita crisps or crusty rolls.

Marinade

¼ cup fresh lemon juice

¼ teaspoon freshly ground pepper

¼ teaspoon salt

¼ teaspoon paprika

⅛ teaspoon dried thyme

1 clove garlic, finely chopped

1 boneless, skinless chicken breast (12 ounces)

1 head butterhead lettuce, torn into generous bite-sized pieces (about 6 cups)

4 slices 95% fat-free turkey bacon, cooked according to package directions and crumbled

16 cherry tomatoes, stemmed and halved

2 hard-boiled eggs, whites only, quartered

1 ounce Roquefort cheese, crumbled

1 avocado, peeled, pitted, and cubed

1. Rinse the chicken, and pat it dry with paper towels.

2. To make the marinade, combine all of the marinade ingredients in a resealable plastic bag, and shake to blend. Add the chicken and turn to coat. Seal the bag, and refrigerate for several hours or overnight, turning the chicken at least once.

3. Line a baking sheet with 1-inch sides with aluminum foil. Remove the chicken from the marinade, discarding the marinade, and transfer the chicken to the baking sheet.

4. Place the chicken under a preheated broiler, 4 inches from the heat source, and broil for 4 to 5 minutes on each side, or until golden brown on the outside and no longer pink on the inside. Allow the chicken to cool for 10 minutes before cutting into thin slices.

5. Combine the chicken, lettuce, bacon, tomatoes, eggs, Roquefort cheese, and avocado in a salad bowl. Add the dressing, and toss gently to coat. Serve immediately.

Kitch's Chicken and Pasta Salad

YIELD: 6 SERVINGS

This salad received an enthusiastic thumbs up from my family! Every bite of this eye-catching salad bursts with flavor. Best of all, this dish is very easy to prepare. Accompany with an assortment of melon wedges.

1 boneless, skinless chicken breast (12 ounces)
4 cans (10.75 ounces each) low-sodium chicken broth
15 peppercorns
1 teaspoon dried thyme
12 ounces bow-tie pasta
½ cup chopped fresh parsley
½ cup thinly sliced scallions
1 package (5 ounces) prewashed baby spinach, stems removed (about 6 cups)

Suggested Dressings

★ 1 recipe Soy Sauce Vinaigrette (page 236)

**NUTRITIONAL FACTS
(per serving, salad only)**

Calories: 357
Carbohydrates: 56.7 g
Cholesterol: 35 mg
Fat: 4.4 g
Calories From Fat: 21.5%
Protein: 25.2 g
Sodium: 669 mg

1. Rinse the chicken, and set aside.

2. Place the broth, peppercorns, and thyme in a large saucepan, and bring to a simmer over medium-high heat. Add the chicken, and simmer uncovered for 10 to 12 minutes, or until the chicken is no longer pink inside. Remove the saucepan from the heat, cover, and allow the chicken to come to room temperature.

3. While the chicken is cooling, cook the pasta according to package directions. Drain, rinse with cool water, and drain again. Set aside.

4. Transfer the cooled chicken to a strainer and drain well, discarding the peppercorns. Cut the chicken into thin slices.

5. Place the pasta in a salad bowl. Over the layer of pasta, create layers of the chicken, parsley, and scallions. Cover and refrigerate for several hours or overnight.

6. Remove the salad from the refrigerator 1 hour before serving. Add the spinach and the vinaigrette, and toss gently to coat. Serve immediately.

Honey-Glazed Chicken Salad With Caramelized Onions

Caramelizing the red onions intensifies their sweetness so that they harmonize more perfectly with the flavors of the honey glaze and the balsamic vinaigrette.

Suggested Dressings

★ 1 recipe Balsamic Vinaigrette (page 215)

1 recipe Maytag Blue Cheese and Balsamic Vinaigrette (page 227)

½ cup commercial fat-free or low-fat balsamic vinaigrette

Honey Marinade

2 tablespoons honey
1 tablespoon hot honey mustard
1 tablespoon dry white wine
1 clove garlic, finely chopped
½ teaspoon freshly ground pepper
¼ teaspoon salt
1 boneless, skinless chicken breast (12 ounces)
2 red bell peppers
1 large red onion, thinly sliced and separated into rings
1 can (6 ounces) unsweetened pineapple juice
6 cups mixed baby greens

Serving Suggestion

For a more artistic presentation, first divide the mixed baby greens among 4 dinner plates. Spoon a serving of caramelized onions over the greens, and top with slices of chicken and roasted red pepper. Finally, drizzle each serving with vinaigrette and garnish with a tomato rose (page 179), if desired.

1. Rinse the chicken, and pat it dry with paper towels.

2. To make the honey marinade, combine all of the marinade ingredients in a resealable plastic bag, and shake to blend. Add the chicken and turn to coat. Seal the bag, and refrigerate for several hours or overnight, turning the chicken at least once.

3. To roast the peppers, place the peppers on a baking sheet that has been lined with aluminum foil. Broil under a preheated broiler, turning the peppers as the skins blacken, for 20 to 25 minutes, or until the skins are charred all over. Once roasted, place in a plastic bag, seal, and allow to steam for 15 minutes. When the peppers are cool enough to handle, peel away the skin and remove the tops and seeds. (Do not rinse the peppers.) Cut the peppers into strips, and set aside.

Time-Saving Tips

❑ Substitute ¼ cup of your favorite commercial honey marinade for the Honey Marinade.

❑ Substitute ½ cup of commercial sweet roasted bell peppers for the home-made roasted peppers.

4. To make the caramelized onions, combine the onion and pineapple juice in a large skillet, and bring to a simmer over moderate heat. Simmer, stirring occasionally, for 30 minutes, or until the onions are golden brown. Set aside.

5. Remove the chicken from the marinade, discarding the marinade. Place the chicken over moderately hot coals on a grill coated with cooking spray. Cover the grill and cook, turning the chicken every 3 minutes, for 6 to 9 minutes, or until golden brown on the outside and no longer pink on the inside. Alternatively, place the chicken under a preheated broiler, 4 inches from the heat source, and broil for 4 to 5 minutes on each side. Allow the chicken to cool for 10 minutes before cutting into thin slices.

6. To serve, combine the chicken, roasted peppers, caramelized onions, and mixed baby greens in a salad bowl. Add the vinaigrette, and toss gently to coat. Serve immediately.

NUTRITIONAL FACTS
(per serving, salad only)

Calories: 207
Carbohydrates: 24.6 g
Cholesterol: 52 mg
Fat: 2.7 g
Calories From Fat: 11.5%
Protein: 22.2 g
Sodium: 248 mg

The Sweetness of Honey

We all know that honey can add sweetness and a distinctive flavor to a variety of dishes, from salads to desserts. But did you know that to produce one pound of honey, bees must touch approximately 2 million blossoms? The kind of blossoms visited by the bees determines the variety of honey produced. Honeys can range from being very clear and colorless to having an intensely dark hue. As a rule, the darker-colored honeys such as buckwheat have a more intense flavor. Looking for a sweeter honey? Try alfalfa, orange blossom, or clover. And for a buttery rich taste, you'll want to sample avocado honey. Finally, a few varieties made from such flowering herbs as thyme and rosemary have an aromatic flavor.

To keep your favorite honey at its best, store it at room temperature. Then dip in whenever you want to add a touch of natural sweetness to salad dressings or any other culinary creation.

Italian Chicken and Pasta Salad

YIELD: **4** SERVINGS

This is the perfect salad to take on a picnic or to an outdoor party. It can be served in a salad bowl, or it can be arranged attractively with the salad in the center of a platter lined with leaves of Bibb lettuce and thinly sliced tomatoes. Serve with Italian bread.

Suggested Dressings

★ 1 recipe Italian Vinaigrette (page 224)

1 recipe Greek Vinaigrette (page 222)

½ cup commercial fat-free or low-fat Italian vinaigrette

½ cup commercial fat-free or low-fat Italian herb and cheese dressing

1 boneless, skinless chicken breast (12 ounces)
2 sprigs fresh thyme
1 bay leaf
6 peppercorns
8 ounces rigatoni or rotini pasta
1 can (13.75 ounces) quartered artichokes hearts, drained
1 yellow bell pepper, diced
1 jar (4 ounces) slivered pimientos, drained
½ cup thinly sliced celery
½ cup diced red onion
¼ cup toasted pine nuts (page 69) (optional)

Time-Saving Tip
❏ Substitute 12 ounces of cubed cooked turkey breast for the chicken.

1. Rinse the chicken. Place enough water to cover the chicken in a medium-sized saucepan, and bring to a simmer over medium-high heat. Add the chicken, thyme, bay leaf, and peppercorns, and simmer uncovered for 10 to 12 minutes, or until the chicken is no longer pink inside. Remove the saucepan from the heat, cover, and allow the chicken to come to room temperature.

2. While the chicken is cooling, cook the pasta according to package directions. Drain, rinse with cool water, and drain again. Set aside.

**NUTRITIONAL FACTS
(per serving, salad only)**
Calories: 354
Carbohydrates: 56.2
Cholesterol: 52 mg
Fat: 2.4 g
Calories From Fat: 12.9%
Protein: 28.7 g
Sodium: 162 mg

3. Transfer the cooled chicken to a strainer and drain well, discarding the thyme, bay leaf, and peppercorns. Cut the chicken into cubes.

4. Combine the chicken, pasta, artichokes, yellow pepper, pimientos, celery, onion, and pine nuts, if desired, in a bowl. Add the dressing, and toss gently to coat. Cover and refrigerate for several hours or overnight.

5. Remove the salad from the refrigerator 1 hour before serving. Blend gently, and serve.

Mediterranean Chicken Salad

The marvelous flavors of the Mediterranean are highlighted in this delicious salad. Set the table with a checkered tablecloth; add a basket of crusty bread, a bottle of red wine, and candles; and imagine yourself enjoying a warm Mediterranean breeze. Better yet, rent a villa in Amalfi and bring the recipe along!

1 boneless, skinless chicken breast (12 ounces)
Olive oil cooking spray
1/4 teaspoon freshly ground pepper
1/8 teaspoon salt
1 head romaine lettuce, torn into generous bite-sized pieces (about 6 cups)
1 small green bell pepper, thinly sliced into rings
1 small red bell pepper, thinly sliced into rings
1 cup julienne strips red onion
1 can (13.75 ounces) quartered artichoke hearts, drained
12 cherry tomatoes, stemmed and halved
2 ounces feta cheese, crumbled
8 pitted Kalamata olives (optional)

Suggested Dressings

★ 1 recipe Greek Vinaigrette (page 222)

1 recipe Italian Vinaigrette (page 224)

1/2 cup commercial fat-free or low-fat Greek vinaigrette

1/2 cup commercial fat-free or low-fat Italian vinaigrette

NUTRITIONAL FACTS
(per serving, salad only)

Calories: 327
Carbohydrates: 41.8 g
Cholesterol: 64 mg
Fat: 7.3 g
Calories From Fat: 18.5%
Protein: 30.6 g
Sodium: 417 mg

1. Rinse the chicken, and pat it dry with paper towels. Lightly coat both sides of the chicken with the cooking spray, and season with pepper and salt.

2. Place the chicken over moderately hot coals on a grill coated with cooking spray. Cover the grill and cook, turning the chicken every 3 minutes, for 6 to 9 minutes, or until golden brown on the outside and no longer pink on the inside. Alternatively, place the chicken under a preheated broiler, 4 inches from the heat source, and broil for 4 to 5 minutes on each side. Allow the chicken to cool for 10 minutes before cutting into thin slices.

3. To serve, place the chicken, lettuce, bell peppers, onion, artichoke hearts, tomatoes, feta cheese, and olives, if desired, in a salad bowl. Add the vinaigrette, and toss gently to coat. Serve immediately.

Mexican Chicken Salad

YIELD: 4 SERVINGS

Suggested Dressings

★ 1 recipe Mexican Vinaigrette (page 228)

1 recipe Southwestern Vinaigrette (page 235)

½ cup commercial fat-free or low-fat Santa Fe blend dressing

Time-Saving Tip
❑ Substitute ¼ cup of your favorite commercial Southwestern marinade for the Spicy Chicken Marinade.

NUTRITIONAL FACTS
(per serving, salad only)
Calories: 226
Carbohydrates: 24.8 g
Cholesterol: 52 mg
Fat: 3.1 g
Calories From Fat: 14.9%
Protein: 24.2 g
Sodium: 217 mg

With its colorful array of spicy ingredients, this exceptional salad has a definite south-of-the-border taste and appearance. Serve with squares of cornbread.

Spicy Chicken Marinade

2 tablespoons fresh lime juice

2 tablespoons fat-free chicken broth

2 tablespoons coarsely chopped fresh cilantro

2 cloves garlic, finely chopped

¼ teaspoon ground cumin

¼ teaspoon chili powder

⅛ teaspoon freshly ground pepper

⅛ teaspoon cayenne pepper

1 boneless, skinless chicken breast (12 ounces)

2 cups prewashed baby spinach, stems removed

2 cups romaine lettuce, torn into generous bite-sized pieces

1½ cups commercial fat-free spicy croutons

2 Roma tomatoes, quartered

1 cup canned whole kernel corn, drained

½ cup julienne strips jicama*

½ cup julienne strips red bell pepper

½ cup thin red onion rings

1 avocado, peeled, pitted, and cubed (optional)

½ cup pitted black olives (optional)

8 canned whole baby sweet corn, drained (optional)

* A root vegetable resembling a turnip, jicama can be found in the produce section of many supermarkets.

1. Rinse the chicken, and pat it dry with paper towels.

2. To make the marinade, combine all of the marinade ingredients in a resealable plastic bag, and shake to blend. Add the chicken and turn to coat. Seal the bag, and refrigerate for several hours or overnight, turning the chicken at least once.

3. Line a baking sheet with 1-inch sides with aluminum foil. Remove the chicken from the marinade, discarding the marinade, and transfer the chicken to the baking sheet.

4. Place the chicken under a preheated broiler, 4 inches from the heat source, and broil for 4 to 5 minutes on each side, or until golden brown on the outside and no longer pink on the inside. Allow the chicken to cool for 10 minutes before cutting into thin slices.

5. To serve, combine the chicken, spinach, lettuce, croutons, tomatoes, corn, jicama, red pepper, onion rings, and avocado and olives, if desired, in a salad bowl. Add the dressing, and toss gently to coat. Divide the salad among 4 individual salad bowls, and garnish each serving with 2 ears of baby sweet corn, if desired. Serve immediately.

YIELD: **4** SERVINGS

Raspberry Marinated Chicken Salad With Papaya

By marinating the chicken in a savory raspberry marinade, you will give it a distinct raspberry flavor—one that can be further intensified by a raspberry vinaigrette. A great salad for raspberry lovers!

Suggested Dressings

★ 1 recipe Raspberry Vinaigrette (page 232)

½ cup commercial fat-free or low-fat raspberry vinaigrette

½ cup commercial fat-free or low-fat poppy seed dressing

Serving Suggestion

For a more artistic presentation, first lightly dress the mixed baby greens with just enough of the dressing to make the greens glisten. Then make a nest of the greens on each of 4 dinner plates, and fan the chicken slices over the greens. Place the papaya and star fruit slices off to one side of the chicken, and drizzle the remaining vinaigrette over each salad. Garnish with the raspberries and scallions.

Marinade
¼ cup raspberry vinegar
1 tablespoon medium-dry red wine, such as Burgundy or zinfandel
1 tablespoon Dijon mustard
1 tablespoon raspberry preserves
1 shallot, minced
¼ teaspoon salt
¼ teaspoon freshly ground pepper
1 boneless, skinless chicken breast (12 ounces)
6 cups mixed baby greens
1 papaya or mango, peeled, seeded, and cut into ¼-inch-thick slices
1 star fruit, thinly sliced
1 pint fresh raspberries
4 scallions, thinly sliced

1. Rinse the chicken, and pat it dry with paper towels.

2. To make the marinade, combine all of the marinade ingredients in a resealable plastic bag, and shake to blend. Add the chicken and turn to coat. Seal the bag, and refrigerate for several hours or overnight, turning the chicken at least once.

3. Line a baking sheet with 1-inch sides with aluminum foil. Remove the chicken from the marinade, discarding the marinade, and transfer the chicken to the baking sheet.

4. Place the chicken under a preheated broiler, 4 inches from the heat source, and broil for 4 to 5 minutes on each side, or until golden brown on the outside and no longer pink on the inside. Allow the chicken to cool for 10 minutes before cutting into thin slices.

NUTRITIONAL FACTS
(per serving, salad only)

Calories: 244
Carbohydrates: 32.7 g
Cholesterol: 52 mg
Fat: 3.3 g
Calories From Fat: 11.7%
Protein: 24.3 g
Sodium: 215 mg

5. To serve, combine the chicken, mixed baby greens, papaya or mango, star fruit, raspberries, and scallions in a salad bowl. Add the dressing, and toss gently to coat. Serve immediately.

Curried Turkey Salad With Grapes and Raisins

If you appreciate the unique flavors of Indian cuisine, you will be delighted by this salad. It can be served surrounded by thinly sliced melons, on a bed of greens, or even topped with a dab of Cranberry Chutney (page 68) and sliced bananas.

1 Vidalia onion or other sweet onion, coarsely chopped
2 cloves garlic, finely chopped
1 teaspoon curry powder
1 cup basmati rice or white rice
2 cups water
2 cups cubed cooked turkey breast (about 12 ounces)
1 cup seedless green grapes, stemmed and halved
¼ cup plus 2 tablespoons golden raisins
2 scallions, thinly sliced

YIELD: 4 SERVINGS

Suggested Dressings
★ 1 recipe Mango Chutney Vinaigrette (page 227)

NUTRITIONAL FACTS
(per serving, salad only)
Calories: 295
Carbohydrates: 50.1 g
Cholesterol: 36 mg
Fat: 2.2 g
Calories From Fat: 6.7%
Protein: 19.4 g
Sodium: 73 mg

1. Coat a large saucepan with nonstick cooking spray, and preheat over medium heat. Add the onion and garlic, and sauté, stirring occasionally, for 9 minutes, or until golden brown. Add the curry powder, and stir-fry for 1 additional minute.

2. Increase the heat to high, stir in the rice and water, and bring to a simmer. Reduce the heat to low, cover, and cook for 20 minutes, or until all of the water has been absorbed. Transfer the rice to a salad bowl, and lightly toss to blend. Allow the rice to cool for 15 minutes.

3. Add the turkey, grapes, raisins, scallions, and dressing to the rice, and toss gently to blend. Cover and refrigerate for several hours.

4. Remove the salad from the refrigerator 1 hour before serving. Toss gently, and serve.

Red Pepper Fettuccine and Chicken Salad

YIELD: 4 SERVINGS

Suggested Dressings

★ 1 recipe Pasta Vinaigrette (page 230)

1 recipe Mexican Vinaigrette (page 228)

½ cup commercial fat-free or low-fat cilantro lime vinaigrette

NUTRITIONAL FACTS
(per serving, salad only)

Calories: 377
Carbohydrates: 57.4 g
Cholesterol: 43 mg
Fat: 9.2 g
Calories From Fat: 45.6%
Protein: 27.4 g
Sodium: 307.5 mg

The wonderfully wide variety of flavored pastas now available gives the creative cook an easy way to add taste and color to a salad. Serve this fettuccine dish with an assortment of melon slices.

3 jalapeño chilies, seeded and minced*
1 boneless, skinless chicken breast (10 ounces)
1 onion, quartered
4 sprigs fresh parsley
6 peppercorns
9 ounces fresh red pepper fettuccine pasta or favorite pasta
4 scallions, thinly sliced
1 avocado, peeled, pitted, and cubed
Fresh parsley or cilantro sprigs (optional)

* To protect your hands from the seeds of the jalapeños, be sure to use rubber or latex gloves while working with the peppers, and wash the knife and cutting board immediately after use.

1. To roast the jalapeños, place the chilies on a baking sheet that has been lined with aluminum foil. Broil under a preheated broiler, turning the chilies as the skins blacken, for 8 to 12 minutes, or until the skins are charred all over. Once roasted, place in a plastic bag, seal, and allow to steam for 15 minutes. When the chilies are cool enough to handle, peel away the skin and remove the tops and seeds. (Do not rinse the peppers.) Cut the chilies into thin slices, and set aside.

2. Rinse the chicken. Place enough water to cover the chicken in a medium-sized saucepan, and bring to a simmer over medium-high heat. Add the chicken, onion, parsley, and peppercorns, and simmer uncovered for 10 to 12 minutes, or until the chicken is no longer pink inside. Remove the saucepan from the heat, cover, and allow the chicken to come to room temperature.

3. While the chicken is cooling, cook the pasta according to package directions. Drain, rinse with cool water, and drain again.

4. Transfer the cooled chicken to a strainer and drain well, discarding the onion, parsley, and peppercorns. Cut the chicken into small cubes.

5. To serve, place the pasta in a salad bowl and separate any strands that may be clinging to one another. Add the chicken, chilies, scallions, avocado, and vinaigrette, and toss gently to coat. Garnish with sprigs of parsley or cilantro, if desired, and serve.

Mandarin Turkey Salad

Featuring teriyaki-flavored turkey and chunks of fresh pineapple, this salad has an alluring Pacific Rim flavor that can be further enhanced by a well-chosen vinaigrette. Add low-fat muffins and a tall glass of iced tea, and the meal is complete.

1 turkey breast tenderloin (12 ounces), cut into 2 pieces
2 tablespoons Sweet Ginger Sesame Hibachi Grill Sauce* or other low-sodium teriyaki marinade
6 cups red leaf lettuce, torn into generous bite-sized pieces
2 cups cubed fresh pineapple (about 1 medium)
4 scallions, thinly sliced
1 tablespoon toasted sesame seeds (page 69) (optional)

* Sweet Ginger Sesame Hibachi Grill Sauce can be found in the Oriental or barbecue sauce section of most supermarkets.

1. Rinse the turkey, and pat it dry with paper towels. Place 1 turkey piece in a large resealable plastic bag. Remove as much air as possible from the bag and seal. Using a meat tenderizer, flatten it into a $1/4$-inch-thick fillet. Repeat with the remaining turkey piece.

2. Brush both sides of the turkey with the grill sauce or marinade.

3. Lightly coat a large nonstick skillet with olive oil cooking spray, and preheat over medium heat. Add the turkey and sauté for 3 minutes on each side, or until golden brown on the outside and no longer pink on the inside. Allow the turkey to cool for 10 minutes before cutting into thin slices.

4. To serve, combine the turkey, lettuce, pineapple, scallions, and sesame seeds, if desired, in a salad bowl. Add the dressing, and toss gently to coat. Serve immediately.

YIELD: 4 SERVINGS

Suggested Dressings

★ 1 recipe Mandarin Dressing (page 226)

$1/2$ cup commercial fat-free or low-fat poppy seed dressing

Serving Suggestion

For a more artistic presentation, first divide the red leaf lettuce among 4 dinner plates. Fan the turkey slices over the top, and distribute the pineapple, scallions, and sesame seeds over the turkey. Finally, drizzle each serving with the dressing, and garnish with a scallion flower (page 42) if desired.

NUTRITIONAL FACTS (per serving, salad only)

Calories: 163
Carbohydrates: 19.5 g
Cholesterol: 37 mg
Fat: 2.2 g
Calories From Fat: 11.8%
Protein: 17.9 g
Sodium: 234 mg

Santa Fe Chicken, Pineapple, and Avocado Salad

This fabulous Southwestern salad is a perfect balance of spicy marinated chicken, sweet pineapple, velvety avocado, and tangy vinaigrette. Serve with corn muffins.

Suggested Dressings

★ 1 recipe Apple Cider Vinaigrette (page 214)

1 recipe Cilantro Vinaigrette (page 219)

½ cup commercial fat-free or low-fat cilantro lime vinaigrette

½ cup commercial fat-free or low-fat Santa Fe blend dressing

Serving Suggestion

For a more artistic presentation, allow the romaine lettuce leaves to remain whole, and arrange the leaves in a spoke design on each of 4 dinner plates. Mound the salad in the center of the lettuce. Finally, garnish each serving with 2 to 3 baked tortilla strips (page 35) that point upward from the center of the salad.

Time-Saving Tips
❏ Substitute ¼ cup of your favorite commercial Southwestern marinade for the homemade marinade.

Marinade

¼ cup fresh lime juice
2 tablespoons coarsely chopped fresh cilantro
¼ teaspoon ground cumin
¼ teaspoon chili powder
¼ teaspoon paprika
¼ teaspoon freshly ground pepper
⅛ teaspoon salt

1 boneless, skinless chicken breast (12 ounces)
1 head romaine lettuce, torn into generous bite-sized pieces (about 6 cups)
1 fresh pineapple, peeled, cored, and cubed
1 avocado, peeled, pitted, and thinly sliced
1 cup julienne strips jicama*
Fresh cilantro sprigs (optional)

* A root vegetable resembling a turnip, jicama can be found in the produce section of many supermarkets.

1. Rinse the chicken, and pat it dry with paper towels.

2. To make the marinade, combine all of the marinade ingredients in a resealable plastic bag, and shake to blend. Add the chicken and turn to coat. Refrigerate for several hours or overnight, turning the chicken at least once.

3. Line a baking sheet with 1-inch sides with aluminum foil. Remove the chicken from the marinade, discarding the marinade, and transfer the chicken to the baking sheet.

4. Place the chicken under a preheated broiler, 4 inches from the heat source, and broil for 4 to 5 minutes on each side, or until golden brown on the outside and no longer pink on the inside. Allow the chicken to cool for 10 minutes before cutting into thin slices.

5. To serve, combine the chicken, lettuce, pineapple, avocado, and jicama in a salad bowl. Add the dressing, and toss gently to coat. Garnish with sprigs of cilantro, if desired, and serve immediately.

NUTRITIONAL FACTS
(per serving, salad only)

Calories: 279
Carbohydrates: 31.6 g
Cholesterol: 52 mg
Fat: 9 g
Calories From Fat: 27.5%
Protein: 22.1 g
Sodium: 128 mg

Spinach and Mushroom Salad With Turkey Bacon

There is nothing I enjoy more than a dinnertime compliment from my children, and this salad generated rave reviews from my finicky group. I hope that you also enjoy this savory combination of healthful ingredients.

6 cups prewashed baby spinach, stems removed

2 cups commercial fat-free seasoned croutons

8 ounces fresh mushrooms, thinly sliced

8 slices 95% fat-free turkey bacon, cooked according to package directions and cut into bite-sized pieces

4 hard-boiled eggs, whites only, quartered

3 Roma tomatoes, quartered

¼ cup grated fat-free Parmesan cheese

1 avocado, peeled, pitted, and cubed (optional)

⅓ cup toasted slivered almonds (page 69) (optional)

¼ cup Crushed Tomato Topping (page 202) (optional)

1. Combine all of the ingredients except for the dressing in a large bowl. Add the dressing, and toss gently to coat.

2. To serve, divide the salad among 4 dinner plates. Garnish each serving with 1 tablespoon of Crushed Tomato Topping, if desired, and serve immediately.

YIELD: 4 SERVINGS

Suggested Dressings

★ 1 recipe Dijon Mustard Vinaigrette (page 221)

1 recipe Cobb Salad Dressing (page 220)

½ cup commercial fat-free or low-fat honey Dijon dressing

½ cup commercial fat-free or low-fat blue cheese dressing

NUTRITIONAL FACTS
(per serving, salad only)

Calories: 119
Carbohydrates: 11.3 g
Cholesterol: 36 mg
Fat: 1.7 g
Calories From Fat: 7.2%
Protein: 15.5 g
Sodium: 426 mg

YIELD: **4 SERVINGS**

Suggested Dressings

★ 1 recipe Epicurean Vinaigrette (page 221)

1 recipe Raspberry Vinaigrette (page 232)

½ cup commercial fat-free or low-fat raspberry vinaigrette

NUTRITIONAL FACTS
(per serving, salad only)

Calories: 240
Carbohydrates: 32.4 g
Cholesterol: 52 mg
Fat: 2.7 g
Calories From Fat: 9.4%
Protein: 21.8 g
Sodium: 79 mg

Smoked Chicken Salad With Grapefruit Compote

Although the preparation of this salad includes many steps, the finished dish is well worth the effort. In fact, the grapefruit compote is so delicious that you might want to double the recipe and serve it as a dessert.

6 cups mixed baby greens

4 scallion flowers (page 42) (optional)

Smoked Chicken

1 ounce loose leaf Chinese black tea*

1 tablespoon firmly packed dark brown sugar

1 star anise, crushed

¼ teaspoon salt

¼ teaspoon freshly ground pepper

1 boneless, skinless chicken breast (12 ounces)

Grapefruit Compote

¼ cup granulated sugar

1 tablespoon medium-dry red wine, such as Burgundy or zinfandel

1 tablespoon port

2 grapefruits, peeled, seeded, and coarsely chopped

* If loose leaf black tea is unavailable, tea bags can be substituted. Open the bags to release the filling.

1. To make the smoked chicken, combine the tea, brown sugar, star anise, salt, and pepper in a small bowl. Place the tea mixture in a large skillet that has been lined with a piece of aluminum foil. Set either a rack or a vegetable steamer lightly coated with cooking spray in the skillet.

2. Rinse the chicken, and place it on the rack in the skillet. Place the skillet over medium heat, cover, and allow to "smoke" for 25 to 30 minutes, or until a meat thermometer registers 170°F and the chicken is no longer pink inside. Allow the chicken to cool for 10 minutes before cutting into thin slices. Cover and set aside.

3. To make the compote, combine the sugar, red wine, and port in a medium-sized saucepan. Bring to a boil over medium heat, and continue to boil for 5 to 6 minutes, or until the mixture reaches a syrupy consistency. Add the grapefruit, and stir to blend well. Cover and set aside at room temperature, or refrigerate for several hours or overnight.

4. To serve, divide the greens among 4 dinner plates. Fan slices of the smoked chicken on top of the greens, and place a spoonful of the compote on both sides of the chicken. Spoon some of the dressing over each serving, and garnish with a scallion flower, if desired. Serve immediately.

Cobb Turkey Salad

This wonderful salad contains a cornucopia of ingredients that beautifully complement one another. If you must limit your sodium intake, keep in mind that it is best not to use commercially prepared turkey and to omit the turkey bacon, because of their high sodium contents. Serve with multigrain French bread.

12 ounces cooked turkey breast, cubed

6 cups prewashed baby spinach, stems removed

4 slices 95% fat-free turkey bacon, cooked according to package directions and crumbled

3 Roma tomatoes, quartered

2 hard-boiled eggs, whites only, quartered

1 ounce Maytag blue cheese or other blue cheese, crumbled

1 avocado, peeled, pitted, and cubed

4 tomato roses (page 179) (optional)

1. Combine the turkey, spinach, bacon, tomatoes, egg whites, blue cheese, and avocado in a salad bowl. Add the dressing, and toss gently to coat.

2. To serve, divide the salad among 4 dinner plates. If desired, garnish each serving with a tomato rose, and serve immediately.

YIELD: 4 SERVINGS

Suggested Dressings

★ 1 recipe Cobb Salad Dressing (page 220)

1 recipe Maytag Blue Cheese and Balsamic Vinaigrette (page 227)

½ cup commercial fat-free or low-fat blue cheese dressing

½ cup commercial fat-free or low-fat Thousand Island dressing

NUTRITIONAL DATA
(per serving, salad only)
Calories: 228
Carbohydrates: 9.1 g
Cholesterol: 58 mg
Fat: 10.5 g
Calories From Fat: 46.5%
Protein: 25.5 g
Sodium: 349 mg

Spicy Chicken, Mandarin Orange, and Mango Salad

YIELD: 4 SERVINGS

Suggested Dressings

★ 1 recipe Oriental Dressing (page 229)

½ cup commercial fat-free or low-fat sweet and sour dressing

Serving Suggestion

For a more artistic presentation, first divide the lettuce among 4 dinner plates. Arrange slices of chicken over the lettuce, and garnish both sides with mango slices and mandarin oranges. Finally, drizzle the dressing over each salad, and garnish with scallion slices.

Time-Saving Tip

❑ Substitute ¼ cup of your favorite commercial Caribbean marinade for the homemade Caribbean Marinade.

NUTRITIONAL FACTS
(per serving, salad only)

Calories: 208
Carbohydrates: 32.7 g
Cholesterol: 34 mg
Fat: 2.3 g
Calories From Fat: 9.5%
Protein: 16.2 g
Sodium: 263 mg

Cooking that fuses the cuisines of different cultures has become very popular, and for good reason. By combining ingredients frequently used in Caribbean cooking with those of the Orient, the result is a salad brimming with a magical array of flavors. In fact, the marinade is so delicious that you will also want to try it with Cornish hens, duck, or even pork. Serve this delectable salad with low-fat mango bread.

Caribbean Marinade

¼ cup fresh lime juice

2 tablespoons coarsely chopped fresh cilantro

1 tablespoon dark brown sugar

1 tablespoon dark rum

1 tablespoon low-sodium soy sauce

1 tablespoon finely chopped fresh ginger

½ teaspoon Asian hot sauce or favorite hot pepper sauce

¼ teaspoon ground cinnamon

¼ teaspoon ground nutmeg

¼ teaspoon ground allspice

⅛ teaspoon salt

1 boneless, skinless chicken breast (12 ounces)

6 cups red leaf lettuce, torn into generous bite-sized pieces

2 mangos or papayas, peeled, pitted, and cut into thin slices

1 can (11 ounces) mandarin oranges, drained

2 scallions, thinly sliced

1. Rinse the chicken, and pat it dry with paper towels.

2. To make the marinade, combine all of the marinade ingredients in a resealable plastic bag, and shake to blend. Add the chicken and turn to coat. Seal the bag, and refrigerate for several hours or overnight, turning the chicken at least once.

3. Line a baking sheet with 1-inch sides with aluminum foil. Remove the chicken from the marinade, discarding the marinade, and transfer the chicken to the baking sheet.

4. Place the chicken under a preheated broiler, 4 inches from the heat source, and broil for 4 to 5 minutes on each side, or until golden brown on the outside and no longer pink on the inside. Allow the chicken to cool for 10 minutes before cutting into thin slices.

5. To serve, combine the chicken, lettuce, mango or papaya, mandarin oranges, and scallions in a salad bowl. Add the dressing, and toss gently to coat. Serve immediately.

Indian Turkey Salad

Yogurt and Cucumber Dressing adds an authentic Indian touch to this melange of vegetables and garbanzo beans. Serve with naan, an Indian flat bread available in health foods stores and Asian markets.

1 cup broccoli florets
1½ cups cubed cooked turkey breast (about 9 ounces)
1 can (1 pound) chickpeas, rinsed and drained
1 cup thinly sliced scallions
2 carrots, peeled and thinly sliced
5 cups prewashed baby spinach, stems removed
½ cup coarsely chopped cashews (optional)

1. Cook the broccoli in a steamer for 1 minute, or just until bright green. Drain well, and allow to come to room temperature.

2. Combine the broccoli, turkey, chickpeas, scallions, and carrots in a salad bowl. Add the dressing, and toss gently to coat. Use immediately, or cover and refrigerate for several hours.

3. To serve, make a wreath of the spinach on each of 4 dinner plates, and spoon the turkey salad in the center of each wreath. Garnish each serving with cashews, if desired, and serve immediately.

YIELD: 4 SERVINGS

Suggested Dressing

★ 1 recipe Yogurt and Cucumber Dressing (page 241)

NUTRITIONAL FACTS (per serving, salad only)

Calories: 242
Carbohydrates: 34.5 g
Cholesterol: 28 mg
Fat: 3 g
Calories From Fat: 10.9%
Protein: 21 g
Sodium: 426 mg

Spicy Couscous, Chicken, and Dried Fruit Salad

YIELD: 4 SERVINGS

Suggested Dressings

★ 1 recipe Lemon and Honey Vinaigrette (page 225)

1 recipe Lemon Vinaigrette (page 225)

½ cup commercial fat-free or low-fat lemon honey dressing

NUTRITIONAL FACTS
(per serving, salad only)

Calories: 330
Carbohydrates: 52.8 g
Cholesterol: 43 mg
Fat: 2.5 g
Calories From Fat: 6.6%
Protein: 27.3 g
Sodium: 271 mg

A staple of North African cuisine, couscous can be enjoyed as a cereal or as an alternative to rice, potatoes, or pasta. It also makes a fabulous salad when combined with chicken, dried fruits, and vegetables.

1 boneless, skinless chicken breast (10 ounces)
1-inch slice fresh ginger, peeled
1 can (14.5 ounces) fat-free chicken broth
¼ cup cold water
½ tablespoon ground ginger
½ tablespoon ground turmeric
½ tablespoon ground cinnamon
8 ounces (1 cup) couscous
¾ cup chopped mixed dried fruit, such as raisins, apricots, and dates
½ cup minced red onion
2 carrots, peeled and minced
⅓ cup toasted slivered almonds (page 69)
2 cantaloupes, halved, peeled, and cut into thin wedges
Four 6-inch cinnamon sticks (optional)

1. Rinse the chicken. Place enough water to cover the chicken in a medium-sized saucepan, and bring to a simmer over medium-high heat. Add the chicken and ginger, and simmer uncovered for 10 to 12 minutes, or until the chicken is no longer pink inside. Remove the saucepan from the heat, cover, and allow the chicken to come to room temperature.

2. While the chicken is cooling, combine the chicken broth, water, ginger, turmeric, and cinnamon in a medium-sized saucepan, and bring to a simmer over high heat. Stir in the couscous, cover the pot, and remove it from the heat. Allow to sit for 5 minutes or until all of the liquid has been absorbed. Fluff the couscous with 2 chopsticks or forks, and allow to cool uncovered for 10 minutes.

3. Transfer the cooled chicken to a strainer and drain well, discarding the ginger. Cut the chicken into small cubes.

4. Combine the chicken, couscous, dried fruit, onion, carrots, and almonds in a salad bowl. Add the dressing, and toss gently to coat. Cover and refrigerate for several hours or overnight.

5. Remove the salad from the refrigerator 1 hour before serving, and toss to blend. To serve, arrange the cantaloupe wedges in a circle on each of 4 dinner plates and spoon a portion of the couscous salad in the center of each serving. If desired, garnish each serving with a cinnamon stick, placing the stick in the center of the salad so that it points upwards.

Turkey, Fruit, and Rice Salad

YIELD: **4** SERVINGS

This salad is so easy to make and so delicious that it is sure to become a favorite. Take it along on a picnic or enjoy it poolside. Serve with fresh fruit slices.

6 ounces (1 cup) favorite long-grain and wild rice mix
1 turkey breast tenderloin (12 ounces), cut into 2 pieces
3 scallions, thinly sliced
3/4 cup chopped mixed dried fruit, such as raisins, apricots, and dates
1/4 cup toasted slivered almonds (page 69) (optional)

1. Cook the rice according to package directions, omitting butter or margarine. Set aside to cool.

2. Rinse the turkey, and pat it dry with paper towels. Place 1 turkey piece in a large resealable plastic bag. Remove as much air as possible from the bag and seal. Using a meat tenderizer, flatten the turkey into a 1/4-inch-thick fillet. Repeat with the remaining turkey piece.

3. Lightly coat a large nonstick skillet with olive oil cooking spray, and preheat over medium heat. Add the turkey, and sauté for 3 minutes on each side, or until golden brown on the outside and no longer pink on the inside. Allow the turkey to cool for 10 minutes before cutting into cubes.

4. Combine the rice, turkey, scallions, dried fruit, and almonds, if desired, in a salad bowl. Add the vinaigrette, and toss gently to coat. Cover and refrigerate for several hours or overnight.

5. Remove the salad from the refrigerator 1 hour before serving. Toss to blend, and serve.

Suggested Dressings

★ 1 recipe White Wine Vinaigrette (page 241)

1 recipe Spicy Vinaigrette (page 236)

NUTRITIONAL FACTS
(per serving, salad only)

Calories: 268
Carbohydrates: 18.9 g
Cholesterol: 37 mg
Fat: 2.1 g
Calories From Fat: 13%
Protein: 21.2 g
Sodium: 616.5 mg

YIELD: **4** SERVINGS

Teriyaki Chicken and Mango Salad

This simple salad is as strikingly attractive as it is delicious. If edible flowers are available, use them to garnish this colorful dish. Serve with low-fat mango bread.

Suggested Dressings

★ 1 recipe Teriyaki Vinaigrette (page 238)

1 recipe Oriental Dressing (page 229)

½ cup commercial fat-free or low-fat poppy seed dressing

Serving Suggestion

For a more artistic presentation, first divide the mixed baby greens among 4 dinner plates. Top each bed of greens with slices of chicken, mango, and mushrooms. Finally, drizzle some dressing over each serving and garnish with the scallions or, if desired, with a scallion flower (page 42).

Teriyaki Marinade

¼ cup low-sodium soy sauce

¼ cup honey

1 teaspoon finely chopped garlic

1 teaspoon finely chopped fresh ginger

1 teaspoon toasted sesame seeds (page 69) (optional)

1 boneless, skinless chicken breast (12 ounces)

3 ounces fresh shiitake mushrooms

6 cups mixed baby greens

2 mangos or papayas, peeled, pitted, and cut into thin slices

2 scallions, thinly sliced

1. To make the marinade, combine all of the marinade ingredients in a resealable plastic bag, and shake to blend. Add the chicken and turn to coat. Seal the bag, and refrigerate for several hours or overnight, turning the chicken at least once.

2. Remove the chicken from the marinade, discarding the marinade. Place the chicken over moderately hot coals on a grill coated with cooking spray. Cover the grill and cook, turning the chicken every 3 minutes, for 6 to 9 minutes, or until golden brown on the outside and no longer pink on the inside. Alternatively, place the chicken under a preheated broiler, 4 inches from the heat source, and broil for 4 to 5 minutes on each side. Allow the chicken to cool for 10 minutes before cutting into thin slices.

3. Remove and discard the stems from shiitake mushrooms. To slice several mushrooms at one time, slightly overlap 3 to 4 mushrooms and cut into thin slices. Repeat with the remaining mushrooms.

4. Lightly coat a medium-sized nonstick skillet with cooking spray, and preheat over medium heat. Add the mushrooms and stir-fry for 1 to 2 minutes, or until fork tender.

NUTRITIONAL FACTS
(per serving, salad only)

Calories: 303
Carbohydrates: 50.8 g
Cholesterol: 52 mg
Fat: 2.9 g
Calories From Fat: 7.9%
Protein: 23.9 g
Sodium: 673 mg

5. To serve, combine the chicken, mushrooms, mixed baby greens, mango or papaya, and scallions in a salad bowl. Add the dressing, and toss gently to coat. Serve immediately.

German Potato and Turkey Kielbasa Salad

German potato salad is a perennial favorite, and the addition of smoked turkey sausage makes it even more satisfying. Of course, even low-fat processed meats will add sodium to your dish, so if you're trying to restrict sodium, cut back on the meat and add more potatoes. Serve with your favorite light German beer.

1½ pounds new potatoes, unpeeled

8 ounces 95% fat-free smoked turkey sausage, cooked according to package directions and thinly sliced

4 slices 95% fat-free turkey bacon, cooked according to package directions and crumbled

1 red bell pepper, diced

¼ cup minced fresh parsley

½ teaspoon caraway seeds

5 cups prewashed baby spinach, stems removed

1. Place enough water to cover the potatoes in a large saucepan, and bring to a boil over medium-high heat. Add the potatoes and simmer uncovered for 25 minutes, or until fork tender. Drain well, and allow to sit for 5 to 10 minutes, or just until cool enough to handle. Cut the potatoes into 1/2-inch-thick slices.

2. Place the potatoes, sausage, bacon, red pepper, and parsley in a salad bowl, and toss gently to blend. Add the caraway seeds and vinaigrette, and toss again to blend.

3. To serve, make a wreath of the spinach on each of 4 dinner plates. Spoon the potato salad in the center of each wreath, and serve immediately. May be served warm or at room temperature.

YIELD: 4 SERVINGS

Suggested Dressings

★ 1 recipe German Potato Salad Vinaigrette (page 222)

½ cup commercial fat-free or low-fat peppercorn ranch dressing

NUTRITIONAL ANALYSIS (per serving, salad only)

Calories: 261
Carbohydrates: 33.2 g
Cholesterol: 50 mg
Fat: 3.5 g
Calories From Fat: 34.1%
Protein: 23.1 g
Sodium: 1,230 mg

YIELD: 4 SERVINGS

Santa Fe Turkey Salad

I enjoyed this salad during a recent trip to Santa Fe. The original recipe called for chicken, but it is equally delicious when prepared with turkey. Serve with grilled polenta.

Suggested Dressings

★ 1 recipe Cilantro Vinaigrette (page 219)

1 recipe Southwestern Vinaigrette (page 235)

½ cup commercial fat-free or low-fat cilantro lime vinaigrette

½ cup commercial fat-free or low-fat peppercorn ranch dressing

Marinade

¼ cup fresh lime juice
2 tablespoons chopped fresh cilantro
3 cloves garlic, chopped
½ teaspoon ground cumin
½ teaspoon chili powder
½ teaspoon cayenne pepper
¼ teaspoon freshly ground pepper

1 turkey breast tenderloin (12 ounces), cut into 2 pieces
6 cups prewashed baby spinach, stems removed
1 cup thin red onion rings
8 ounces fresh mushrooms, thinly sliced
12 cherry tomatoes, stemmed and halved
1½ ounces feta cheese, crumbled

Time-Saving Tip

❏ Substitute ¼ cup of your favorite commercial Southwestern marinade for the homemade marinade.

NUTRITIONAL FACTS
(per serving, salad only)

Calories: 166
Carbohydrates: 11.2 g
Cholesterol: 47 mg
Fat: 4.7 g
Calories From Fat: 24.5%
Protein: 21.4 g
Sodium: 210 mg

1. Rinse the turkey, and pat it dry with paper towels. Place 1 turkey piece in a large resealable plastic bag. Remove as much air as possible from the bag and seal. Using a meat tenderizer, flatten the turkey into a 1/4-inch-thick fillet. Repeat with the remaining turkey piece.

2. To make the marinade, combine all of the marinade ingredients in a resealable plastic bag, and shake to blend. Add the turkey and turn to coat. Seal the bag, and refrigerate for several hours or overnight, turning the turkey at least once.

3. Remove the turkey from the marinade, discarding the marinade. Place the turkey over moderately hot coals on a grill coated with cooking spray. Cover the grill and cook, turning the turkey every 3 minutes, for 6 to 9 minutes, or until golden brown on the outside and no longer pink on the inside. Alternatively, place the turkey under a preheated broiler, 4 inches from the heat source, and broil for 5 to 6 minutes on each side. Allow the turkey to cool for 10 minutes before cutting into thin slices.

4. To serve, combine the turkey, spinach, onion, mushrooms, tomatoes, and feta cheese in a salad bowl. Add the dressing, and toss gently to coat. Serve immediately.

Thanksgiving Turkey and Sweet Potato Salad

This is the ideal salad to make a day or two after your Thanksgiving feast. After a second night of turkey and fixings, sandwiches for lunch, and turkey soup, this dish will provide a light and refreshing change of tastes and textures.

2 sweet potatoes or yams (1 pound each), peeled and thinly sliced

1 cup frozen peas

6 cups red leaf lettuce

2 cups thinly sliced cooked turkey breast (about 12 ounces)

2 scallions, thinly sliced

½ cup Cranberry Chutney (page 68) (optional)

YIELD: 4 SERVINGS

Suggested Dressings

★ 1 recipe Raspberry Vinaigrette (page 232)

1 recipe Honey Dijon Vinaigrette (page 223)

½ cup commercial fat-free or low-fat raspberry vinaigrette

½ cup commercial fat-free or low-fat honey French dressing

NUTRITIONAL FACTS
(per serving, salad only)

Calories: 349
Carbohydrates: 63.5 g
Cholesterol: 36 mg
Fat: 1.6 g
Calories From Fat: 4%
Protein: 21.3 g
Sodium: 77 mg

1. Place enough water to cover the sweet potatoes in a large saucepan, and bring to a boil over high heat. Add the potatoes, and boil uncovered for 10 to 12 minutes, or just until fork tender. Drain well, and allow to come to room temperature.

2. While the potatoes are cooking, cook the peas according to package directions. Drain well, and allow to come to room temperature.

3. To serve, first divide the lettuce among 4 dinner plates. Arrange the sweet potato slices in a circle around the lettuce. Arrange the turkey slices over the lettuce, and distribute the peas and scallions over the turkey. Finally, drizzle the dressing over each serving, and, if desired, garnish with a dollop of Cranberry Chutney. Serve immediately.

Making Cranberry Chutney

Want to give your Thanksgiving Turkey and Sweet Potato Salad (page 67) the ultimate crowning touch? Try this easy recipe for Cranberry Chutney. This chutney is also a sensational accompaniment to the holiday turkey.

Cranberry Chutney

1 cup granulated sugar
1 cup cold water
½ cup chopped onion
¼ cup white distilled vinegar
4 whole cloves
1 teaspoon ground cinnamon
½ teaspoon salt
2 cups fresh or frozen (thawed) cranberries
½ cup dark raisins
½ cup chopped pitted dates
¼ cup chopped preserved ginger
¼ cup firmly packed dark brown sugar

1. Combine the sugar, water, onion, vinegar, cloves, cinnamon, and salt in a large saucepan, and bring the mixture to a boil over medium heat. Simmer over medium heat, stirring occasionally, for 5 minutes.

2. Stir all of the remaining ingredients into the sugar mixture. Continue to simmer, stirring occasionally, for 12 minutes, or until the cranberries begin to pop open.

3. Remove the saucepan from the heat, and allow the chutney to come to room temperature. Do not cover the saucepan. Transfer the chutney to a covered container, and refrigerate until ready to use.

Turkey and Dried Cherry Salad

*This delicious salad was created when friends brought us
holiday gifts of dried cherries and pecans.*

1 turkey breast tenderloin (12 ounces), cut into 2 pieces

6 cups mixed baby greens

¾ cup dried cherries (3 ounces)

1 cup thin red onion rings

¼ cup coarsely chopped pecans (optional)

1. Rinse the turkey, and pat it dry with paper towels. Place 1 turkey piece in a large resealable plastic bag. Remove as much air as possible from the bag and seal. Using a meat tenderizer, flatten the turkey into a ¼-inch-thick fillet. Repeat with the remaining turkey piece.

2. Lightly coat a large nonstick skillet with olive oil cooking spray, and preheat over medium heat. Add the turkey and sauté for 3 minutes on each side, or until golden brown on the outside and no longer pink on the inside. Allow the turkey to cool for 10 minutes before cutting into thin slices.

3. To serve, combine the turkey, mixed baby greens, cherries, onion rings, and pecans, if desired, in a salad bowl. Add the dressing, and toss gently to coat. Serve immediately.

YIELD: 4 SERVINGS

Suggested Dressings

★ 1 recipe Raspberry Vinaigrette (page 232)

½ cup commercial fat-free or low-fat raspberry vinaigrette

½ cup commercial fat-free or low-fat poppy seed dressing

Time-Saving Tip
❏ Substitute 1¼ cups of slivered cooked turkey breast for the turkey tenderloin.

**NUTRITIONAL FACTS
(per serving, salad only)**
Calories: 200
Carbohydrates: 11.2 g
Cholesterol: 36 mg
Fat: 1.9 g
Calories From Fat: 13.5%
Protein: 19.4 g
Sodium: 57 mg

Toasting Nuts and Seeds

Toasting intensifies the flavor of all nuts and seeds, allowing you to use a smaller amount without sacrificing flavor. This is a great way to reduce fat without reducing taste.

To toast nuts or seeds, simply arrange them in a single layer in a shallow pan, and bake in a preheated 350°F oven for 10 to 15 minutes, or until golden brown. Watch carefully, as once they begin to toast, they can quickly burn!

YIELD: 2 SERVINGS

Valentine's Day Chicken Salad

Cooked beets cut into hearts with a heart-shaped cookie cutter add a whimsical touch to this special salad. Light the candles and serve the salad with a French baguette and a bottle of your favorite wine.

Suggested Dressings

★ ¼ cup Raspberry Vinaigrette (page 232)

¼ cup commercial low-fat or fat-free raspberry vinaigrette

¼ cup commercial low-fat or fat-free poppy seed dressing

Serving Suggestion

For a more artistic presentation, first arrange a bed of mixed baby greens and endive on each of 2 dinner plates. Fan the chicken slices over the top, and place 2 whole hearts of palm so that they radiate out from under one edge of each chicken fan. Sprinkle diced beets over each salad. Then garnish the side of each salad with the beet hearts and, if desired, the slice of cheese. Finally, drizzle dressing over each serving.

Marinade

2 tablespoons raspberry vinegar
½ tablespoon medium-dry red wine, such as Burgundy or zinfandel
½ tablespoon Dijon mustard
½ tablespoon raspberry preserves
1 shallot, minced
⅛ teaspoon salt
⅛ teaspoon freshly ground pepper

1 boneless, skinless chicken breast half (6 ounces)
1 beet (12–16 ounces, or 3 inches in diameter)
4 cups mixed baby greens
1 Belgian endive, chopped
½ cup sliced canned hearts of palm, drained
1 ounce goat cheese (such as Montrachet), halved (optional)

1. Rinse the chicken, and pat it dry with paper towels.

2. To make the marinade, combine all of the marinade ingredients in a resealable plastic bag, and shake to blend. Add the chicken and turn to coat. Seal the bag, and refrigerate for several hours or overnight, turning the chicken at least once.

3. Place enough water to cover the beet in a medium-sized saucepan, and bring to a boil over high heat. Reduce the heat to medium, add the beet, and simmer uncovered for 50 to 60 minutes, or until fork tender. Drain well, and set aside until cool enough to handle.

4. Peel away the outer covering of the beet and remove the ends. Cut the remaining beet into ½-inch-thick slices. Using a 2 ½-inch heart-shaped cookie cutter, cut out at least 4 hearts, and dice the remaining beet. (If using small beets, use a smaller cookie cutter.) Cover and set aside.

5. Line a baking sheet with 1-inch sides with aluminum foil. Remove the chicken from the marinade, discarding the marinade, and transfer the chicken to the baking sheet.

6. Place the chicken under a preheated broiler, 4 inches from the heat source, and broil for 4 to 5 minutes on each side, or until golden brown on the outside and no longer pink on the inside. Allow the chicken to cool for 10 minutes before cutting into thin slices.

7. Combine the chicken, diced beets, mixed baby greens, endive, and hearts of palm in a salad bowl. Add the dressing, and toss gently to coat.

8. To serve, divide the salad between 2 dinner plates, and garnish each serving with beet valentine hearts and, if desired, a slice of goat cheese. Serve immediately.

NUTRITIONAL FACTS
(per serving, salad only)

Calories: 372
Carbohydrates: 63.1 g
Cholesterol: 52 mg
Fat: 3.6 g
Calories From Fat: 8%
Protein: 29.6 g
Sodium: 399 mg

Beet Savvy

Beets are indigenous to the Mediterranean region. The Romans ate only the leaves of the beet, but it wasn't long before the fleshy root of the plant was found to be even more delicious.

At the market, look for small- to medium-sized beets with smooth, unblemished skins, and fresh, crisp greens. To store beets, remove most of the greens, leaving about 2 inches, and place the beets in a sealed plastic bag in the refrigerator. The beets should remain fresh for up to three weeks.

YIELD: **4** SERVINGS

Sautéed Turkey, Asparagus, and Red Pepper Salad

The diverse ingredients in this light and artful salad result in an impressively pleasing blend of flavors. Serve with crusty rolls.

Suggested Dressings

★ 1 recipe Champagne Vinaigrette (page 218)

1 recipe Tarragon Vinaigrette (page 238)

½ cup favorite commercial fat-free or low-fat white wine vinaigrette

½ cup commercial fat-free or low-fat lemon Dijon dressing

Serving Suggestion

For a more artistic presentation, first divide the mixed baby greens among 4 dinner plates. Arrange the turkey slices over the top. Then arrange whole asparagus spears so that they radiate out from under one side of the turkey, and arrange the pears slices so that they radiate from the other side. Finally, randomly distribute red pepper strips and onion rings over the top, and drizzle the dressing over each salad.

Marinade
¼ cup fresh lemon juice
1 clove garlic, finely chopped
¼ teaspoon salt
¼ teaspoon freshly ground pepper
⅛ teaspoon dried thyme
1 turkey breast tenderloin (12 ounces), cut into 2 pieces
24 fresh asparagus spears (1 pound), tough ends removed, or 1 can (15 ounces) asparagus spears, drained
6 cups mixed baby greens
1 red bell pepper, cut into julienne strips
1 cup thin red onion rings
2 ripe pears, cored and thinly sliced

1. Rinse the turkey, and pat it dry with paper towels. Place 1 turkey piece in a large resealable plastic bag. Remove as much air as possible from the bag and seal. Using a meat tenderizer, flatten the turkey into a ¼-inch-thick fillet. Repeat with the remaining turkey piece.

2. To make the marinade, combine all of the marinade ingredients in a resealable plastic bag, and shake to blend. Add the turkey and turn to coat. Seal the bag, and refrigerate for several hours or overnight, turning the turkey at least once.

3. Remove the turkey from the marinade, discarding the marinade. Lightly coat a large nonstick skillet with olive oil cooking spray, and preheat over medium heat. Add the turkey and sauté for 3 minutes on each side, or until golden brown on the outside and no longer pink on the inside. Allow the turkey to cool for 10 minutes before cutting into thin slices. Set aside.

4. Cut the asparagus into 2-inch lengths. If using fresh asparagus, cook in a steamer for 2 to 3 minutes, or just until fork tender. Drain well, and allow to come to room temperature.

5. To serve, combine the turkey, asparagus, mixed baby greens, red pepper, onion rings, and pears in a salad bowl. Add the dressing, and toss gently to coat. Serve immediately.

NUTRITIONAL FACTS
(per serving, salad only)

Calories: 213
Carbohydrates: 28 g
Cholesterol: 50 mg
Fat: 4.1 g
Calories From Fat: 13.5%
Protein: 19.4 g
Sodium: 64 mg

Turkey, Pear, and Dried Cherry Salad

This combination of sautéed turkey tenderloin, pears, and cherries is a great taste sensation—especially when topped with a raspberry vinaigrette. Serve with low-fat zucchini bread.

1 turkey breast tenderloin (12 ounces), cut into 2 pieces
6 cups mixed baby greens
2 pears, cored and thinly sliced
3/4 cup dried cherries (3 ounces)
2 scallions, thinly sliced
Edible flowers (optional)

1. Rinse the turkey, and pat it dry with paper towels. Place 1 turkey piece in a large resealable plastic bag. Remove as much air as possible from the bag and seal. Using a meat tenderizer, flatten the turkey into a 1/4-inch-thick fillet. Repeat with the remaining turkey piece.

2. Lightly coat a large nonstick skillet with olive oil cooking spray, and preheat over medium heat. Add the turkey and sauté for 3 minutes on each side, or until golden brown on the outside and no longer pink on the inside. Allow the turkey to cool for 10 minutes before cutting into thin slices.

3. To serve, first divide the mixed baby greens among 4 dinner plates. Fan slices of the turkey over the greens, and arrange the pear slices so that they radiate out from under the turkey. Randomly sprinkle the cherries and scallions over the salad. Finally, drizzle the dressing over each salad, and serve immediately. Garnish with edible flowers, if available.

YIELD: 4 SERVINGS

Suggested Dressings

★ 1 recipe Raspberry Vinaigrette (page 232)

1/2 cup commercial fat-free or low-fat raspberry vinaigrette

1/2 cup commercial fat-free or low-fat honey Dijon dressing

Time-Saving Tip
❏ Substitute 1 1/4 cups of slivered cooked turkey breast for the turkey tenderloin.

NUTRITIONAL FACTS
(per serving, salad only)

Calories: 243
Carbohydrates: 38.3 g
Cholesterol: 37 mg
Fat: 2.3 g
Calories From Fat: 12.4%
Protein: 19.5 g
Sodium: 55 mg

Teriyaki Turkey Salad With Papaya

Papayas are exceedingly high in vitamin C, and have a delectably sweet taste. Including them in a teriyaki salad is a wonderfully pleasing way to take your vitamins. Serve with low-fat mango muffins.

Suggested Dressings

★ 1 recipe Raspberry Vinaigrette (page 232)

1 recipe Mandarin Dressing (page 226)

½ cup commercial fat-free or low-fat raspberry vinaigrette

½ cup commercial fat-free or low-fat poppy seed dressing

1 turkey breast tenderloin (12 ounces), cut into 2 pieces
2 tablespoons Sweet Ginger Sesame Hibachi Grill Sauce* or other low-sodium teriyaki marinade
3 ounces fresh shiitake mushrooms
6 cups mixed baby greens
2 papayas or mangos, peeled, seeded, and thinly sliced
1 cup fresh raspberries

* Sweet Ginger Sesame Hibachi Grill Sauce is available in the Oriental or barbecue sauce section of most supermarkets.

Serving Suggestion

For a more artistic presentation, first lightly dress the mixed baby greens with just enough dressing to make the greens glisten, and make a nest of them in the center of each of 4 dinner plates. Alternate slices of turkey and papaya around the greens, and distribute the mushrooms over the greens. Finally, drizzle the remaining dressing over each salad and garnish with fresh raspberries.

1. Rinse the turkey, and pat it dry with paper towels. Place 1 turkey piece in a large resealable plastic bag. Remove as much air as possible from the bag and seal. Using a meat tenderizer, flatten the turkey into a 1/4-inch-thick fillet. Repeat with the remaining turkey piece.

2. Brush both sides of the turkey with the grill sauce or marinade, and set aside.

3. Remove and discard the stems from the shiitake mushrooms. To slice several mushrooms at one time, slightly overlap 3 or 4 mushrooms and cut into thin slices. Repeat with the remaining mushrooms.

4. Lightly coat a large nonstick skillet with cooking spray, and preheat over medium heat. Add the mushrooms, and stir-fry for 1 to 2 minutes, or until fork tender. Transfer the mushrooms to a dish, and allow to come to room temperature.

5. Add the turkey to the same skillet, and sauté over medium heat for 3 minutes on each side, or until golden brown on the outside and no longer pink on the inside. Allow the turkey to cool for 10 minutes before cutting into thin slices.

NUTRITIONAL FACTS
(per serving, salad only)

Calories: 241
Carbohydrates: 40.7 g
Cholesterol: 36 mg
Fat: 1.8 g
Calories From Fat: 6.7%
Protein: 19.5 g
Sodium: 263 mg

6. To serve, combine the turkey, mushrooms, mixed baby greens, papaya or mango, and raspberries in a salad bowl. Add the dressing, and toss gently to coat. Serve immediately.

Getting the Most From Papayas

The tropical papaya—which is sometimes called a pawpaw—has an elongated shape, similar to that of an avocado. Beneath the greenish-yellow skin, the flesh can be yellow-orange or even a striking salmon color. When ripe, the papaya has a sweet-tart flavor.

Although the skin of some papayas is spotted, this does not affect their taste. A better indication of good flavor is a fruit that is heavy for its size and gives just a little when lightly pressed. In addition, the peel should be mostly yellow, and the fruit should have a fresh, pleasing aroma. You are most likely to find high-quality papayas during May and June, when the fruit is at its peak.

When using a papaya in a salad, always remove the peel. You will probably also want to remove the seeds. But keep in mind that the seeds are edible, so if you're adventurous, you may want to use them as a salad garnish!

Turkey, Mushroom, and Orange Pepper Salad

YIELD: 4 SERVINGS

*This salad is a marvelous union of colorful and tasty ingredients.
Serve with melon wedges.*

Suggested Dressings

★ 1 recipe Honey Dijon
Vinaigrette (page 223)

1 recipe Balsamic and
Walnut Oil Vinaigrette
(page 215)

½ cup commercial fat-free
or low-fat honey Dijon
vinaigrette

| 1 turkey breast tenderloin (12 ounces), cut into 2 pieces |
| 2 tablespoons low-sodium teriyaki marinade |
| 3 ounces fresh shiitake mushrooms |
| 8 ounces green beans, trimmed |
| 6 cups mixed baby greens |
| 1 small orange bell pepper, cut into julienne strips |
| 4 scallions, thinly sliced |

Serving Suggestion

For a more artistic presentation, first lightly dress the mixed baby greens with 2 tablespoons of the vinaigrette, and mound the greens in the center of each of 4 dinner plates. Arrange the remaining salad components by alternating sections of turkey, green beans, orange pepper, and mushrooms in a circle around the greens. Finally, drizzle the remaining vinaigrette over each salad and garnish with the scallions.

1. Rinse the turkey, and pat it dry with paper towels. Place 1 turkey piece in a large resealable plastic bag. Remove as much air as possible from the bag and seal. Using a meat tenderizer, flatten the turkey into a 1/4-inch-thick fillet. Repeat with the remaining turkey piece.

2. Brush both sides of the turkey with the grill sauce or marinade, and set aside.

3. Remove and discard the stems from shiitake mushrooms. To slice several mushrooms at one time, slightly overlap the mushrooms and cut into thin slices. Repeat with the remaining mushrooms.

4. Lightly coat a large nonstick skillet with cooking spray, and preheat over medium heat. Add the mushrooms and stir-fry for 1 to 2 minutes, or until fork tender. Transfer the mushrooms to a dish, and allow to come to room temperature.

NUTRITIONAL FACTS
(per serving, salad only)

Calories: 193
Carbohydrates: 25.6 g
Cholesterol: 37 mg
Fat: 2.3 g
Calories From Fat: 9.9%
Protein: 21.2 g
Sodium: 294 mg

5. Add the turkey to the same skillet, and sauté over medium heat for 3 minutes on each side, or until golden brown on the outside and no longer pink on the inside. Allow the turkey to cool for 10 minutes before cutting into thin slices.

6. Place enough water to cover the green beans in a large saucepan, and bring to a boil over high heat. Add the green beans and continue to boil for 5 minutes, or until fork tender. Drain well, and allow to come to room temperature.

7. To serve, combine the turkey, mushrooms, green beans, mixed baby greens, orange pepper, and scallions in a salad bowl. Add the vinaigrette, and toss gently to coat. Serve immediately.

Southwestern Grilled Turkey Salad

YIELD: 4 SERVINGS

Experience the lively flavors of the Southwest by tossing tender leaves of spinach with spicy marinated turkey, black beans, alfalfa sprouts, and scallions. Serve with squares of grilled polenta.

Suggested Dressings

★ 1 recipe Roasted Red Pepper Dressing (page 233)

1 recipe Southwestern Vinaigrette (page 235)

½ cup commercial fat-free or low-fat Santa Fe blend dressing

½ cup commercial fat-free or low-fat Vidalia onion-tomato dressing

Marinade

¼ cup fresh lime juice

2 tablespoons finely chopped fresh cilantro

1 clove garlic, finely chopped

¼ teaspoon ground cumin

¼ teaspoon cayenne pepper

¼ teaspoon paprika

¼ teaspoon chili powder

⅛ teaspoon ground coriander

⅛ teaspoon freshly ground pepper

1 turkey breast tenderloin (12 ounces), cut into 2 pieces

6 cups prewashed baby spinach, stems removed

1 can (15 ounces) black beans, rinsed and drained

1½ cups alfalfa sprouts

3 scallions, thinly sliced

Serving Suggestion

For a more artistic presentation, first divide the spinach among 4 dinner plates. Make a circle of the turkey slices by slightly overlapping them on the spinach. Place the black beans in the center of the circle, and spoon the dressing over each serving. Finally, mound the alfalfa sprouts on top and garnish with the scallions.

1. Rinse the turkey, and pat it dry with paper towels. Place 1 turkey piece in a large resealable plastic bag. Remove as much air as possible from the bag and seal. Using a meat tenderizer, flatten the turkey into a ¼-inch-thick fillet. Repeat with the remaining turkey piece.

2. To make the marinade, combine all of the marinade ingredients in a resealable plastic bag, and shake to blend. Add the turkey and turn to coat. Seal the bag, and refrigerate for several hours or overnight, turning the turkey at least once.

3. Remove the turkey from the marinade, discarding the marinade. Place the turkey over moderately hot coals on a grill coated with cooking spray. Cover the grill and cook, turning the turkey every 3 minutes, for 6 to 9 minutes, or until the turkey is golden brown on the outside and no longer pink on the inside. Alternatively, place the turkey under a preheated broiler, 4 inches from the

NUTRITIONAL FACTS
(per serving, salad only)

Calories: 240
Carbohydrates: 31.1 g
Cholesterol: 36 mg
Fat: 2 g
Calories From Fat: 7.1%
Protein: 26.5 g
Sodium: 94 mg

heat source, and broil for 5 to 6 minutes on each side. Allow the turkey to cool for 10 minutes before cutting into thin slices.

4. To serve, combine the turkey, spinach, black beans, alfalfa sprouts, and scallions in a salad bowl. Add the dressing, and toss gently to coat. Serve immediately.

Mouth-Watering Beef, Lamb, and Pork Salads

For many people, nothing is more delicious or satisfying than a beef, lamb, or pork dish. Yet most meat dishes provide more fat and cholesterol than a healthy diet should include. How can you have your steak and eat it, too? First start with a lean cut of meat; then toss it with other flavorful main course salad ingredients. Once you have enjoyed spectacular Beef Tenderloin Salad, exotic Pacific Rim Pork and Orzo Salad, or hearty Ham-and-Cheese Potato Salad, you will never miss plain steaks or chops again—especially when you see that this chapter provides over twenty healthy and delicious ways to enjoy these great foods. So put away your steak knife, and grab a salad fork. Main course salads never tasted so good!

Taco Salad

One of the original main course salads, this colorful creation brings south-of-the-border flavors to the salad bowl. Serve with corn bread.

2 large cloves garlic, finely chopped
1 Vidalia onion or other sweet onion, chopped
12 ounces 95% lean ground beef
1 tablespoon chili powder
1 tablespoon fresh lime juice
8 cups romaine lettuce, torn into generous bite-sized pieces
1 can (8.75 ounces) kidney beans, rinsed and drained
1 cup (2 ounces) coarsely crushed baked tortilla chips
1 cup shredded fat-free or low-fat Cheddar cheese
1 avocado, peeled, pitted, and cut into ½-inch cubes (optional)
½ cup sliced ripe olives (optional)
½ cup fat-free or low-fat sour cream
4 sprigs fresh cilantro (optional)

1. Coat a large nonstick skillet with olive oil cooking spray, and preheat over medium heat. Add the garlic and onion, and stir-fry for 5 minutes, or until translucent.

2. Increase the heat to medium-high, and add the ground beef to the skillet. Cook for 6 to 8 minutes, or until no longer red, breaking up the meat with a fork.

3. Add the chili powder and lime juice to the skillet, and stir to blend well. Cook for 1 additional minute. Then remove the skillet from the heat, and allow to come to room temperature.

4. Combine the beef mixture, lettuce, kidney beans, tortilla chips, cheese, and avocado and olives, if desired, in a large bowl. Add just enough dressing to coat the ingredients, and toss well.

5. To serve, divide the salad among 4 dinner plates. Top each serving with a dollop of sour cream, and garnish with a sprig of cilantro, if desired. Serve immediately.

Suggested Dressings

★ 1 recipe Salsa Dressing (page 234)

1 recipe Southwestern Vinaigrette (page 235)

½ cup commercial fat-free or low-fat Santa Fe blend dressing

½ cup commercial fat-free or low-fat Vidalia onion-tomato dressing

Serving Suggestion

For a more artistic presentation, first arrange 6 whole romaine lettuce leaves in a spoke design on each of 4 dinner plates. Mound the salad in the center of the lettuce, and spoon a dollop of sour cream over each serving. Garnish with any remaining dressing and a sprig of cilantro. Finally, arrange 2 to 3 whole tortilla chips in the center of the salad, pointing upwards.

NUTRITIONAL FACTS
(per serving, salad only)
Calories: 418
Carbohydrates: 33.3 g
Cholesterol: 93 mg
Fat: 13.3 g
Calories From Fat: 50.9%
Protein: 45 g
Sodium: 655 mg

Beef Tenderloin Salad

YIELD: 4 SERVINGS

Serve this spectacular salad when having friends over for a casual dinner. Although the beef tenderloin is part of what makes this salad so special, lean store-bought roast beef can be used instead—a substitution that sacrifices only a little of the flavor, but greatly reduces both the fat content and the prep time. Serve mugs of gazpacho as a first course, followed by the salad, a whole wheat French baguette, and your favorite red wine.

Suggested Dressings

★ 1 recipe Maytag Blue Cheese and Balsamic Vinaigrette (page 227)

1 recipe Balsamic Vinaigrette (page 215)

1 recipe Balsamic and Walnut Oil Vinaigrette (page 215)

½ cup commercial fat-free or low-fat balsamic vinaigrette

½ cup commercial fat-free or low-fat red wine vinaigrette

1 beef tenderloin (10 ounces), all visible fat removed
¼ teaspoon freshly ground pepper
⅛ teaspoon salt
1 pound new potatoes, halved
3 ounces fresh shiitake mushrooms
6 cups mixed baby greens
1 cup julienne strips red onion
1 red bell pepper, cut into julienne strips
1 can (14 ounces) hearts of palm, drained and sliced ¼ inch thick

Serving Suggestion

For a more artistic presentation, first divide the mixed baby greens among 4 dinner plates, piling the greens in the center of each plate. Fan slices of beef over one side of the greens, and arrange the potatoes and mushrooms over the other side. Randomly distribute the onion, red pepper, and hearts of palm over the salad. Finally, drizzle the vinaigrette over each serving.

1. Rinse the tenderloin, and pat it dry with paper towels. Sprinkle both sides with the pepper and salt.

2. Place the tenderloin in a roasting pan, and bake in a preheated 400°F oven for 20 to 25 minutes, or until a meat thermometer inserted in the center of the meat registers 145°F or the beef is done to taste. Allow the beef to cool for 10 minutes before cutting into thin slices. Set aside.

3. Cook the potatoes in a large steamer for 20 to 25 minutes, or until fork tender. Drain well, and allow to come to room temperature.

4. Remove and discard the stems from the shiitake mushrooms. To slice several mushrooms at one time, slightly overlap 3 to 4 mushrooms and cut into thin slices. Repeat with the remaining mushrooms.

5. Lightly coat a medium-sized nonstick skillet with olive oil cooking spray, and preheat over medium heat. Add the mushrooms and stir-fry for 1 to 2 minutes, or until fork tender. Allow the mushrooms to come to room temperature.

Time-Saving Tip

❏ Substitute 10 ounces of sliced lean commercial roast beef for the flank steak.

6. To serve, combine the beef, potatoes, mushrooms, mixed baby greens, onion, red pepper, and hearts of palm in a salad bowl. Add the vinaigrette, and toss gently to coat. Serve immediately.

NUTRITIONAL FACTS
(per serving, salad only)
Calories: 453
Carbohydrates: 62.1 g
Cholesterol: 50 mg
Fat: 16.9 g
Calories From Fat: 31.3%
Protein: 21.2 g
Sodium: 142 mg

The Temptingly Tender Tenderloin

The most tender cuts of beef come from the muscles of the animal that are used the least. One such cut is the beef tenderloin, which originates in the short loin. It is also one of the most expensive cuts of beef, and for good reason—it is exceptionally tender and intensely flavored.

For best results, choose a tenderloin that is bright cherry red in color. If the beef is packaged, there should not be any excess moisture or discoloration on the surface of the meat. When preparing your tenderloin, cook it until the internal temperature reaches 145°F, a temperature that indicates medium doneness. Well-done meat should be avoided, as it tends to be less flavorful and tender.

Caribbean Flank Steak Salad

YIELD: 4 SERVINGS

In this salad, the Caribbean marinade not only tenderizes the flank steak, but intensifies its flavor, as well.

Suggested Dressings

★ 1 recipe Caribbean Dressing (page 217)

Serving Suggestion

For a more artistic presentation, first divide the greens among 4 dinner plates, making a slightly off-center bed of greens on each plate. Fan slices of flank steak over the greens, and arrange the broccoli and red pepper around the beef slices. Randomly distribute the onion over the top, and drizzle dressing over each serving. Finally, garnish the open side of the plate with mango and star fruit slices and a sprig of fresh mint or cilantro.

Caribbean Marinade

¼ cup fresh lime juice
2 tablespoons coarsely chopped fresh cilantro
1 tablespoon dark brown sugar
1 tablespoon dark rum
1 tablespoon low-sodium soy sauce
1 tablespoon finely chopped fresh ginger
½ teaspoon Asian hot sauce or favorite hot pepper sauce
¼ teaspoon ground cinnamon
¼ teaspoon ground nutmeg
¼ teaspoon ground allspice
⅛ teaspoon salt

1 flank steak (12 ounces), all visible fat removed
2 cups broccoli florets
3 cups red leaf lettuce, torn into generous bite-sized pieces
3 cups curly endive (frisée), torn into generous bite-sized pieces
1 red bell pepper, cut into julienne strips
1 cup julienne strips red onion

1. Rinse the steak, and pat it dry with paper towels. Pierce the steak all over with a fork.

2. To make the marinade, combine all of the marinade ingredients in a resealable plastic bag, and shake to blend. Add the steak and turn to coat. Seal the bag, and refrigerate for several hours or overnight, turning the steak at least once.

3. Line a baking sheet with 1-inch sides with aluminum foil. Remove the steak from the marinade, discarding the marinade, and transfer the steak to the baking sheet.

4. Place the steak under a preheated broiler, 4 inches from the heat source, and broil for 5 to 6 minutes on each side, or until a meat thermometer inserted in the center of the steak registers 145°F or the steak is done to taste. Allow the steak to cool for 10 minutes before cutting into thin slices. Set aside.

5. Cook the broccoli in a steamer for 2 minutes, or until bright green. Drain, rinse with cold water, and drain again.

6. To serve, combine the flank steak, broccoli, lettuce, curly endive, red pepper, and onion in a salad bowl. Add the dressing, and toss gently to coat. Serve immediately.

NUTRITIONAL FACTS
(per serving, salad only)

Calories: 276
Carbohydrates: 20.6 g
Cholesterol: 43 mg
Fat: 9.8 g
Calories From Fat: 31%
Protein: 28.2 g
Sodium: 346 mg

Flank Steak Tips

The flank steak is a lean cut of beef, making it a perfect ingredient for main course salads. However, if not prepared properly, flank steak can be less tender than many other cuts. The following guidelines will give you the best results when using flank steak in your main course salads.

• Always marinate flank steak before cooking it, as the marinating process will break down the fibers of the meat, increasing its tenderness.

• Cook the flank steak quickly and serve it medium-rare—again, to avoid toughness and chewiness. A meat thermometer should read 145°F when inserted in the thickest portion of the steak.

• Always slice flank steak against the grain, and cut it as thinly as possible. If the recipe instructs you to slice the beef before cooking, first place it in the freezer for 30 minutes. This will make the meat firmer, enabling you to more easily cut it into thin slices.

Suggested Dressings

★ 1 recipe Southwestern
Vinaigrette (page 235)

1 recipe Cilantro
Vinaigrette (page 219)

1 recipe Mexican
Vinaigrette (page 228)

½ cup commercial fat-free
or low-fat Santa Fe blend
dressing

½ cup commercial fat-free
or low-fat cilantro lime
vinaigrette

NUTRITIONAL FACTS
(per serving, salad only)

Calories: 208
Carbohydrates: 11.8 g
Cholesterol: 39 mg
Fat: 7.7 g
Calories From Fat: 32.1%
Protein: 24.6 g
Sodium: 485 mg

Beef Fajita Salad

This salad is a delightful medley of flavors, including those of marinated beef, sautéed vegetables, and a delicious array of condiments. If you are trying to limit your sodium intake, make sure to choose a low-sodium commercial salsa. Better yet, top it with Roasted Vegetable Salsa (page 192)!

Marinade

¼ cup unsweetened pineapple juice
2 tablespoons low-sodium soy sauce
¼ teaspoon freshly ground pepper
⅛ teaspoon salt

1 flank steak (10 ounces), all visible fat removed
1 large red onion, thinly sliced and separated into rings
1 large green bell pepper, thinly sliced into rings
1 head romaine lettuce, torn into generous bite-sized pieces (about 6 cups)
¼ cup fat-free sour cream
¼ cup shredded fat-free Cheddar cheese
½ cup low-sodium salsa or Roasted Vegetable Salsa (page 192)
¼ cup sliced black olives (optional)
4 sprigs fresh cilantro (optional)

1. Rinse the steak, and pat it dry with paper towels. Cut the steak into thin slices.

2. To make the marinade, combine all of the marinade ingredients in a resealable plastic bag, and shake to blend. Add the beef and turn to coat. Seal the bag, and refrigerate for several hours or overnight, turning the beef at least once.

3. Lightly coat a large nonstick skillet with cooking spray, and pre-heat over medium-high heat. Add the onion and green pepper, and stir-fry for 5 minutes.

4. Remove the steak from the marinade, discarding the marinade, and add the beef to the skillet. Stir-fry for an additional 5 to 7 minutes, or until the vegetables are fork tender and the beef is done to taste.

5. To serve, divide the romaine lettuce among 4 dinner plates. Arrange the beef mixture over the lettuce, and drizzle with some of the dressing. Top each serving with 1 tablespoon of sour cream, 1 tablespoon of Cheddar, 2 tablespoons of salsa, and, if desired, 1 tablespoon of black olives. Garnish with sprigs of cilantro, if desired, and serve immediately.

YIELD: 4 SERVINGS

Flank Steak and Crispy Onion Salad

When sweet onions are allowed to cook slowly, they become crisp and richly flavored. Pair these morsels with savory marinated meat, and you have an intensely satisfying salad.
Serve with a French baguette.

Suggested Dressings

★ 1 recipe Champagne Vinaigrette (page 218)

1 recipe Balsamic Vinaigrette (page 215)

½ cup commercial fat-free or low-fat red wine vinaigrette

½ cup commercial fat-free or low-fat balsamic vinaigrette

Red Wine Vinegar Marinade

2 tablespoons red wine vinegar
1½ tablespoons low-sodium soy sauce
½ tablespoon dry mustard
½ teaspoon freshly ground pepper
2 cloves garlic, chopped

1 flank steak (12 ounces), all visible fat removed
1 large Vidalia onion or other sweet onion, thinly sliced and separated into rings
1 pound new potatoes, halved
6 cups Bibb lettuce, torn into generous bite-sized pieces
12 yellow or red cherry tomatoes, stemmed and halved
1 red bell pepper, cut into julienne strips

Serving Suggestion

For a more artistic presentation, first divide the Bibb lettuce among 4 dinner plates, making a bed of lettuce in the center of each plate. Fan slices of the flank steak in the center of the lettuce, and arrange the potatoes and cherry tomatoes on each side. Distribute the crispy onions on top of the steak, and top with the red pepper. Finally, drizzle the vinaigrette over each salad, and, if desired, garnish each serving with a tomato rose (page 179).

1. Rinse the steak, and pat it dry with paper towels. Pierce the steak all over with a fork.

2. To make the marinade, combine all of the marinade ingredients in a resealable plastic bag, and shake to blend. Add the steak and turn to coat. Refrigerate for several hours or overnight, turning the steak at least once.

3. While the steak is marinating, lightly coat a large nonstick skillet with olive oil cooking spray, and preheat over medium heat. Arrange the onion rings in the pan so that they're slightly overlapping one another, and cook for 20 minutes without turning. Turn the onions, and continue to cook, stirring occasionally, for 20 minutes or until crisp and golden brown. Set aside.

4. Cook the potatoes in a large steamer for 20 to 25 minute, or until fork tender. Drain well, and allow to come to room temperature.

Top Left: Pork Tenderloin and
Wild Rice Salad (page 116)

Top Right: Raspberry Grilled
Lamb Salad (page 106)

Bottom: Vietnamese Beef
Salad (page 103)

Top Left: Greek Spinach Salad With Lamb (page 104)

Top Right: Caribbean Flank Steak Salad (page 84)

Bottom: Ginny's Pork and Dried Cherry Salad (page 114)

5. Line a baking sheet with 1-inch sides with aluminum foil. Remove the steak from marinade, discarding the marinade, and transfer the steak to the baking sheet.

6. Place the steak under a preheated broiler, 4 inches from the heat source, and broil for 5 to 6 minutes on each side, or until a meat thermometer inserted in the center of the steak registers 145°F or the steak is done to taste. Allow the steak to cool for 10 minutes before cutting into thin slices.

7. To serve, combine the steak, crispy onions, potatoes, lettuce, cherry tomatoes, and red pepper in a salad bowl. Add the vinaigrette, and toss gently to coat. Serve immediately.

NUTRITIONAL FACTS
(per serving, salad only)

Calories: 379
Carbohydrates: 45.2 g
Cholesterol: 43 mg
Fat: 11 g
Calories From Fat: 24.6%
Protein: 30.6 g
Sodium: 339 mg

The Venerable Vidalia

The Vidalia is a seasonal onion that grows in a specific geographical area of Georgia, and is available from late April through June. Only the onions grown in this area—an area consisting of twenty counties designated by the state of Georgia—can be called Vidalia onions.

These large onions are highly prized because they are both sweet and juicy. When choosing Vidalia onions for use in your salads, look for onions that are heavy for their size and have a dry, papery skin. Then, to keep your onions at their best, place them in a brown paper bag, and store in a cool, dry place with good circulation. Stored this way, your onions should remain fresh for up to two months.

YIELD: 4 SERVINGS

Suggested Dressings

★ 1 recipe Caper
Vinaigrette (page 217)

1 recipe Red Wine
Vinaigrette (page 232)

½ cup commercial fat-free
or low-fat red wine
vinaigrette

½ cup commercial fat-free
or low-fat balsamic
vinaigrette

Serving Suggestion

For a more artistic presentation, first make a wreath of the mixed baby greens on each of 4 dinner plates, and arrange the caramelized onions in the center of each wreath. Alternate sections of flank steak, roasted red peppers, whole asparagus spears, and shiitake mushrooms around the caramelized onions, slightly tucking them under the onions and allowing them to overlap the greens. Finally, drizzle vinaigrette over each serving.

Steak, Asparagus, and Caramelized Onion Salad

Caramelized onions not only add an interesting flavor to this salad, but also provide a nice contrast in texture, color, and taste. Serve with wedges of mango.

Red Wine Vinegar Marinade

2 tablespoons red wine vinegar
1½ tablespoons low-sodium soy sauce
½ tablespoon dry mustard
½ teaspoon freshly ground pepper
2 cloves garlic, peeled and chopped

1 flank steak (10 ounces), all visible fat removed
2 red bell peppers
1 large red onion, thinly sliced and separated into rings
1 can (6 ounces) unsweetened pineapple juice
3 ounces fresh shiitake mushrooms
24 fresh asparagus spears (1 pound), tough ends removed, or 1 can (15 ounces) asparagus spears, drained
6 cups mixed baby greens

1. Rinse the steak, and pat it dry with paper towels. Pierce the steak all over with a fork.

2. To make the marinade, combine all of the marinade ingredients in a resealable plastic bag, and shake to blend. Add the steak and turn to coat. Refrigerate for several hours or overnight, turning the steak at least once.

3. To roast the peppers, place the peppers on a baking sheet that has been lined with aluminum foil. Broil under a preheated broiler, turning the peppers as the skins blacken, for 20 to 25 minutes, or until the skins are charred all over. Once roasted, place in a plastic bag, seal, and allow to steam for 15 minutes. When the peppers are cool enough to handle, peel away the skin and remove the tops and seeds. (Do not rinse the peppers.) Cut the peppers into strips, and set aside.

4. To make the caramelized onions, combine the onion rings and pineapple juice in a large skillet, and bring to a simmer over medium heat. Simmer, stirring occasionally, for 20 to 30 minutes, or until all of the juice has been absorbed. Allow the onions to come to room temperature.

5. Remove and discard the stems from the shiitake mushrooms. To slice several mushrooms at one time, slightly overlap 3 to 4 mushrooms and cut into thin slices. Repeat with the remaining mushrooms.

6. Lightly coat a medium-sized nonstick skillet with olive oil cooking spray, and preheat over medium heat. Add the mushrooms, and stir-fry for 1 to 2 minutes, or until fork tender. Allow the mushrooms to come to room temperature.

7. Cut the asparagus in half. If using fresh asparagus, place enough water to cover the asparagus in a large skillet, and bring to a boil over medium-high heat. Add the asparagus and simmer for 1 to 2 minutes, or until almost fork tender. Drain the asparagus and immediately immerse them in a large bowl filled with ice water. Drain well, and set aside.

8. Line a baking sheet with 1-inch sides with aluminum foil. Remove the steak from the marinade, discarding the marinade, and transfer the steak to the baking sheet.

9. Place the steak under a preheated broiler, 4 inches from the heat source, and broil for 5 to 6 minutes on each side, or until a meat thermometer inserted in the center of the steak registers 145°F or the steak is done to taste. Allow the steak to cool for 10 minutes before cutting into thin slices.

10. To serve, combine the steak, roasted peppers, caramelized onions, mushrooms, asparagus, and mixed baby greens in a salad bowl. Add the vinaigrette, and toss gently to coat. Serve immediately.

Time-Saving Tip
❏ Substitute ½ cup of commercial sweet roasted bell peppers for the homemade roasted peppers.

NUTRITIONAL FACTS
(per serving, salad only)
Calories: 282
Carbohydrates: 32.5 g
Cholesterol: 36 mg
Fat: 8.1 g
Calories From Fat: 24.5%
Protein: 24 g
Sodium: 291 mg

Suggested Dressings

★ 1 recipe Tarragon
Vinaigrette (page 238)

1 recipe Champagne
Vinaigrette (page 218)

½ cup commercial fat-free
or low-fat red wine
vinaigrette

½ cup commercial fat-free
or low-fat balsamic
vinaigrette

Time-Saving Tips

❑ Substitute ½ cup of
commercial sweet roasted
bell peppers for the home-
made roasted peppers.

❑ Substitute 12 ounces of
sliced lean commercial
roast beef for the flank
steak.

Steak, Roasted Potato, and Red Pepper Salad

*Use your favorite marinade to flavor and tenderize the flank steak.
Once broiled, the flank steak will contribute an intense flavor
to the combination of potatoes, peppers, and dressing.
Serve with a French baguette.*

1 flank steak (12 ounces), all visible fat removed
¼ cup commercial low-sodium marinade
2 large red bell peppers
1 tablespoon extra virgin olive oil
1 teaspoon freshly ground pepper
½ teaspoon paprika
¼ teaspoon salt
2 pounds new potatoes, halved
2 cups thinly sliced arugula, stems removed
2 cups red leaf lettuce, torn into bite-sized pieces
2 scallions, thinly sliced

1. Rinse the steak, and pat it dry with paper towels. Pierce the steak all over with a fork.

2. Place the steak and marinade in a resealable plastic bag. Seal the bag, turn to coat, and refrigerate for several hours or overnight, turning the steak at least once.

3. To roast the peppers, place the peppers on a baking sheet that has been lined with aluminum foil. Broil under a preheated broiler, turning the peppers as the skins blacken, for 20 to 25 minutes, or until the skins are charred all over. Once roasted, place in a plastic bag, seal, and allow to steam for 15 minutes. When the peppers are cool enough to handle, peel away the skin and remove the tops and seeds. (Do not rinse the peppers.) Cut the peppers into strips, and set aside.

4. Combine the olive oil, pepper, paprika, and salt in a medium-sized bowl. Add the potatoes, and turn to coat. Coat a large baking pan with olive oil cooking spray, and arrange the potatoes in the pan in a single layer. Bake in a preheated 425°F oven, turning the potatoes every 15 minutes, for 45 minutes, or until fork tender and golden brown. Allow the potatoes to cool to room temperature.

5. Line a baking sheet with 1-inch sides with aluminum foil. Remove the steak from the marinade, discarding the marinade, and transfer the steak to the baking sheet.

6. Place the steak under a preheated broiler, 4 inches from the heat source, and broil for 5 to 6 minutes on each side, or until a meat thermometer inserted in the center of the steak registers 145°F or the steak is done to taste. Allow the steak to cool for 10 minutes before cutting into thin slices.

7. To serve, combine the steak, roasted peppers, roasted potatoes, arugula, red leaf lettuce, and scallions in a salad bowl. Add the vinaigrette, and toss gently to coat. Serve immediately.

NUTRITIONAL FACTS
(per serving, salad only)
Calories: 410
Carbohydrates: 44.5 g
Cholesterol: 43 mg
Fat: 13.5 g
Calories From Fat: 28.8%
Protein: 30.9 g
Sodium: 453 mg

Serving Suggestion

For a more artistic presentation, first divide the arugula and red leaf lettuce among 4 dinner plates, mounding them in the center of each plate. Arrange a section of flank steak so that it slightly over-laps one side of the greens, and repeat with another section of flank steak on the other side. Arrange the roasted potatoes and roasted peppers in the open spaces, and sprinkle the scallions over the top. Finally, drizzle vinaigrette over each salad, and, if desired, garnish each serving by placing long strands of chives so that they point upwards from the center of the salad.

Grilled Flank Steak and Tangerine Salad

YIELD: 4 SERVINGS

Flank steak cooked on the grill always seem to taste better because of both the wonderful smoky flavor and the joy of being able to cook outdoors. As a bonus, this recipe pairs the steak with tart and juicy tangerines—a union that is truly delectable. Start the meal with mugs of gazpacho.

Suggested Dressings

★ 1 recipe Southwestern Vinaigrette (page 235)

1 recipe Mexican Vinaigrette (page 228)

½ cup commercial fat-free or low-fat cilantro lime vinaigrette

½ cup commercial fat-free or low-fat Santa Fe blend dressing

Marinade

2 tablespoons fresh lime juice
2 tablespoons fat-free chicken broth
2 cloves garlic, chopped
¼ teaspoon ground cumin
¼ teaspoon cayenne pepper
¼ teaspoon chili powder
⅛ teaspoon freshly ground pepper

1 flank steak (10 ounces), all visible fat removed
6 cups prewashed baby spinach, stems removed
3 seedless tangerines, peeled and segmented
1 cup julienne strips red onion
1 red bell pepper, cut into julienne strips
1 avocado, peeled, pitted, and cubed (optional)
4 tomato roses (page 179) (optional)

Time-Saving Tip

❑ Substitute ¼ cup of your favorite commercial marinade for the home-made marinade.

NUTRITIONAL FACTS
(per serving, salad only)

Calories: 199
Carbohydrates: 12.4 g
Cholesterol: 36 mg
Fat: 7.8 g
Calories From Fat: 34.3%
Protein: 21.4 g
Sodium: 101 mg

1. Rinse the flank steak, and pat it dry with paper towels. Pierce the steak all over with a fork.

2. To make the marinade, combine all of the marinade ingredients in a resealable plastic bag, and shake to blend. Add the steak and turn to coat. Refrigerate for several hours or overnight, turning the steak at least once.

3. Remove the steak from marinade, discarding the marinade. Place the steak over moderately hot coals on a grill coated with cooking spray, and sear for 1 minute on each side. Then cover the grill and cook for 5 to 6 minutes on each side, or until a meat thermometer inserted in the center of the steak registers 145°F or the steak is done to taste. Alternatively, place the steak under a pre-heated broiler, 4 inches from the heat source, and broil for 5 to 6 minutes on each side. Allow the steak to cool for 10 minutes before cutting into thin slices.

4. Combine the flank steak, spinach, tangerines, onion, red pepper, and avocado, if desired, in a salad bowl. Add the vinaigrette, and toss gently to coat.

5. To serve, divide the salad among 4 dinner plates. Garnish each serving with a tomato rose, if desired, and serve immediately.

Ripening an Avocado

Avocados add a velvety texture and a mild but distinctive flavor to a variety of dishes. Sometimes, though, it's difficult to find an avocado that is as ripe as you'd like it to be. Fortunately, there is a way to ripen your avocado quickly and easily. Simply place the avocado in a wool sock and keep it in a dark, enclosed pantry or closet for two days. Once ripened, the avocado may be stored in the vegetable bin of your refrigerator for up to two weeks.

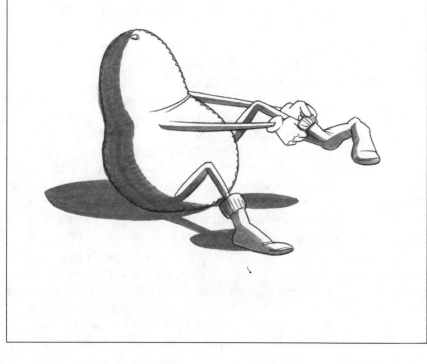

YIELD: 4 SERVINGS

Grilled Steak, Eggplant, and Red Pepper Salad

As far as my family is concerned, anything cooked on the grill tastes great, and this salad confirms their conviction. The flank steak, eggplant, and red peppers incorporate the smoky aroma from the grill, and are then further enhanced by a savory vinaigrette. Start the meal with mugs of your favorite chilled soup and serve the salad with grilled polenta.

Suggested Dressings

★ 1 recipe Caper Vinaigrette (page 217)

1 recipe Italian Vinaigrette (page 224)

½ cup commercial fat-free or low-fat balsamic vinaigrette

½ cup commercial fat-free or low-fat Italian vinaigrette

½ cup commercial fat-free or low-fat Greek vinaigrette

1 flank steak (12 ounces), all visible fat removed
¼ cup commercial fat-free Italian dressing
4 red bell peppers
3–4 Japanese eggplants (1 pound), stemmed and halved
Olive oil cooking spray
6 cups prewashed baby spinach, stems removed
4 sprigs parsley (optional)

Time-Saving Tip
❏ Substitute 1 cup of commercial sweet roasted bell peppers for the home-made roasted peppers.

1. Rinse the steak, and pat it dry with paper towels. Pierce the steak all over with a fork.

2. Place the steak and the Italian dressing in a resealable plastic bag. Seal the bag, turn to coat, and refrigerate for several hours or overnight, turning the steak at least once.

3. To grill the red peppers, place the peppers over moderately hot coals on a grill coated with cooking spray. Cover the grill and cook for 14 to 20 minutes, or until the skins are charred all over, turning the peppers as the skins blacken. Alternatively, place the peppers under a preheated broiler, and broil for 20 to 25 minutes. Once the skins have blackened, place the peppers in a plastic bag, seal, and allow to steam for 15 minutes. When the peppers are cool enough to handle, peel away the skin and remove the tops and seeds. (Do not rinse the peppers.) Cut the peppers into cubes and set aside.

4. To grill the eggplant, first lightly coat the eggplant halves with olive oil cooking spray. Place them over moderately hot coals on a grill coated with cooking spray, cover, and cook for 4 to 5 minutes on each side, or until fork tender and golden brown. Alternatively, place the eggplant under a preheated broiler, and broil for 4 to 5 minutes on each side. Cut the eggplant into cubes and set aside.

5. Remove the steak from the marinade, discarding the marinade. Place the steak over moderately hot coals on a grill coated with cooking spray, and sear for 1 minute on each side. Then cover the grill and cook for 5 to 6 minutes on each side, or until a meat thermometer inserted in the center of the steak registers 145°F or the steak is done to taste. Alternatively, place the steak under a preheated broiler, 4 inches from the heat source, and broil for 5 to 6 minutes on each side. Allow the steak to cool for 10 minutes before cutting into thin slices.

6. To serve, make a bed of the spinach on each of 4 dinner plates. Arrange slices of the flank steak over the spinach, and top with the grilled peppers and eggplant. Drizzle some of the vinaigrette over each salad, and, if desired, garnish with a sprig of parsley. Serve immediately.

NUTRITIONAL FACTS
(per serving, salad only)
Calories: 242
Carbohydrates: 15.6 g
Cholesterol: 43 mg
Fat: 9.4 g
Calories From Fat: 33.8%
Protein: 25.8 g
Sodium: 545 mg

The Beauty of Japanese Eggplant

Japanese eggplants vary in shape from long and slender to short and plump. Some are a rich purple in color, while others are creamy white or even striped. Unlike the larger varieties of eggplant commonly found in supermarkets, Japanese eggplants have a thin skin and a mildly sweet flesh. Because they are not bitter, these eggplants do not require peeling or salting.

When choosing Japanese eggplants, look for fruits that are heavy for their size and have a shiny skin. Stored in a cool dry place, your eggplants should stay fresh for one or two days.

YIELD: **4** SERVINGS

Kathy's Steak, Maytag Blue, and Fettuccine Salad

This recipe can be made with either beef tenderloin or flank steak. Either way, it is divine and lends itself to combinations with almost any of your favorite pastas and vegetables.

Suggested Dressings

★ 1 recipe Honey Dijon Vinaigrette (page 223)

1 recipe Balsamic Vinaigrette (page 215)

½ cup commercial fat-free or low-fat honey Dijon vinaigrette

½ cup commercial fat-free or low-fat honey French dressing

Serving Suggestion

For a more artistic presentation, first make a bed of the fettuccine on each of 4 dinner plates. Arrange slices of flank steak and grilled peppers over the fettuccine, and sprinkle with the blue cheese. Tuck tomato slices off to one side partially under the fettuccine, and repeat with the cucumber slices on the other side. Finally, drizzle the dressing over each serving.

Marinade

2 tablespoons red wine vinegar
1½ tablespoons low-sodium soy sauce
1 tablespoon Worcestershire sauce
½ tablespoon dry mustard
½ teaspoon freshly ground pepper
2 cloves garlic, chopped

1 flank steak (10 ounces), all visible fat removed
1 red bell pepper
1 yellow bell pepper
1 orange bell pepper
8 ounces fettuccine pasta
1½ ounces Maytag blue cheese or other blue cheese, crumbled
3 Roma tomatoes, thinly sliced
1 small cucumber, unpeeled and thinly sliced

1. Rinse the steak, and pat it dry with paper towels. Pierce the steak all over with a fork.

2. To make the marinade, combine all of the marinade ingredients in a resealable plastic bag, and shake to blend. Add the steak and turn to coat. Refrigerate for several hours or overnight, turning the steak at least once.

3. To grill the peppers, place the peppers over moderately hot coals on a grill coated with cooking spray. Cover the grill and cook for 14 to 20 minutes, or until the skins are charred all over, turning the peppers as the skins blacken. Alternatively, place the peppers under a preheated broiler, and broil for 20 to 25 minutes. Once the skins have blackened, place the peppers in a plastic bag, seal, and allow to steam for 15 minutes. When the peppers are cool enough to handle, peel away the skin and remove the tops and seeds. (Do not rinse the peppers.) Slice the peppers into wide strips and set aside.

4. Remove the steak from the marinade, discarding the marinade. Place the steak over moderately hot coals on a grill coated with cooking spray, and sear for 1 minute on each side. Then cover the grill and cook for 5 to 6 minutes on each side, or until a meat thermometer inserted in the center of the steak registers 145°F or the steak is done to taste. Alternatively, place the steak under a preheated broiler, 4 inches from the heat source, and broil for 5 to 6 minutes on each side. Allow the steak to cool for 10 minutes before cutting into thin slices. Set aside.

5. Cook the fettuccine according to package directions. Drain, rinse with cool water, and drain again.

6. To serve, combine the steak, grilled peppers, fettuccine, blue cheese, tomatoes, and cucumber in a salad bowl. Add the dressing, and toss gently to coat. Serve immediately.

Time-Saving Tip
❏ Substitute ¾ cup of commercial sweet roasted bell peppers for the homemade roasted peppers.

NUTRITIONAL FACTS
(per serving, salad only)
Calories: 438
Carbohydrates: 56.6 g
Cholesterol: 44 mg
Fat: 11.2 g
Calories From Fat: 39.5%
Protein: 30 g
Sodium: 505 mg

In Praise of Maytag Blue

On October 11, 1941, the first vat of Maytag blue cheese was made at the Maytag Dairy Farms in Newton, Iowa. Yes, there is a relationship between the dairy and the company that manufactures washing machines; the cheese company was established by the son of the founder of the famous appliance firm.

A process for making an American blue cheese had been developed at Iowa State University, and was adopted by the dairy. This time-consuming method of making the cheese by hand in small batches and then carefully aging it is still being used today to make Maytag blue — and the resulting cheese is well worth the effort. Maytag blue cheese has been acclaimed by food experts as the finest American blue, in part because it is creamier than most other blues. Use this exceptional cheese to add a distinctive flavor and a decadently creamy texture to your favorite main course salads.

YIELD: **4** SERVINGS

Roast Beef and Potato Salad

A gourmet delight, this salad also offers a wonderful opportunity to impress friends and family with your artistry. Serve with French bread.

Suggested Dressings

★ 1 recipe Anchovy and Mustard Vinaigrette (page 213)

1 recipe Dijon Mustard Vinaigrette (page 221)

½ cup commercial fat-free or low-fat Italian herb and cheese dressing

½ cup commercial fat-free or low-fat lemon Dijon dressing

2 red bell peppers
1 pound new potatoes, halved
8 ounces green beans, trimmed and cut into 2-inch lengths
3 ounces fresh shiitake mushrooms
2 tablespoons finely chopped fresh parsley
6 cups mixed baby greens
12 ounces cooked lean roast beef, thinly sliced
4 Roma tomatoes, quartered

Time-Saving Tip

❏ Substitute ½ cup of commercial sweet roasted bell peppers for the homemade roasted peppers.

1. To roast the peppers, place the peppers on a baking sheet that has been lined with aluminum foil. Broil under a preheated broiler, turning the peppers as the skins blacken, for 20 to 25 minutes, or until the skins are charred all over. Once roasted, place in a plastic bag, seal, and allow to steam for 15 minutes. When the peppers are cool enough to handle, peel away the skin and remove the tops and seeds. (Do not rinse the peppers.) Cut the peppers into strips, and set aside.

2. Cook the potatoes in a large steamer for 20 minutes. Add the green beans, and cook for an additional 7 to 8 minutes, or until the vegetables are fork tender. Drain well, and allow to come to room temperature.

3. Remove and discard the stems from the shiitake mushrooms. To slice several mushrooms at one time, slightly overlap 3 to 4 mushrooms and cut into thin slices. Repeat with the remaining mushrooms.

4. Lightly coat a medium-sized nonstick skillet with olive oil cooking spray, and preheat over medium heat. Add the mushrooms and stir-fry for 1 to 2 minutes, or until fork tender. Allow the mushrooms to come to room temperature.

5. Combine the potatoes, green beans, mushrooms, and parsley in a medium-sized bowl. Add just enough dressing to coat the vegetables, tossing gently. Cover the bowl and set aside at room temperature.

6. To serve, combine the potato mixture, roasted peppers, mixed baby greens, roast beef, and tomatoes in a salad bowl. Add the remaining dressing, and toss gently to coat. Serve immediately.

Serving Suggestion

For a more artistic presentation, first make a wreath of the mixed baby greens on each of 4 dinner plates. Mound the potato mixture in the center of the wreath, and arrange slices of beef on one side of the potatoes, and slices of red pepper on the other side. Instead of quartering the tomatoes, thinly slice each one to within 1/4-inch of the bottom, and gently separate the slices to make a fan. Place a tomato fan next to each mound of potato salad, slightly tucking the bottom of the fan under the potatoes. Finally, drizzle the remaining dressing over each salad.

NUTRITIONAL FACTS
(per serving, salad only)

Calories: 236
Carbohydrates: 38.7 g
Cholesterol: 30 mg
Fat: 0.5 g
Calories From Fat: 2.7%
Protein: 17.4 g
Sodium: 800 mg

Thai Beef and Spinach Salad

Thai cooking has become extremely popular, and for good reason. This recipe captures the exotic flavors and wonderful combinations of vegetables and meats that are typical of this appealing cuisine.

Suggested Dressings

★ 1 recipe Oriental Dressing (page 229)

1 recipe Spicy Vinaigrette (page 236)

½ cup commercial fat-free or low-fat Oriental dressing

Marinade

½ cup unsweetened pineapple juice
2 tablespoons hot honey mustard
1½ tablespoons kecap manis* or soy sauce
¼ teaspoon Asian hot sauce or favorite hot pepper sauce

1 flank steak (10 ounces), all visible fat removed
4 cups prewashed baby spinach, stems removed
1½ cups bean sprouts
1 cup thinly sliced bok choy
1 red bell pepper, cut into julienne strips
1 can (7 ounces) whole sweet baby corn, drained
4 scallions, thinly sliced

Time-Saving Tip

❏ Substitute ¼ cup of your favorite low-sodium teriyaki marinade for the homemade marinade.

* A sweet Indonesian soy sauce, kecap manis can be found in Asian food stores.

1. Rinse the steak, and pat it dry with paper towels. Pierce the steak all over with a fork.

2. To make the marinade, combine all of the marinade ingredients in a resealable plastic bag, and shake to blend. Add the steak and turn to coat. Seal the bag, and refrigerate for several hours or overnight, turning the steak at least once.

NUTRITIONAL FACTS
(per serving, salad only)

Calories: 246
Carbohydrates: 18.2 g
Cholesterol: 36 mg
Fat: 8.4 g
Calories From Fat: 29.7%
Protein: 26.4 g
Sodium: 443 mg

3. Line a baking sheet with 1-inch sides with aluminum foil. Remove the steak from marinade, discarding the marinade, and transfer the steak to the baking sheet.

4. Place the steak under a preheated broiler, 4 inches from the heat source, and broil for 5 to 6 minutes on each side, or until a meat thermometer inserted in the center of the steak registers 145°F or the steak is done to taste. Allow the steak to cool for 10 minutes before cutting into thin slices.

5. To serve, combine the steak, spinach, bean sprouts, bok choy, red pepper, corn, and scallions in a salad bowl. Add the dressing, and toss gently to coat. Serve immediately.

Vietnamese Beef Salad

YIELD: **4** SERVINGS

*Jo Gail Wenzel, co-author of my first cookbook, "The Prune Gourmet,"
received this fabulous recipe from a Vietnamese woman. It is
a delicately flavored and artfully composed combination
of stir-fried beef and onions presented on a bed of
watercress and tomatoes, with crisp marinated
onions scattered over the top.*

1 flank steak (12 ounces), all visible fat removed

2 large Vidalia onions or other sweet onions,
thinly sliced and separated into rings, divided

2 cloves garlic, finely chopped

1½ tablespoons low-sodium soy sauce

1 large bunch (or 2 small bunches) watercress,
large stems removed

2 large tomatoes, cut into thin wedges

Suggested Dressing

★ 1 recipe Vietnamese
Vinaigrette (page 240)

NUTRITIONAL FACTS
(per serving, salad only)

Calories: 200
Carbohydrates: 5.7 g
Cholesterol: 43 mg
Fat: 9 g
Calories From Fat: 40.5%
Protein: 23.9 g
Sodium: 292 mg

1. Rinse the beef, and pat it dry with paper towels. Cut it into thin slices, and set aside.

2. Combine half of the onions and all of the vinaigrette in a non-metal dish, and toss gently to blend. Cover and refrigerate for several hours, stirring the onions at least twice.

3. Coat a large nonstick skillet with cooking spray, and preheat over medium-high heat. Add the garlic, and stir-fry for 1 minute.

4. Add the steak slices to the skillet, and stir-fry for 3 to 4 minutes, or until done to taste. Add the soy sauce, and toss gently to blend.

5. Add the remaining onions to the skillet, and stir-fry for 3 to 4 minutes, or until the onions are soft.

6. To serve, line the rim of a large platter with the watercress. Arrange the tomato wedges over the watercress, allowing the tips of the watercress to show. Spoon the flank steak mixture in the center.

7. Remove the marinated onions from the vinaigrette, reserving the vinaigrette, and distribute the onions over the beef mixture. Sprinkle 1 tablespoon of the reserved vinaigrette over the entire salad, and pass the remaining vinaigrette. Serve immediately.

Greek Spinach Salad With Lamb

The addition of flavorful and tender lamb—a traditional favorite in Greece—makes this Greek salad both delicious and unusual. Serve with warm pita bread.

Suggested Dressings

★ 1 recipe Greek Vinaigrette (page 222)

1 recipe Lemon Vinaigrette (page 225)

1 recipe Red Wine Vinaigrette (page 232)

½ cup commercial fat-free or low-fat Greek vinaigrette

½ cup commercial fat-free or low-fat lemon Dijon dressing

Marinade

2 tablespoons fresh lemon juice
1 tablespoon dry white wine
2 cloves garlic, chopped
1 teaspoon dried oregano
¼ teaspoon dried dill
¼ teaspoon salt
¼ teaspoon freshly ground pepper

10 ounces boned, butterflied leg of lamb, all visible fat removed
6 cups prewashed spinach, stems removed and cut into generous bite-sized pieces
4 Roma tomatoes, quartered
1 Spanish onion, thinly sliced and separated into rings
1 green bell pepper, thinly sliced into rings
1 ounce feta cheese, crumbled
4 pepperoncini
4 pitted Kalamata olives (optional)

Time-Saving Tip
❏ Substitute ¼ cup of your favorite commercial Greek marinade or vinaigrette for the homemade marinade.

NUTRITIONAL FACTS
(per serving, salad only)

Calories: 226
Carbohydrates: 19.2 g
Cholesterol: 45 mg
Fat: 11.8 g
Calories From Fat: 44.1%
Protein: 14.3 g
Sodium: 264 mg

1. Rinse the lamb, and pat it dry with paper towels.

2. To make the marinade, combine all of the marinade ingredients in a resealable plastic bag, and shake to blend. Add the lamb and turn to coat. Refrigerate for several hours or overnight, turning the lamb at least once.

3. Remove the lamb from the marinade, discarding the marinade. Place the lamb on a baking pan, and bake in a preheated 350°F oven for 50 to 60 minutes, or until a meat thermometer inserted in the center of the meat registers 160°F. Allow the lamb to cool for 10 minutes before cutting into thin slices.

4. To serve, combine the spinach, tomatoes, onion, green pepper, and feta cheese in a salad bowl. Add just enough vinaigrette to make the greens glisten, tossing gently. Divide the salad among 4 dinner plates, and fan slices of lamb over each serving. Garnish with a pepperoncini and, if desired, an olive. Drizzle the remaining vinaigrette over each salad, and serve immediately.

YIELD: 4 SERVINGS

Raspberry Grilled Lamb Salad

In this salad, a raspberry marinade lends the lamb a subtle raspberry flavor. You can enhance the flavor still more by cloaking the salad in a raspberry vinaigrette. Serve with crusty bread.

Suggested Dressings

★ 1 recipe Raspberry Vinaigrette (page 232)

1 recipe Maytag Blue Cheese and Balsamic Vinaigrette (page 227)

½ cup commercial fat-free or low-fat raspberry vinaigrette

½ cup commercial blush wine vinaigrette

Raspberry Marinade

2 tablespoons raspberry vinegar
2 tablespoons fat-free chicken broth
⅛ teaspoon salt
⅛ teaspoon freshly ground pepper
12 ounces boned, butterflied leg of lamb, all visible fat removed
1 Vidalia onion or other sweet onion, thinly sliced and separated into rings
6 cups mixed baby greens
1½ ounces feta cheese, crumbled
Fresh raspberries (optional)

NUTRITIONAL FACTS
(per serving, salad only)

Calories: 209
Carbohydrates: 5.7 g
Cholesterol: 56 mg
Fat: 13.9 g
Calories From Fat: 59.6%
Protein: 15.5 g
Sodium: 239 mg

1. Rinse the lamb, and pat it dry with paper towels.

2. To make the marinade, combine all of the marinade ingredients in a plastic resealable bag, and shake to blend. Add the lamb and turn to coat. Refrigerate for several hours or overnight, turning the lamb at least once.

3. Combine the onions and just enough of the vinaigrette to lightly coat in a nonmetal dish, and toss gently to blend. Cover and set aside at room temperature.

4. Remove the lamb from the marinade, discarding the marinade. Place the lamb over moderately hot coals on a grill coated with cooking spray, and sear for 1 minute on each side. Then cover the grill and cook for 8 to 9 minutes on each side, or until a meat thermometer inserted in the center of the meat registers 160°F. Alternatively, roast the lamb in a preheated 350°F oven for 50 to 60 minutes. Allow the lamb to cool for 10 minutes before cutting into thin slices.

5. To serve, divide the mixed baby greens among 4 dinner plates. Arrange the lamb, onions, and feta cheese over the greens, and drizzle with the remaining vinaigrette. Garnish each serving with fresh raspberries, if desired, and serve immediately.

Chinese Pork, Asparagus, and Pasta Salad

This exquisite salad is a masterpiece of colors and flavors. Chilled melon soup makes a marvelous complementary starter.

Marinade

2 tablespoons low-sodium soy sauce

1 tablespoon bourbon

1 tablespoon honey

1 clove garlic, chopped

1/8 teaspoon salt

1/8 teaspoon Asian hot sauce or favorite hot pepper sauce

1 pork tenderloin (12 ounces), all visible fat removed

24 fresh asparagus spears (1 pound), tough ends removed, or 1 can (15 ounces) asparagus spears, drained

8 ounces bow-tie pasta or fresh Chinese egg noodles

1 red bell pepper, minced

1. Rinse the tenderloin, and pat it dry with paper towels.

2. To make the marinade, combine all of the marinade ingredients in a resealable plastic bag, and shake to blend. Add the tenderloin and turn to coat. Seal the bag, and refrigerate for several hours or overnight, turning the tenderloin at least once.

3. Remove the tenderloin from the marinade, discarding the marinade, and transfer the tenderloin to a roasting pan. Bake in a preheated 350°F oven for 35 to 40 minutes, or until a meat thermometer inserted in the center of the meat registers 155°F or the meat is no longer pink inside. Allow the tenderloin to cool for 10 minutes before carving into thin slices. Set aside.

4. Cut the asparagus into 2-inch lengths. If using fresh asparagus, cook in a steamer for 2 to 3 minutes, or just until fork tender. Drain well, and allow to come to room temperature.

5. Cook the pasta according to package directions. Drain, rinse with cool water, and drain again.

6. To serve, combine pork, asparagus, pasta, and red pepper in large salad bowl. Add dressing, and toss gently to coat. Serve immediately.

YIELD: 4 SERVINGS

Suggested Dressings

★ 1 recipe Spicy Vinaigrette (page 236)

1 recipe Oriental Dressing (page 229)

1/2 cup commercial fat-free or low-fat sweet and sour dressing

Serving Suggestion

For a more artistic presentation, first divide the pasta among 4 dinner plates. Fan slices of pork over the pasta, and tuck whole asparagus spears under the pork. Randomly distribute the red pepper over the pork. Finally, drizzle the dressing over the salad.

Time-Saving Tip

❑ Substitute 1/4 cup of your favorite commercial low-sodium teriyaki marinade for the homemade marinade.

NUTRITIONAL FACTS
(per serving, salad only)
Calories: 338
Carbohydrates: 60.8 g
Cholesterol: 55 mg
Fat: 3 g
Calories From Fat: 19.4%
Protein: 25.6 g
Sodium: 359 mg

Pacific Rim Pork and Orzo Salad

Suggested Dressings

★ 1 recipe Oriental Dressing (page 229)

1 recipe Spicy Vinaigrette (page 236)

½ cup commercial fat-free or low-fat Oriental dressing

Time-Saving Tip

❏ Substitute ¼ cup of your favorite low-sodium teriyaki marinade for the homemade marinade.

While vacationing in Maui, I enjoyed the cuisine of the Pacific Rim featured at many of the excellent local restaurants. This salad, with its melange of marinated pork, orzo, bean sprouts, shiitake mushrooms, and scallions, has a marvelous flavor when accented with an Oriental-style dressing.

Marinade
2 tablespoons low-sodium soy sauce
1 tablespoon bourbon
1 tablespoon honey
1 clove garlic, chopped
⅛ teaspoon salt
⅛ teaspoon Asian hot sauce or favorite hot pepper sauce

1 pork tenderloin (12 ounces), all visible fat removed
8 ounces orzo pasta*
3 ounces fresh shiitake mushrooms
¾ cup bean sprouts
4 scallions, thinly sliced
6 cups prewashed baby spinach, stems removed
¼ cup shredded carrots (optional)

* Orzo can be found in the pasta or rice section of most supermarkets.

1. Rinse the tenderloin, and pat it dry with paper towels.

2. To make the marinade, combine all of the marinade ingredients in a resealable plastic bag, and shake to blend. Add the tenderloin and turn to coat. Seal the bag, and refrigerate for several hours or overnight, turning the tenderloin at least once.

3. Remove the tenderloin from the marinade, discarding the marinade, and transfer the tenderloin to a roasting pan. Bake in a preheated 350°F oven for 35 to 40 minutes, or until a meat thermometer inserted in the center of the meat registers 155°F or the meat is no longer pink inside. Allow the tenderloin to cool for 10 minutes before cutting into thin slices. Set aside.

4. Cook the orzo according to package directions. Drain well, rinse with cool water, and drain again. Set aside.

5. Remove and discard the stems from the shiitake mushrooms. To slice several mushrooms at one time, slightly overlap 3 to 4 mushrooms and cut into thin slices. Repeat with the remaining mushrooms.

6. Lightly coat a medium-sized nonstick skillet with cooking spray, and preheat over medium heat. Add the mushrooms and stir-fry for 1 to 2 minutes, or just until fork tender. Allow the mushrooms to come to room temperature.

7. Combine the pork, orzo, mushrooms, bean sprouts, and scallions in a large bowl. Add the dressing, and toss gently to coat. Cover and refrigerate for several hours or overnight.

8. To serve, remove the salad from the refrigerator, and toss gently to blend. Then divide the spinach among 4 dinner plates, and spoon the salad in the center of the greens. Garnish each serving with shredded carrots, if desired, and serve immediately.

NUTRITIONAL FACTS
(per serving, salad only)
Calories: 313
Carbohydrates: 51.5 g
Cholesterol: 37 mg
Fat: 3 g
Calories From Fat: 8.5%
Protein: 21.7 g
Sodium: 581 mg

YIELD: **4** SERVINGS

Suggested Dressings

★ 1 recipe Balsamic and
Walnut Oil Vinaigrette
(page 215)

1 recipe Maytag Blue
Cheese and Balsamic
Vinaigrette (page 227)

½ cup commercial fat-free
or low-fat blue cheese
dressing

NUTRITIONAL FACTS
(per serving, salad only)

Calories: 264
Carbohydrates: 35.1 g
Cholesterol: 40 mg
Fat: 4.5 g
Calories From Fat: 15.3%
Protein: 21.5 g
Sodium: 1,230 mg

Easter Ham, Asparagus, and New Potato Salad

*This salad is a marvelous way to use leftover ham from a bountiful
Easter dinner. Deliciously light and satisfying, this is
perfect after a holiday indulgence!*

24 fresh asparagus spears (1 pound), tough ends removed, or
1 can (15 ounces) asparagus spears, drained

2 pounds new potatoes

1 head red leaf lettuce, separated into individual leaves

12 ounces lean ham, cubed (about 2 cups)

3 scallions, thinly sliced

1. Cut the asparagus into 4-inch lengths. If using fresh asparagus,
place enough water to cover the asparagus in a large skillet, and
bring to a boil over medium-high heat. Add the asparagus and
simmer over medium-high heat for 1 to 2 minutes, or until almost
fork tender. Drain the asparagus and immediately immerse them
in a large bowl filled with ice water. Drain well, and set aside.

2. Cook the potatoes in a large steamer for 20 to 25 minutes, or until fork tender. Drain well, and allow to come to room temperature.

3. To serve, combine the asparagus, potatoes, red leaf lettuce, ham,
and scallions in a salad bowl. Add the dressing, and toss gently to
coat. Serve immediately.

Serving Suggestion

For a more artistic presentation, first make a bed of red leaf lettuce
on each of 4 dinner plates. Then fan slices of ham over the center of
each bed. Arrange whole asparagus spears so that they radiate out
from under one side of the ham, and arrange the potatoes on the
other side. Finally, drizzle vinaigrette over each serving and garnish with the scallions.

Ham-and-Cheese Potato Salad

Eating this salad is like eating a deli sandwich with potato salad on the side. It is perfect autumn fare to enjoy while cheering for the home football team.

1 pound new potatoes, sliced ½-inch thick
¼ cup minced fresh parsley
12 ounces lean ham, cubed (about 2 cups)
3 ounces fat-free Cheddar cheese, cubed
1¼ cups julienne strips red onion
5 cups chicory
4 Roma tomatoes, thinly sliced

1. Cook the potatoes in a large steamer for 20 minutes, or until fork tender. Drain well.

2. Transfer the warm potatoes to a medium-sized bowl. Add the parsley and just enough of the dressing to coat, and toss gently to mix. Loosely cover and set aside for 1 hour, or until the potatoes have reached room temperature.

3. Add the ham, cheese, onion, and remaining vinaigrette to the potato mixture, and toss gently to coat. Cover and refrigerate for several hours or overnight.

4. To serve, make a wreath of chicory leaves on each of 4 dinner plates. Mound the potato salad in the center, and arrange the tomato slices off to one side, overlapping the slices and tucking them partly under the salad. Serve immediately.

YIELD: 4 SERVINGS

Suggested Dressings

★ 1 recipe Potato Salad Vinaigrette (page 231)

½ cup commercial fat-free or low-fat slaw dressing

½ cup commercial fat-free or low-fat blue cheese dressing

NUTRITIONAL FACTS
(per serving, salad only)

Calories: 293
Carbohydrates: 35.7 g
Cholesterol: 36 mg
Fat: 5.1 g
Calories From Fat: 14.9%
Protein: 29.7 g
Sodium: 1,336 mg

Don't Spare the Asparagus

Asparagus add color, a distinctive flavor, and a decorative shape to salads. For best results, though, it's important to know how to select and prepare these delicate vegetables.

When buying fresh asparagus in the spring, choose spears that are pencil thin. As the season for asparagus progresses, the fatter ones will taste best. Choose firm stalks that have tips with tightly closed buds. Because asparagus begin to lose their sweetness as soon as they are cut, take notice of the stem end to assure that it has been freshly cut and does not appear to be dried out.

Before cooking your asparagus, hold onto both ends of each spear, and snap. The spear will naturally break where it is tough and fibrous, leaving only the tender portion of the vegetable.

YIELD: **4** SERVINGS

Pork, Mushroom, and Red Pepper Salad

This easy-to-make dish can be prepared with leftover pork. However, I prefer to marinate a pork roast the day I am going to serve it. Either way, the salad is both delicious and satisfying.

Suggested Dressings

★ 1 recipe Honey Dijon Vinaigrette (page 223)

1 recipe Oriental Dressing (page 229)

½ cup commercial fat-free or low-fat honey Dijon vinaigrette

½ cup commercial fat-free or low-fat Oriental dressing

Time-Saving Tip
❑ Substitute ¼ cup of your favorite low-sodium teriyaki marinade for the homemade marinade.

Marinade

2 tablespoons low-sodium soy sauce
1 tablespoon dark brown sugar
1 tablespoon rum
¼ teaspoon ground ginger
¼ teaspoon Asian hot sauce or favorite hot pepper sauce
⅛ teaspoon dry mustard
⅛ teaspoon paprika
⅛ teaspoon salt
⅛ teaspoon freshly ground pepper

1 pork tenderloin (12 ounces), all visible fat removed
3 ounces fresh shiitake mushrooms
6 cups mixed baby greens
1 orange bell pepper, cut into julienne strips
2 tablespoons chopped pecans (optional)

1. Rinse the tenderloin, and pat it dry with paper towels.

2. To make the marinade, combine all of the marinade ingredients in a resealable plastic bag, and shake to blend. Add the tenderloin and turn to coat. Seal the bag, and refrigerate for several hours or overnight, turning the tenderloin at least once.

3. Remove the tenderloin from the marinade, discarding the marinade, and transfer the tenderloin to a roasting pan. Bake in a preheated 350°F oven for 35 to 40 minutes, or until a meat thermometer inserted in the center of the meat registers 155°F or the meat is no longer pink inside. Allow the tenderloin to cool for 10 minutes before cutting into thin slices. Set aside.

4. Remove and discard the stems from the shiitake mushrooms. To slice several mushrooms at one time, slightly overlap 3 to 4 mushrooms and cut into thin slices. Repeat with the remaining mush-rooms.

5. Lightly coat a medium-sized nonstick skillet with cooking spray, and preheat over medium heat. Add the mushrooms and stir-fry for 1 to 2 minutes, or just until fork tender. Allow the mushrooms to come to room temperature.

6. To serve, combine the pork, mushrooms, mixed baby greens, bell pepper, and pecans, if desired, in a salad bowl. Add the dressing, and toss gently to coat. Serve immediately.

NUTRITIONAL FACTS
(per serving, salad only)

Calories: 211
Carbohydrates: 24 g
Cholesterol: 55 mg
Fat: 3.4 g
Calories From Fat: 14.3%
Protein: 21.79 g
Sodium: 413 mg

Ginny's Pork and Dried Cherry Salad

This special salad would be an appropriate choice for a formal luncheon. Or enjoy it at any time as a light entrée.

Suggested Dressings

★ 1 recipe Raspberry Vinaigrette (page 232)

1 recipe Balsamic and Walnut Oil Vinaigrette (page 215)

½ cup commercial fat-free or low-fat raspberry vinaigrette

Marinade

2 tablespoons low-sodium soy sauce
1 tablespoon bourbon
1 tablespoon honey
1 clove garlic, peeled and chopped
⅛ teaspoon salt
⅛ teaspoon Asian hot sauce or favorite hot pepper sauce

1 pork tenderloin (12 ounces), all visible fat removed
24 fresh asparagus spears (1 pound), tough ends removed, or 1 can (15 ounces) asparagus spears, drained
6 cups mixed baby greens
1 cup dried cherries
¼ cup plus 2 tablespoons broken walnuts (optional)
Edible flowers (optional)

Time-Saving Tip

❑ Substitute ¼ cup of your favorite low-sodium teriyaki marinade for the homemade marinade.

NUTRITIONAL FACTS
(per serving, salad only)

Calories: 258
Carbohydrates: 33 g
Cholesterol: 44 mg
Fat: 3.4 g
Calories From Fat: 19.3%
Protein: 22.5 g
Sodium: 366 mg

1. Rinse the tenderloin, and pat it dry with paper towels.

2. To make the marinade, combine all of the marinade ingredients in a resealable plastic bag, and shake to blend. Add the tenderloin, and turn to coat. Refrigerate for several hours or overnight, turning the tenderloin at least once.

3. Remove the tenderloin from the marinade, discarding the marinade, and transfer it to a roasting pan. Bake in a preheated 350°F oven for 35 to 40 minutes, or until a meat thermometer inserted in the center of the meat registers 155°F or the meat is no longer pink inside. Allow the tenderloin to cool for 10 minutes before cutting into thin slices. Set aside.

4. If using fresh asparagus, cook them in a steamer for 4 minutes, or until almost fork tender. Drain well, and allow to come to room temperature.

5. To serve, divide the mixed baby greens among 4 dinner plates. Fan the pork slices over each bed of greens, and tuck the asparagus spears under the pork, off to one side. Sprinkle the cherries and, if desired, the walnuts over the salad, and drizzle some of the vinaigrette over each serving. Garnish with edible flowers, if desired, and serve immediately.

Yuletide Pork and Cranberry Salad

This festive salad would make a fitting dinner after a joyful day of opening gifts and sharing holiday spirit with family and good friends. Serve this light and colorful creation with low-fat pumpkin muffins.

1 pork tenderloin (12 ounces), all visible fat removed

¼ teaspoon freshly ground pepper

⅛ teaspoon salt

1 box (9 ounces) frozen peas and pearl onions

6 cups red leaf lettuce, torn into generous bite-sized pieces

1 red bell pepper, cut into julienne strips

1 cup sweetened dried cranberries (craisins)

1. Rinse the tenderloin, and pat it dry with paper towels. Sprinkle both sides with the pepper and salt.

2. Place the tenderloin in a roasting pan, and bake in a preheated 350°F oven for 35 to 40 minutes, or until a meat thermometer inserted in the center of the meat registers 155°F or the meat is no longer pink inside. Allow the tenderloin to cool for 10 minutes before cutting into thin slices. Set aside.

3. Cook the peas and onions according to package directions. Drain well, and allow to come to room temperature.

4. To serve, combine the pork, peas and onions, lettuce, red pepper, and cranberries in a large salad bowl. Add the vinaigrette, and toss gently to coat. Serve immediately.

YIELD: 4 SERVINGS

Suggested Dressings

★ 1 recipe Maytag Blue Cheese and Balsamic Vinaigrette (page 227)

1 recipe Balsamic and Walnut Oil Vinaigrette (page 215)

½ cup commercial fat-free or low-fat balsamic vinaigrette

Serving Suggestion

For a more artistic presentation, first make a bed of the red leaf lettuce on each of 4 dinner plates. Arrange the pork slices over the center of the greens, and distribute the peas and onions and red pepper over the top. Finally, drizzle the vinaigrette over each serving and garnish with the dried cranberries.

NUTRITIONAL FACTS
(per serving, salad only)
Calories: 281
Carbohydrates: 41.8 g
Cholesterol: 44 mg
Fat: 3.5 g
Calories From Fat: 15.4%
Protein: 23.5 g
Sodium: 281 mg

Pork Tenderloin and Wild Rice Salad

In this salad, marinated pork tenderloin is perfectly complemented by flavorful and crunchy wild rice.

YIELD: 4 SERVINGS

Suggested Dressings

★ 1 recipe Citrus Vinaigrette (page 219)

½ cup commercial fat-free or low-fat Oriental vinaigrette

Time-Saving Tips

❑ Substitute ¼ cup of your favorite low-sodium teriyaki marinade for the homemade marinade.

❑ Substitute 2 cups of diced or thinly sliced cooked pork for the marinated pork tenderloin.

Marinade
¼ cup hoisin sauce*
1 teaspoon low-sodium teriyaki marinade
1 teaspoon rice wine
1 teaspoon minced garlic
¼-inch piece fresh ginger, peeled and halved
1 pork tenderloin (10 ounces), all visible fat removed
1 cup wild rice
2 shallots, finely chopped
3 cups fat-free chicken broth
1 red bell pepper, diced
2 scallions, thinly sliced
1 orange, peeled, seeded, and coarsely chopped
2 tablespoons chopped pecans (optional)

* A sweet and spicy condiment, hoisin sauce can be found in the Asian section of most supermarkets.

1. Rinse the tenderloin, and pat it dry with paper towels.

2. To make the marinade, combine all of the marinade ingredients in a resealable plastic bag, and shake to blend. Add the tenderloin and turn to coat. Seal the bag, and refrigerate for several hours or overnight, turning the tenderloin at least once.

3. Remove the tenderloin from the marinade, discarding the marinade, and transfer the tenderloin to a roasting pan. Bake in a preheated 350°F oven for 35 to 40 minutes, or until a meat thermometer inserted in the center of the meat registers 155°F or the meat is no longer pink inside. Allow the tenderloin to cool for 10 minutes before cutting into small cubes.

4. While the tenderloin is cooking, place the wild rice in a fine-sieved strainer, and rinse with cold water. Set aside to drain.

5. Lightly coat a medium-sized nonstick saucepan with cooking spray, and preheat over medium heat. Add the shallots and sauté for 2 minutes, stirring frequently. Add the wild rice and chicken broth to the pan. Increase the heat to medium-high, and bring the mixture to a boil. Simmer uncovered over medium-high heat for 35 to 40 minutes, or just until the grains begin to open. Transfer the wild rice to a strainer and rinse with cold water. Drain well.

6. Combine the pork, wild rice, red pepper, scallions, orange, and pecans, if desired, in a salad bowl. Add just enough vinaigrette to coat the salad, reserving any remaining vinaigrette. Cover and refrigerate until ready to serve.

7. Stir the salad, and add any additional vinaigrette if necessary. Serve immediately.

Serving Suggestion

For a more artistic presentation, first arrange 6 radicchio leaves around the edge of each of 4 dinner plates, and mound the salad in the center of the leaves. Peel and segment 2 oranges, and garnish both sides of the salad with the orange segments.

NUTRITIONAL FACTS
(per serving, salad only)

Calories: 324
Carbohydrates: 45.1 g
Cholesterol: 39 mg
Fat: 5.4 g
Calories From Fat: 13.6%
Protein: 31.5 g
Sodium: 495 mg

YIELD: **4** SERVINGS

Suggested Dressings

★ 1 recipe Oriental Dressing (page 229)

½ cup commercial fat-free or low-fat Oriental dressing

Time-Saving Tip

❑ Substitute ¼ cup of your favorite low-sodium teriyaki marinade for the homemade marinade.

NUTRITIONAL FACTS
(per serving, salad only)

Calories: 247
Carbohydrates: 31.6 g
Cholesterol: 55 mg
Fat: 3.6 g
Calories From Fat: 12.6%
Protein: 23.8 g
Sodium: 402 mg

Oriental Pork Salad

This pork salad is a cornucopia of colors, textures, and flavors.
For variety, try substituting chicken for the pork.
Serve with low-fat papaya bread.

Marinade

2 tablespoons low-sodium soy sauce

1 tablespoon bourbon

1 tablespoon honey

1 clove garlic, chopped

⅛ teaspoon salt

⅛ teaspoon Asian hot sauce or favorite hot pepper sauce

1 pork tenderloin (12 ounces), all visible fat removed

6 cups mixed baby greens

1 can (11 ounces) mandarin oranges, drained

1 orange bell pepper, cut into julienne strips

4 carrots, peeled and cut into julienne strips

1 small yellow squash, cut into julienne strips

4 scallions, thinly sliced

1. Rinse the tenderloin, and pat it dry with paper towels.

2. To make the marinade, combine all of the marinade ingredients in a resealable plastic bag, and shake to blend. Add the tenderloin and turn to coat. Seal the bag, and refrigerate for several hours or overnight, turning the tenderloin at least once.

3. Remove the tenderloin from the marinade, discarding the marinade, and transfer the tenderloin to a roasting pan. Bake in a preheated 350°F oven for 35 to 40 minutes, or until a meat thermometer inserted in the center of the meat registers 155°F or the meat is no longer pink inside. Allow the tenderloin to cool for 10 minutes before cutting into thin slices.

4. To serve, divide the mixed baby greens among 4 dinner plates. Randomly distribute the pork slices, mandarin oranges, bell pepper, carrots, yellow squash, and scallions over the greens. Drizzle some of the dressing over each salad, and serve immediately.

Spicy Pork and Potato Salad

YIELD: 4 SERVINGS

This tangy creation is very similar to the popular Salad Niçoise, except that it features the wonderfully exotic flavors of India. For a delicious change of pace, try substituting lamb for the pork. Serve this salad with naan—Indian flat bread.

Suggested Dressings

★ 1 recipe Curry Vinaigrette (page 220)

Marinade

½ cup unsweetened pineapple juice

2 tablespoons hot honey mustard

1½ tablespoons kecap manis* or soy sauce

¼ teaspoon Asian hot sauce or favorite hot pepper sauce

1 pork tenderloin (12 ounces), all visible fat removed

1 pound new potatoes, sliced ½ inch thick

2 scallions, thinly sliced

2 tablespoons chopped fresh cilantro

1 shallot, finely chopped

4 carrots, peeled and cut into julienne strips

24 fresh asparagus spears (1 pound), tough ends removed, or 1 can (15 ounces) asparagus, drained

6 cups prewashed baby spinach, stems removed

NUTRITIONAL FACTS
(per serving, salad only)

Calories: 255
Carbohydrates: 32.8 g
Cholesterol: 55 mg
Fat: 4.1 g
Calories From Fat: 13.9%
Protein: 24.2 g
Sodium: 450 mg

* A sweet Indonesian soy sauce, kecap manis can be found in Asian food stores.

1. Rinse the tenderloin, and pat it dry with paper towels.

2. To make the marinade, combine all of the marinade ingredients in a resealable plastic bag, and shake to blend. Add the tenderloin and turn to coat. Seal the bag, and refrigerate for several hours or overnight, turning the tenderloin at least once.

3. Remove the tenderloin from the marinade, discarding the marinade, and transfer the tenderloin to a roasting pan. Bake in a preheated 350°F oven for 35 to 40 minutes, or until a meat thermometer inserted in the center of the meat registers 155°F or the meat is no longer pink inside. Allow the tenderloin to cool for 10 minutes before cutting into thin slices. Set aside.

4. Cook the potatoes in a large steamer for 20 to 25 minutes, or until fork tender. Drain well, and allow to come to room temperature.

5. Combine the potatoes, scallions, cilantro, shallot, and 3 table-spoons of the dressing in a large salad bowl, and toss gently to mix. Cover the bowl and set aside at room temperature for 1 to 2 hours.

6. While the potato mixture is marinating, cook the carrots in a steamer for 4 minutes. If using fresh asparagus, cut the asparagus in half and add them to the steamer. Cook for 2 additional minutes, or until the vegetables are fork tender. Drain well, and allow to come to room temperature.

7. Add the pork, carrots, and asparagus to the potato mixture, and toss gently to combine. Add the remaining dressing, and toss gently to coat.

8. To serve, divide the spinach among 4 dinner plates, and spoon the salad in the center of the greens. Serve immediately.

Satisfying
Seafood Salads

The variety of ocean bounty that is now available year-round from coast to coast has created a generation of seafood lovers. If you are a devotee of seafood, you will be delighted by the recipes in this chapter. Here, you will discover that the tuna salad we all remember from our childhood has grown up into such mouthwatering delights as Mediterranean Grilled Tuna Salad, and Tuna, Avocado, and Spinach Salad. Other gifts from the sea are featured in such dishes as the refreshing Shrimp and Mandarin Orange Salad, and the zesty Caesar Salad With Grilled Salmon. Once you have sampled just a few of these novel yet simple-to-prepare creations, I predict you will become "hooked" on main course seafood salads.

Balsamic Vinegar-Glazed Salmon Salad

Salmon reaches a new dimension when enlivened with a reduced balsamic glaze. It is then further enhanced by a bed of citrus-kissed spinach. Serve with low-fat poppy seed bread.

1 skinless salmon fillet (12 ounces)

⅓ cup balsamic vinegar

6 cups prewashed baby spinach, stems removed

1 papaya or mango, peeled, seeded, and cut into cubes

1. Rinse the salmon fillet, and pat it dry with paper towels. Cut the fillet into thin strips.

2. Coat a large nonstick skillet with olive oil cooking spray, and preheat over medium-high heat. Add the salmon and stir-fry for 1 to 2 minutes, or until no longer red inside. Transfer the salmon to a dish, cover loosely with aluminum foil, and set aside.

3. Add the balsamic vinegar to the same skillet, and reduce the heat to medium. Simmer, stirring occasionally, for 3 to 4 minutes, or until the vinegar becomes syrupy.

4. Return the salmon to the skillet, and turn to coat with the glaze. Remove the skillet from the heat, and set aside.

5. Combine the spinach and dressing in a large bowl, and toss gently to coat.

6. To serve, divide the spinach among 4 dinner plates. Top each bed of spinach with some of the salmon, and randomly arrange the papaya or mango cubes over the fish. Serve immediately.

YIELD: 4 SERVINGS

Suggested Dressings

★ 1 recipe Citrus Vinaigrette (page 219)

1 recipe Lemon Vinaigrette (page 225)

½ cup commercial fat-free or low-fat lemon Dijon dressing

NUTRITIONAL FACTS
(per serving, salad only)

Calories: 135
Carbohydrates: 8.4 g
Cholesterol: 44 mg
Fat: 3.2 g
Calories From Fat: 20.9%
Protein: 19 g
Sodium: 107 mg

Caesar Salad With Grilled Salmon

YIELD: 4 SERVINGS

Suggested Dressings

★ 1 recipe Caesar
Dressing (page 216)

½ cup commercial fat-free
or low-fat Caesar dressing

½ cup commercial fat-free
or low-fat Caesar Italian
dressing

NUTRITIONAL FACTS
(per serving, salad only)

Calories: 174
Carbohydrates: 10.9 g
Cholesterol: 60 mg
Fat: 3.8 g
Calories From Fat: 19.2%
Protein: 25.4 g
Sodium: 411 mg

*On a recent trip to Seattle, I was served this wonderful salad at a
seafood restaurant. Now I enjoy this delicious and
satisfying dish in my own home.*

1 skinless salmon fillet (12 ounces)
Olive oil cooking spray
⅛ teaspoon salt
⅛ teaspoon freshly ground pepper
6 cups prewashed baby spinach, stems removed
12 cherry tomatoes, stemmed and halved
½ cup grated fat-free Parmesan cheese
4 anchovy fillets, drained
1 cup commercial fat-free Caesar-flavored croutons (optional)
1 avocado, peeled, pitted, and thinly sliced (optional)

1. Rinse the salmon, and pat it dry with paper towels.

2. Lightly coat both sides of the salmon with the olive oil cooking
spray, and season with the salt and pepper. Place the salmon over
moderately hot coals on a grill coated with cooking spray. (If available, use a grilling grid coated with cooking spray.*) Cover the grill
and cook for 10 minutes, or until the salmon is no longer red
inside. Alternatively, cook the salmon in a microwave oven by
placing the salmon and 2 tablespoons of water in a covered
microwave-safe dish. Microwave on high power for 7 to 9 minutes.
Allow the salmon to cool for 10 minutes before cutting into cubes.

3. To serve, combine the salmon, spinach, tomatoes, Parmesan
cheese, and anchovies in a salad bowl. If desired, add the croutons
and avocado. Add the dressing, and toss gently to coat. Serve
immediately.

* A grilling grid is a flat porcelain-enameled steel grate with multiple holes.
When placed directly on the cooking grate of a grill, it is excellent for grilling
vegetables, seafood, or other foods that are too small or fragile to cook over a
conventional grate.

Hail Caesar!

Although Julius Caesar was a great statesman and general, he did not invent the Caesar Salad. Instead, it was invented in the 1920s by Caesar Cardini, the owner of an Italian restaurant in Tijuana, Mexico. The now-famous dish was originally known as the "aviator's salad," but Mr. Cardini later renamed it "Caesar's Salad."

Greek Salmon and Pasta Salad

YIELD: 4 SERVINGS

Greek salad is a Mediterranean specialty that combines wonderful spices, condiments, and vegetables. The addition of salmon and pasta turns this delight into an exceptional meal. Serve with warm pita bread.

1 skinless salmon fillet (12 ounces)

2 tablespoons cold water

6 ounces ziti pasta

1 orange bell pepper, thinly sliced into strips

1 cup thin red onion rings

1½ ounces feta cheese, crumbled

½ cup pitted Kalamata olives (optional)

2 Roma tomatoes, quartered

4 cups prewashed baby spinach, stems removed

Suggested Dressings

★ 1 recipe Greek Vinaigrette (page 222)

1 recipe Red Wine Vinaigrette (page 232)

½ cup commercial fat-free or low-fat Greek vinaigrette

½ cut commercial fat-free or low-fat red wine vinaigrette

NUTRITIONAL FACTS
(per serving, salad only)

Calories: 250
Carbohydrates: 37.3 g
Cholesterol: 36 mg
Fat: 3.7 g
Calories From Fat: 30%
Protein: 18.3 g
Sodium: 154 mg

1. Rinse the salmon, and place the salmon and the water in a covered microwave-safe dish. Microwave on high power for 7 to 9 minutes, or until no longer red inside. Allow the salmon to cool for 10 minutes before cutting into cubes.

2. While the salmon is cooling, cook the pasta according to package directions. Drain, rinse with cool water, and drain again. Allow the pasta to come to room temperature.

3. Combine the salmon, pasta, bell pepper, onion rings, feta cheese, and olives, if desired, in a salad bowl. Add the vinaigrette, and toss gently to coat. Cover and refrigerate until ready to serve.

4. Remove the salad from the refrigerator 1 hour before serving. Add the tomatoes, and toss gently.

5. To serve, make a wreath of the spinach on each of 4 dinner plates. Mound the salmon salad in the center of each wreath, and serve immediately.

Salmon, Avocado, and Papaya Salad

YIELD: **4 SERVINGS**

This designer salad is artfully composed of colorful slices of orange-tinted salmon and papaya combined with green avocado, all against a background of mixed baby greens. A tangy dressing boldly dresses the salad to complete the dazzling composition.

Suggested Dressings

★ 1 recipe Lime Vinaigrette (page 226)

1 recipe Lemon Vinaigrette (page 225)

½ cup commercial fat-free or low-fat lemon Dijon dressing

1 skinless salmon fillet (12 ounces)
2 tablespoons cold water
6 cups mixed baby greens
2 papayas or mangos, peeled, seeded, and thinly sliced
1 avocado, peeled, pitted, and thinly sliced

1. Rinse the salmon, and place the salmon and the water in a covered microwave-safe dish. Microwave on high power for 7 to 9 minutes, or until the salmon is no longer red inside. Allow the salmon to cool for 10 minutes before cutting into cubes.

2. To serve, combine the salmon, mixed baby greens, papaya or mango, and avocado in a salad bowl. Add the dressing, and toss gently to coat. Serve immediately.

NUTRITIONAL FACTS
(per serving, salad only)

Calories: 213
Carbohydrates: 15.2 g
Cholesterol: 44 mg
Fat: 8.9 g
Calories From Fat: 36.6%
Protein: 19.7 g
Sodium: 85 mg

Serving Suggestion

For a more artistic presentation, instead of cubing the salmon, cut it into 4 portions. Divide the mixed baby greens among 4 dinner plates, and place a piece of salmon on each bed of greens. Create a contrasting design of the papaya and avocado by fanning 2 to 3 slices of papaya interspersed with slices of avocado beside each portion of salmon. Finally, drizzle the dressing over each salad, and garnish with a scallion flower (page 42), if desired.

Salmon, Avocado, Feta, and Onion Salad

YIELD: 4 SERVINGS

This salmon salad boasts an unusual array of contrasting ingredients and flavors that amazingly come together to form a tantalizing entrée. Serve with warm pita bread.

1 skinless salmon fillet (12 ounces)
2 tablespoons cold water
6 cups prewashed baby spinach, stems removed
1 avocado, peeled, pitted, and thinly sliced
1 cup thin red onion rings
1½ ounces feta cheese, crumbled
1 tablespoon capers, rinsed and drained

1. Rinse the salmon, and place the salmon and the water in a covered microwave-safe dish. Microwave on high power for 7 to 9 minutes, or until the salmon is no longer red inside. Allow the salmon to cool for 10 minutes before cutting into bite-sized pieces.

2. To serve, combine the salmon, spinach, avocado, onion rings, feta cheese, and capers in a salad bowl. Add the vinaigrette, and toss gently to coat. Serve immediately.

Suggested Dressings

★ 1 recipe Lemon Vinaigrette (page 225)

1 recipe Greek Vinaigrette (page 222)

½ cup commercial fat-free or low-fat Greek vinaigrette

NUTRITIONAL FACTS
(per serving, salad only)

Calories: 214
Carbohydrates: 8.4 g
Cholesterol: 54 mg
Fat: 11.2 g
Calories From Fat: 45.8%
Protein: 21.4 g
Sodium: 228 mg

Salmon Savvy

Salmon is a firm, pink-fleshed fish with a butter-smooth flavor. Both Atlantic and Pacific varieties are available. Atlantic salmon has more flavor, especially if caught in Scotland or Ireland. Today, however, most salmon are actually farm-raised. Pacific salmon are usually harvested wild, though, and so are available during only the spring and summer months.

When you choose a salmon fillet, look for one that has a translucent appearance, is brilliant in color, and has a firm flesh with a moist sheen on its surface. Refrigerate your salmon as soon as you get it home, and use it on the day of purchase.

Salmon Salad With Roasted Red Pepper Purée

YIELD: 4 SERVINGS

Suggested Dressings

★ 1 recipe Balsamic Vinaigrette (page 215)

1 recipe Caper Vinaigrette (page 217)

½ cup commercial fat-free or low-fat balsamic vinaigrette

Time-Saving Tip
❑ Substitute ¾ cup of commercial sweet roasted bell peppers for the home-made roasted peppers.

NUTRITIONAL FACTS
(per serving, salad only)

Calories: 141
Carbohydrates: 8.9 g
Cholesterol: 44 mg
Fat: 3.3 g
Calories From Fat: 20.8%
Protein: 19.6 g
Sodium: 152 mg

When poached salmon is combined with diced red onions and tomatoes, placed on a bed of spinach, and topped with a flavorful roasted red pepper purée, the result is both colorful and delicious. If there is insufficient time to prepare the purée, you'll find that the salad is excellent even when unadorned.

Roasted Red Pepper Purée

3 large red bell peppers

1 teaspoon balsamic vinegar

¼ teaspoon ground cumin

⅛ teaspoon salt

⅛ teaspoon freshly ground pepper

1 skinless salmon fillet (12 ounces)

2 tablespoons cold water

1 cup diced red onion

1 cup diced seeded tomato

6 cups prewashed baby spinach, stems removed

4 sprigs fresh parsley (optional)

1. To roast the peppers, place the peppers on a baking sheet that has been lined with aluminum foil. Broil under a preheated broiler, turning the peppers as the skins blacken, for 20 to 25 minutes, or until the skins are charred all over. Once roasted, place in a plastic bag, seal, and allow to steam for 15 minutes. When the peppers are cool enough to handle, peel away the skin and remove the tops and seeds. (Do not rinse the peppers.)

2. Place the roasted peppers in the work bowl of a food processor fitted with a metal blade, and process until puréed. Add the remaining purée ingredients, and process until well blended. Transfer the purée to a covered container, and set aside at room temperature for up to 1 hour, or refrigerate for several hours or overnight.

3. Rinse the salmon, and place the salmon and the water in a covered microwave-safe dish. Microwave on high power for 7 to 9 minutes, or until the salmon is no longer red inside. Allow the salmon to cool for 10 minutes before cutting into small cubes.

4. Combine the salmon, onion, and tomato in a medium-sized bowl, and toss gently to blend. Set aside.

5. Combine the spinach and vinaigrette in a medium-sized bowl, and toss gently to coat. Set aside.

6. If the roasted red pepper purée was refrigerated, allow to come to room temperature.

7. To serve, divide the spinach among 4 dinner plates. Place a mound of the salmon mixture on each bed of spinach, and spoon the purée over each serving. Garnish with a sprig of parsley, if desired, and serve immediately.

Southwestern Rubbed Salmon Salad

I frequently use spice-infused rubs to transform simple fare into mouth-watering creations. In this salad, a rub puts a Southwestern spin on a simple salad of salmon, spinach, pineapple, and avocado. Serve with grilled polenta.

Suggested Dressings

★ 1 recipe Southwestern Vinaigrette (page 235)

1 recipe Cilantro Vinaigrette (page 219)

½ cup commercial fat-free or low-fat Santa Fe blend dressing

½ cup commercial Southwest Caesar dressing

Serving Suggestion

For a more artistic presentation, first make a bed of the spinach on each of 4 dinner plates. Slice the salmon, and arrange the slices over the spinach. Arrange the pineapple and avocado cubes on either side of the salmon, and drizzle the dressing over each serving. Finally, garnish with baked tortilla strips (page 35), if desired.

NUTRITIONAL FACTS
(per serving, salad only)

Calories: 211
Carbohydrates: 13.9 g
Cholesterol: 44 mg
Fat: 9.4 g
Calories From Fat: 38.4%
Protein: 19.9 g
Sodium: 245 mg

Southwestern Rub

1 tablespoon packed dark brown sugar
2 teaspoons cumin
1 teaspoon ground coriander
1 teaspoon dry mustard
½ teaspoon freshly ground pepper
¼ teaspoon salt
⅛ teaspoon cayenne pepper
1 skinless salmon fillet (12 ounces)
6 cups prewashed baby spinach, stems removed
2 cups cubed fresh pineapple
1 avocado, peeled, pitted, and cubed

1. To make the rub, combine all of the rub ingredients in a jar with a tight-fitting lid, and shake well to mix.

2. Rinse the salmon, and pat it dry with paper towels. Press the rub onto both sides of the fillet.

3. Place the salmon over moderately hot coals on a grill coated with cooking spray. (If available, use a grilling grid coated with cooking spray.*) Cover the grill and cook for 10 minutes, or until the salmon is no longer red inside. Alternatively, place the salmon under a preheated broiler and broil for 4 minutes on each side. Allow to cool for 10 minutes before cutting into cubes.

4. To serve, combine the salmon, spinach, pineapple, and avocado in a salad bowl. Add the dressing, and toss gently to coat. Serve immediately.

* A grilling grid is a flat porcelain-enameled steel grate with multiple holes. When placed directly on the cooking grate of a grill, it is excellent for grilling seafood or other foods that are too fragile to cook over a conventional grate.

Caribbean Shrimp and Mango Salad

Caribbean cuisine has recently become very popular, and for good reason. The intense fruit and spice flavors of the tropics add zest to almost any dish. This salad incorporates many of the same ingredients found in a Cobb salad, but adds a new twist in the form of a piquant Caribbean dressing. Serve with low-fat papaya bread.

12 ounces medium shrimp, peeled and deveined
6 cups prewashed baby spinach, stems removed
4 slices 95% fat-free turkey bacon, cooked according to package directions and crumbled
1 large mango or papaya, peeled, pitted, and cut into cubes
1 cup diced red bell pepper
1 cup diced red onion
1 ounce Maytag blue cheese or other blue cheese, crumbled

1. Rinse the shrimp. Place enough water to cover the shrimp in a medium-sized saucepan, and bring to a boil over high heat. Add the shrimp and boil for 1 to 2 minutes, or until the shrimp turn pink. Drain well, and allow to come to room temperature.

2. To serve, combine the shrimp, spinach, bacon, mango or papaya, red pepper, onion, and blue cheese in a salad bowl. Add the dressing, and toss gently to coat. Serve immediately.

Suggested Dressings

★ 1 recipe Caribbean Dressing (page 217)

Time-Saving Tip
❏ Substitute 12 ounces of precooked shrimp for the home-cooked shrimp.

NUTRITIONAL FACTS
(per serving, salad only)
Calories: 220
Carbohydrates: 21.3 g
Cholesterol: 150 mg
Fat: 4.4 g
Calories From Fat: 21.8%
Protein: 25.1 g
Sodium: 497 mg

Cubing a Mango

The mango has a large, flat pit in the middle of the fruit. This pit can make cubing a mango a little tricky.

The easiest way to cube the flesh of a mango and separate the flesh from the pit is to first stand the fruit upright. Then use a sharp knife to cut downwards on either side of the pit, so that you've divided the mango into three parts, with the pit in the central section. Take each of the outside sections, one at a time, and score the flesh of the mango in a grid pattern, being careful not to cut through the skin. Then turn each section inside out, so that the flesh is on the outside. Slice the flesh away, cutting as close to the skin as possible, and you'll have a neatly cubed mango.

YIELD: 4 SERVINGS

Salmon, Red Pepper, and Onion Salad

The inspiration for this salad came from my passion for Indian cuisine. The salmon is marinated with Indian spices, and then, after cooking, is combined with red pepper and onions. Serve with naan, an Indian flatbread that is available in most Asian food stores.

Time-Saving Tip

❏ Substitute ⅓ cup of your favorite Indian marinade for the homemade marinade.

**NUTRITIONAL FACTS
(per serving, salad only)**

Calories: 183
Carbohydrates: 15.7 g
Cholesterol: 44 mg
Fat: 5.2 g
Calories From Fat: 24.9%
Protein: 19.7 g
Sodium: 202 mg

Marinade

¼ cup plus 2 tablespoons unsweetened pineapple juice

1½ tablespoons finely chopped fresh ginger

1½ teaspoons ground coriander

1½ teaspoons ground cumin

¼ teaspoon cayenne pepper

¼ teaspoon salt

1 skinless salmon fillet (12 ounces)

½ tablespoon canola oil

1 clove garlic, thinly sliced

1 cup very thin rings Vidalia or other sweet onion

2 tablespoons fresh lemon juice

1 large red bell pepper, cut into julienne strips

2 scallions, thinly sliced

2 tablespoons coarsely chopped fresh cilantro

1. Rinse the salmon, and pat it dry with paper towels.

2. To make the marinade, combine all of the marinade ingredients in a microwave-safe dish, and stir to blend. Add the salmon and turn to coat. Cover the dish with plastic wrap and refrigerate for 30 minutes, turning the salmon after 15 minutes.

3. Transfer the salmon to a plate and strain the marinade, reserving 2 tablespoons. Return the reserved marinade and the salmon to the dish, cover, and microwave on high power for 7 to 9 minutes, or until the salmon is no longer red inside. Allow the salmon to cool for 10 minutes before cutting into cubes.

4. While the salmon is cooling, lightly coat a small nonstick skillet with cooking spray, and preheat over medium heat. Add the canola oil and garlic, and stir-fry for 2 to 3 minutes, or until the garlic is golden. Remove the skillet from heat and set aside.

5. Combine the onion and lemon juice in a salad bowl, and turn to coat. Set aside for 5 minutes.

6. Add the salmon, red pepper, scallions, and cilantro to the salad bowl, and toss gently to blend. Add the garlic and toss once more. Cover and refrigerate for several hours or overnight.

7. Stir the chilled salad, and serve immediately.

Shrimp and Mushroom Salad

For exquisite color and taste, you can't top this showstopping salad. It is beautiful whether served in a crystal bowl, or artfully arranged in the center of a wreath of baby greens.

12 ounces medium shrimp, peeled and deveined

8 ounces fresh mushrooms, thinly sliced

1 red bell pepper, cut into julienne strips

2 scallions, thinly sliced

2 tablespoons coarsely chopped fresh cilantro

1. Rinse the shrimp. Place enough water to cover the shrimp in a medium-sized saucepan, and bring to a boil over high heat. Add the shrimp and boil for 1 to 2 minutes, or until the shrimp turn pink. Drain well, and allow to come to room temperature.

2. Combine the shrimp, mushrooms, red pepper, scallions, and cilantro in a salad bowl. Add the dressing, and toss gently to coat. Cover and refrigerate for several hours.

3. Stir the chilled salad, and serve immediately.

YIELD: 4 SERVINGS

Suggested Dressings

★ 1 recipe Lime Vinaigrette (page 226)

1 recipe Citrus Vinaigrette (page 219)

½ cup commercial fat-free or low-fat lemon Dijon dressing

Time-Saving Tip
❑ Substitute 12 ounces of precooked shrimp for the home-cooked shrimp.

**NUTRITIONAL FACTS
(per serving, salad only)**
Calories: 289
Carbohydrates: 50.4 g
Cholesterol: 129 mg
Fat: 2.3 g
Calories From Fat: 6.4%
Protein: 24.3 g
Sodium: 138 mg

Shrimp and Avocado Salad

YIELD: 4 SERVINGS

This dish was inspired by a friend's description of a fabulous salad she enjoyed at a Seattle restaurant. The artful contrast of pink shrimp, orange mango, red tomato, and green avocado is nothing short of spectacular in appearance.

Suggested Dressings

★ 1 recipe Raspberry Vinaigrette (page 232)

1 recipe Citrus Vinaigrette (page 219)

½ cup commercial fat-free or low-fat raspberry vinaigrette

½ cup commercial fat-free or low-fat poppy seed dressing

12 ounces medium shrimp, peeled and deveined

12 leaves lamb's lettuce, torn into generous bite-sized pieces

2 cups bean sprouts

1 mango or papaya, peeled, pitted, and cubed

1 avocado, peeled, pitted, and cubed

1 cup stemmed and halved cherry tomatoes

1 cup thin red onion rings

Time-Saving Tip
❏ Substitute 12 ounces of precooked shrimp for the home-cooked shrimp.

1. Rinse the shrimp. Place enough water to cover the shrimp in a large saucepan, and bring to a boil over high heat. Add the shrimp and boil for 1 to 2 minutes, or until the shrimp turn pink. Drain well, and allow to come to room temperature.

2. To serve, combine the shrimp, lettuce, bean sprouts, mango or papaya, avocado, tomatoes, and onion rings in a salad bowl. Add the vinaigrette, and toss gently to coat. Serve immediately.

**NUTRITIONAL FACTS
(per serving, salad only)**

Calories: 263
Carbohydrates: 23.1 g
Cholesterol: 129 mg
Fat: 7.7 g
Calories From Fat: 27.9%
Protein: 21.7 g
Sodium: 162 mg

Serving Suggestion

For a more artistic presentation, make the shrimp salad as described above, omitting the lettuce. Add just enough vinaigrette to lightly coat, and toss gently to blend. Arrange 2 to 3 lamb's lettuce leaves on each of 4 dinner plates, so that the leaves slightly overlap one another and their points are almost in the center of each plate. Spoon the shrimp salad in the center of each plate so that it slightly overlaps the points of the leaves. Thinly slice 2 peaches and 1 avocado, and garnish one side of the salad with the peach slices, and the other with the avocado slices. Drizzle the remaining dressing over the lettuce leaves.

Shrimp and Mandarin Orange Salad

This quick-and-easy salad is ideal to prepare when time is of the essence. The toasted sesame seeds and almonds add crunch and flavor, and the dressing adds zest to the shrimp and spinach. Serve with crusty rolls.

12 ounces medium shrimp, peeled and deveined
6 cups prewashed baby spinach, stems removed
1 can (11 ounces) mandarin oranges, drained
1 star fruit, sliced
2 scallions, thinly sliced
1½ tablespoons toasted slivered almonds (page 69)
1 tablespoon toasted sesame seeds (page 69)
4 scallion flowers (page 42) (optional)

Suggested Dressings

★ 1 recipe Red Wine Vinaigrette (page 232)

1 recipe Honey Dijon Vinaigrette (page 223)

½ cup commercial fat-free or low-fat red wine vinaigrette

½ cup commercial fat-free or low-fat honey Dijon dressing

1. Rinse the shrimp, and pat them dry with paper towels.

2. Lightly coat a medium-sized nonstick skillet with cooking spray, and preheat over medium-high heat. Add the shrimp and stir-fry for 2 to 3 minutes, or until the shrimp turn pink. Allow the shrimp to come to room temperature.

3. Combine the shrimp, spinach, mandarin oranges, star fruit, scallions, almonds, and sesame seeds in a salad bowl. Add the dressing, and toss gently to coat.

4. To serve, divide the salad among 4 dinner plates, and garnish each serving with a scallion flower, if desired. Serve immediately.

Time-Saving Tip

❑ Substitute 12 ounces of precooked shrimp for the home-cooked shrimp.

NUTRITIONAL FACTS
(per serving, salad only)

Calories: 174
Carbohydrates: 13.4 g
Cholesterol: 129 mg
Fat: 4.7 g
Calories From Fat: 23.8%
Protein: 20.7 g
Sodium: 177 mg

Shrimp Talk

Shrimp make a delicious addition to salads. But keep in mind that, like all seafood, shrimp are highly perishable. So it is important to select fresh, high-quality shrimp; to store them properly; and to use them as soon as possible.

If buying shrimp in their shells, look for shiny, tight-fitting shells. If the shrimp have already been shelled, make sure that they are dry and firm. Always avoid any shrimp with black discolorations along the head or belly, as well as shrimp that have an ammonia odor. For best results, buy your seafood the day you plan to use it, and store it in the coldest part of the refrigerator until needed.

Shrimp and Rice Salad

This is a perfect salad to tuck into your picnic basket. Just add a variety of sliced melons and a loaf of crusty bread.

Suggested Dressings

★ 1 recipe Caper Vinaigrette (page 217)

1 recipe Italian Vinaigrette (page 224)

½ cup commercial fat-free or low-fat Italian vinaigrette

½ cup commercial fat-free or low-fat Greek vinaigrette

Time-Saving Tip
❑ Substitute 1 pound of precooked shrimp for the home-cooked shrimp.

NUTRITIONAL FACTS
(per serving, salad only)
Calories: 276
Carbohydrates: 41.7 g
Cholesterol: 166 mg
Fat: 1.6 g
Calories From Fat: 5.1%
Protein: 25 g
Sodium: 304 mg

1 cup long-grain rice
1 pound medium shrimp, peeled and deveined
1 red bell pepper, minced
1 can (13 ounces) quartered artichoke hearts, drained
½ cup minced red onion
¼ cup chopped fresh parsley
1 can (4 ounces) sliced black olives, drained (optional)

1. Cook the rice according to package directions, omitting butter and margarine. Allow the rice to come to room temperature.

2. While the rice is cooking, rinse the shrimp. Place enough water to cover the shrimp in a medium-sized saucepan, and bring to a boil over high heat. Add the shrimp and boil for 1 to 2 minutes, or until the shrimp turn pink. Drain well, and allow to come to room temperature.

3. Combine the rice, shrimp, red pepper, artichoke hearts, onion, parsley, and olives, if desired, in a salad bowl. Add the vinaigrette, and toss gently to coat. Cover and refrigerate for several hours or overnight.

4. Remove the salad from the refrigerator 1 hour before serving. Toss gently to blend, and serve immediately.

Rice Tips

Rice adds both a distinctive flavor and a contrasting texture to salads, in addition to making your dish more satisfying. For best results, though, you'll want your rice to be as fluffy as possible before you toss it into your salad. A quick and easy way to fluff rice after it has been cooked is to separate the grains with a pair of chopsticks held slightly apart. After the rice has come to room temperature, add the remaining salad ingredients and the vinaigrette.

Shrimp and Pasta Salad

This salad combines shrimp, pasta, and an array of vegetables to make a fabulous dish that bursts with savory flavors. Serve on a ring of thinly sliced tomatoes with bits of parsley randomly placed between some of the slices.

6 ounces ziti pasta
8 ounces medium shrimp, peeled and deveined
1 cup broccoli florets
12 sun-dried tomatoes (packaged without oil)
2 cups thinly sliced prewashed spinach, stems removed
1 can (13 ounces) quartered artichoke hearts, drained

1. Cook the pasta according to package directions. Drain, rinse with cool water, and drain again. Set aside.

2. Rinse the shrimp. Place enough water to cover the shrimp in a medium-sized saucepan, and bring to a boil over high heat. Add the shrimp and boil for 1 to 2 minutes, or until the shrimp turn pink. Drain well, and allow to come to room temperature.

3. Cook the broccoli in a steamer for 1 minute. Drain well, and allow to come to room temperature.

4. Place the sun-dried tomatoes in a small heatproof bowl, and add enough boiling water to cover. Allow to sit for 5 to 15 minutes, or until the tomatoes are soft. Drain well, and thinly slice.

5. Combine the pasta, shrimp, broccoli, tomatoes, spinach, and artichokes in a salad bowl. Add the dressing, and toss gently to coat. Cover and refrigerate for several hours.

6. Remove the salad from the refrigerator 1 hour before serving. Toss gently to blend, and serve immediately.

Serving Suggestion

For a more artistic presentation, first thinly slice 4 tomatoes, and make a wreath of the slices on each of 4 dinner plates. Mound the salad in the center of each wreath, and randomly place bits of parsley between some of the tomato slices.

YIELD: 4 SERVINGS

Suggested Dressings

★ 1 recipe Tarragon Vinaigrette (page 238)

1 recipe Italian Vinaigrette (page 224)

½ cup commercial fat-free or low-fat classic herb vinaigrette

½ cup commercial fat-free or low-fat Italian Parmesan dressing

Time-Saving Tip

❑ Substitute 8 ounces of precooked shrimp for the home-cooked shrimp.

NUTRITIONAL FACTS
(per serving, salad only)

Calories: 318
Carbohydrates: 54.8 g
Cholesterol: 129 mg
Fat: 1.9 g
Calories From Fat: 10.1%
Protein: 29.9 g
Sodium: 324 mg

YIELD: **4** SERVINGS

Shrimp and Saffron Rice Salad

Reminiscent of Spanish paella, this shrimp and saffron rice salad will make you feel as though you're sitting in a café overlooking the Costa del Sol. All that is needed to complete the fantasy is a pitcher of sangria and a warm gentle breeze.

Serving Suggestion

For a more artistic presentation, make the rice salad as described above, but reserve 8 of the cooked shrimp. Line four 2-cup custard cups with plastic wrap, and fill each with the salad, packing it down as much as possible. Turn 1 custard cup upside-down in the middle of each of 4 dinner plates, and carefully remove the cup and the plastic wrap. Make a wreath of the arugula leaves around half of the rice, and garnish the other half of the rice with 2 of the reserved shrimp.

1 cup frozen peas
1 large Vidalia onion or other sweet onion, coarsely chopped
2 cloves garlic, finely chopped
2 teaspoons extra virgin olive oil, divided
1 cup arborio rice*
12 ounces medium shrimp, peeled and deveined
¼ cup plus 2 tablespoons fat-free chicken broth, divided
½ teaspoon saffron threads
½ teaspoon freshly ground pepper
¼ teaspoon salt
4 cups packed arugula leaves, tough stems removed
4 tomato roses (page 179) (optional)

* A starchy short-grain rice often used to make risotto, arborio rice can be found in the rice section of many supermarkets and specialty stores.

1. Cook the peas according to package directions. Drain well, and allow to come to room temperature.

2. Coat a medium-sized nonstick skillet with olive oil cooking spray, and preheat over medium heat. Add the onion, garlic, and 1 teaspoon of the olive oil, and stir to blend. Cook, stirring occasionally, for 25 to 30 minutes, or until the onion and garlic are golden and tender.

3. While the onion and garlic are cooking, cook the rice according to package directions. Allow to come to room temperature.

4. Place the cooked rice, onion, and garlic in a salad bowl, and stir gently to blend. Set aside.

5. Rinse the shrimp, and pat them dry with paper towels. Preheat the same skillet used earlier over medium heat, and add the shrimp. Stir-fry for 3 minutes, or until the shrimp turn pink. Add the shrimp to the rice mixture, and toss gently to blend.

Time-Saving Tip

❏ Substitute 12 ounces of precooked shrimp for the home-cooked shrimp.

6. Place 2 tablespoons of the chicken broth in a small saucepan, and cook over medium heat until warm. Place the warmed chicken broth and the saffron in a small dish, and allow to sit for 15 minutes to bring out the flavor and color of the saffron.

7. Place the remaining $1/4$ cup of chicken broth, the remaining teaspoon of olive oil, and the pepper and salt in another small dish, and stir to blend well.

8. Add the saffron mixture, chicken broth mixture, and peas to the rice mixture, and toss gently to blend. Cover and refrigerate for several hours or overnight.

9. Remove the salad from the refrigerator 1 hour before serving, and stir gently to blend. Make a wreath of the arugula leaves on each of 4 dinner plates. Spoon the rice mixture in the center of each wreath, and garnish with a tomato rose, if desired. Serve immediately.

NUTRITIONAL FACTS
(per serving, salad only)

Calories: 322
Carbohydrates: 45.9 g
Cholesterol: 129 mg
Fat: 4 g
Calories From Fat: 11.3%
Protein: 24.2 g
Sodium: 361 mg

Saffron—The Priceless Spice

Saffron, the most expensive spice in the world, is actually the dried stigma of the blue flower Crocus sativus. It is grown in Spain, Turkey, and India. Each flower produces three very small, deep yellow-orange stigma threads that can be removed only by hand. To produce one pound of saffron, between 70,000 and 225,000 flowers must be processed this way.

Is saffron worth the price? This valued ingredient adds a golden color as well as a subtle but exotic aroma and flavor to dishes. And, fortunately, a little saffron goes a long way.

Shrimp and Wild Rice Salad

YIELD: 4 SERVINGS

Honey Dijon Vinaigrette accents the flavors of the crunchy wild rice, shrimp, and vegetables in this colorful salad. I like to serve it on a bed of spinach leaves garnished with slices of mango, kiwi fruit, and star fruit.

Suggested Dressings

★ 1 recipe Honey Dijon Vinaigrette (page 223)

½ cup commercial fat-free or low-fat honey Dijon dressing

Serving Suggestion

For a more artistic presentation, make a bed of spinach leaves on each of 4 dinner plates, and mound the shrimp salad in the center of each spinach bed. Thinly slice 1 star fruit, 1 kiwi fruit, and 1 mango, and arrange some of the slices to the side of each wreath.

1 cup wild rice
2 carrots, peeled and thinly sliced
1 cup broccoli florets
10 ounces small shrimp, peeled and deveined
¾ cup dark raisins
1 red bell pepper, diced
¼ cup thinly sliced scallions
¼ cup coarsely chopped pecans (optional)

1. Cook the rice according to package directions, omitting butter or margarine. Allow the rice to come to room temperature.

2. While the rice is cooking, cook the carrots in a steamer for 2 minutes. Add the broccoli, and cook for 1 additional minute, or until the broccoli is bright green. Drain well, and allow to come to room temperature.

3. Rinse the shrimp. Place enough water to cover the shrimp in a medium-sized saucepan, and bring to a boil over high heat. Add the shrimp and boil for 1 to 2 minutes, or just until the shrimp turn pink. Drain well, and allow to come to room temperature.

4. Combine the rice, carrots and broccoli, shrimp, raisins, red pepper, scallions, and pecans, if desired, in a salad bowl. Add the dressing, and toss gently to blend. Cover and refrigerate for several hours or overnight.

5. Remove the salad from the refrigerator 1 hour before serving. Toss to blend, and serve immediately.

Time-Saving Tip

❏ Substitute 10 ounces of precooked shrimp for the home-cooked shrimp.

NUTRITIONAL FACTS
(per serving, salad only)

Calories: 326
Carbohydrates: 58.4 g
Cholesterol: 138 mg
Fat: 1.6 g
Calories From Fat: 4.2%
Protein: 23.4 g
Sodium: 184 mg

Shrimp, Green Bean, and Fava Bean Salad

YIELD: 4 SERVINGS

The fava bean—also called a broad bean—is a legume frequently used in Middle Eastern, Italian, Chinese, and North American cuisines. This bean deliciously intermingles with the flavors of shrimp and green beans when dressed in a citrus vinaigrette. Serve with warm pita bread.

12 ounces medium shrimp, peeled and deveined
8 ounces green beans, trimmed and cut into 2-inch pieces
1 can (15 ounces) fava beans, rinsed and drained
4 cups mixed baby greens

1. Rinse the shrimp. Place enough water to cover the shrimp in a medium-sized saucepan, and bring to a boil over high heat. Add the shrimp and boil for 1 to 2 minutes, or until the shrimp turn pink. Drain well, and allow to come to room temperature.

2. Cook the green beans in a steamer for 5 minutes, or just until tender and bright green. Drain well, and allow to come to room temperature.

3. To serve, combine the shrimp, green beans, fava beans, and mixed baby greens in a salad bowl. Add the dressing, and toss gently to coat. Serve immediately. (If you don't intend to serve the salad for several hours, reserve the greens when tossing the salad, cover, and refrigerate for several hours or overnight. Toss in the greens directly before serving.)

Suggested Dressings

★ 1 recipe Citrus Vinaigrette (page 219)

1 recipe Lemon Vinaigrette (page 225)

½ cup commercial fat-free or low-fat lemon Dijon dressing

Time-Saving Tip
❏ Substitute 12 ounces of precooked shrimp for the home-cooked shrimp.

NUTRITIONAL FACTS
(per serving, salad only)
Calories: 194
Carbohydrates: 18.9 g
Cholesterol: 129 mg
Fat: 2.3 g
Calories From Fat: 10.4%
Protein: 25.3 g
Sodium: 202 mg

YIELD: **4 SERVINGS**

Shrimp, Mango, and Avocado Salad

With its array of vibrant colors and its striking design, this salad makes a spectacular presentation. And its intriguing taste insures rave reviews. Serve with low-fat poppy seed muffins.

Time-Saving Tip
❏ Substitute 12 ounces of precooked shrimp for the home-cooked shrimp.

NUTRITIONAL FACTS
(per serving, salad only)

Calories: 266
Carbohydrates: 32.5 g
Cholesterol: 129 mg
Fat: 7.7 g
Calories From Fat: 24.5%
Protein: 20.7 g
Sodium: 265 mg

Rice Vinegar Marinade

⅓ cup rice vinegar

2 tablespoons fat-free chicken broth

1 tablespoon light corn syrup

¼ teaspoon salt

¼ teaspoon freshly ground pepper

1 cup diced red onion

12 ounces medium shrimp, peeled and deveined

6 cups mixed baby greens

3 mangos or papayas, peeled, pitted, and thinly sliced

1 avocado, peeled, pitted, and diced

1. To make the marinade, combine all of the marinade ingredients in a salad bowl, and stir to blend well. Add the red onion, and stir to blend well. Set aside.

2. Rinse the shrimp. Place enough water to cover the shrimp in a medium-sized saucepan, and bring to a boil over high heat. Add the shrimp and boil for 1 to 2 minutes, or until the shrimp turn pink. Drain well, and allow to come to room temperature.

3. Add the shrimp to the salad bowl mixture, and toss gently to mix. Cover and refrigerate for several hours or overnight, turning the shrimp and onions at least once.

4. Transfer the shrimp and onions to a strainer, and drain off and discard the marinade.

5. To serve, make a wreath of the mixed baby greens on each of 4 dinner plates. On each plate, arrange a circle of the mango or papaya slices inside the wreath so that they slightly overlap the greens, and spoon the shrimp and onions in the center of the wreath. Garnish the top of each salad with the avocado, and serve immediately.

Shrimp Salad With Fruit Salsa

The strawberry and mango salsa adds sensational taste as well as eye-catching color to this shrimp salad. The salsa is also delicious on poached salmon or a savory Southwestern chicken dish.

Time-Saving Tip
❑ Substitute 12 ounces of precooked shrimp for the home-cooked shrimp.

Fruit Salsa

12 large strawberries, hulled and diced

1 small mango or papaya, peeled, pitted, and diced

¼ cup diced yellow bell pepper

1 tablespoon coarsely chopped fresh cilantro

1 jalapeño chili, seeded and finely chopped*

2 tablespoons fresh lime juice

1 tablespoon rice vinegar

12 ounces medium shrimp, peeled and deveined

6 cups mixed baby greens

4 sprigs fresh cilantro (optional)

**NUTRITIONAL FACTS
(per serving, salad only)**
Calories: 237
Carbohydrates: 35.6 g
Cholesterol: 129 mg
Fat: 3.1 g
Calories From Fat: 11.1%
Protein: 20.3 g
Sodium: 132 mg

* To protect your hands from the seeds of the jalapeños, be sure to use rubber or latex gloves when working with the peppers, and wash the knife and cutting board immediately after use.

1. To make the salsa, combine all of the salsa ingredients in a medium-sized bowl, and stir gently to blend. Cover and refrigerate for up to 6 hours.

2. Rinse the shrimp. Place enough water to cover the shrimp in a medium-sized saucepan, and bring to a boil over high heat. Add the shrimp and boil for 1 to 2 minutes, or until the shrimp turn pink. Drain well, and allow to come to room temperature.

3. To serve, first stir the salsa gently to mix well. Arrange a bed of mixed baby greens on each of 4 dinner plates, and place the shrimp in the center of the greens. Spoon the salsa over each serving, garnish with a sprig of cilantro, if desired, and serve immediately.

YIELD: **4** SERVINGS

Suggested Dressing

★ 1 recipe Oriental Plum
   Dressing (page 230)

NUTRITIONAL FACTS
(per serving, salad only)
Calories: 342
Carbohydrates: 51.3 g
Cholesterol: 129 mg
Fat: 3 g
Calories From Fat: 8.2%
Protein: 24.3 g
Sodium: 393 mg

Shrimp, Vermicelli, and Vegetable Salad

Because of the artful contrast between the white vermicelli, green snow peas, orange peppers, and pink shrimp, this salad is a real showstopper. Best of all, it makes a sensational meal!

Marinade

2 tablespoons rice wine
1 tablespoon coarsely chopped fresh ginger
¼ teaspoon salt

12 ounces medium shrimp, peeled and deveined
8 ounces bean thread vermicelli (cellophane noodles), broken into 3- to 4-inch strands
1 teaspoon Oriental sesame oil
8 ounces fresh snow peas, strings removed
1 orange bell pepper, diced
½ teaspoon finely chopped fresh ginger
½ teaspoon finely chopped garlic
1 tablespoon thinly sliced scallions

1. Rinse the shrimp, and pat them dry with paper towels.

2. To make the marinade, combine all of the marinade ingredients in a resealable plastic bag, and shake to blend. Add the shrimp and turn to coat. Seal the bag, and refrigerate for 30 minutes.

3. While the shrimp are marinating, cook the vermicelli according to package directions. Drain, rinse with cool water, and drain again.

4. Place the vermicelli in a medium-sized bowl, and separate any strands that may be clinging to one another. Add the sesame oil, and toss to blend well. Set aside.

5. Cook the snow peas in a steamer for 2 minutes, or until bright green. Drain well, and allow to come to room temperature.

6. Coat a large nonstick skillet or wok with cooking spray, and preheat over medium-high heat. Add the orange pepper, and stir-fry for 2 minutes or until crisp-tender. Transfer the orange pepper to a dish, and set aside.

7. Add the ginger and garlic to the same skillet, and stir-fry for 1 minute.

8. Add the shrimp *along with the marinade* to the skillet, and stir-fry along with the ginger and garlic for 3 to 4 minutes, or until the shrimp turn pink.

9. To serve, make a large wreath of the vermicelli noodles on a 10- or 11-inch round platter. Arrange a circle of the snow peas on the inside of the wreath, placing the snow peas so that they slightly overlap both the pasta and one another. (About half of the pasta should be visible.) Spoon the shrimp mixture in the center of the wreath, and randomly distribute the diced pepper over the snow peas and pasta. Pour the dressing over the shrimp, and garnish with the scallions. Serve immediately.

YIELD: **4** SERVINGS

Spicy Shrimp, Mango, and Red Pepper Salad

Although precooked shrimp can be used in this salad, I prefer to marinate fresh shrimp and then stir-fry them in ginger and garlic to heighten their flavor. I hope you will agree that the results are well worth the effort.

Suggested Dressings

★ 1 recipe Oriental Dressing (page 229)

1 recipe Mandarin Dressing (page 226)

½ cup commercial fat-free or low-fat Oriental dressing

½ cup commercial fat-free or low-fat sweet and sour dressing

Serving Suggestion

For a more artistic presentation, first mix the lettuce and boy choy, and make a bed of the greens on each of 4 dinner plates. Arrange a row of the shrimp down the center of the greens, and place mango slices on both sides of shrimp. Randomly distribute the red pepper over the mango, and drizzle the dressing over each salad. Finally, garnish each serving with the scallions or with a scallion flower (page 42).

NUTRITIONAL FACTS
(per serving, salad only)

Calories: 217
Carbohydrates: 25.8 g
Cholesterol: 130 mg
Fat: 3.7 g
Calories From Fat: 15.3%
Protein: 20.6 g
Sodium: 157 mg

Marinade

2 tablespoons medium-dry sherry
2 tablespoons hoisin sauce*
¼ teaspoon Oriental sesame oil
12 ounces medium shrimp, peeled and deveined
1 tablespoon finely chopped fresh ginger
1 tablespoon finely chopped garlic
4 cups red leaf lettuce, torn into generous bite-sized pieces
2 cups thinly sliced bok choy
2 mangos or papayas, peeled, pitted, and thinly sliced
1 red bell pepper, cut into julienne strips
2 scallions, thinly sliced

* A sweet and spicy condiment, hoisin sauce can be found in the Asian section of most supermarkets.

1. Rinse the shrimp, and pat them dry with paper towels.

2. To make the marinade, combine all of the marinade ingredients in a resealable plastic bag, and shake to blend. Add the shrimp and turn to coat. Seal the bag, and refrigerate for up to 6 hours, turning the shrimp at least once.

3. Coat a medium-sized nonstick skillet with cooking spray, and preheat over medium-high heat. Add the ginger and garlic, and stir-fry for 1 minute. Add the shrimp *along with the marinade*, and stir-fry for 3 to 5 minutes, or until the shrimp turn pink.

4. Combine the shrimp, lettuce, bok choy, mangos or papayas, red pepper, and scallions in a salad bowl. Add the dressing, and toss gently to coat. Serve immediately.

Italian Seafood and Tortellini Salad

YIELD: 6 SERVINGS

This light and zesty melange of seafood, vegetables, and pasta is perfect summer fare. Make it in advance to allow the flavors to blend, and enjoy it on your patio or deck. Serve with a loaf of crusty bread.

6 ounces medium shrimp, peeled and deveined
6 ounces bay scallops
8 ounces favorite low-fat tortellini
1 red bell pepper, cut into ½-inch squares
1 green bell pepper, cut into ½-inch squares
1 cup diced red onion
1 can (13 ounces) quartered artichoke hearts, drained
¼ cup minced fresh parsley
24 radicchio leaves
6 sprigs parsley (optional)

Suggested Dressings

★ 1 recipe Italian Vinaigrette (page 224)

1 recipe Caper Vinaigrette (page 217)

½ cup commercial fat-free or low-fat Italian vinaigrette

½ cup commercial fat-free or low-fat lemon Dijon dressing

Time-Saving Tip
❑ Substitute 6 ounces of precooked shrimp for the home-cooked shrimp.

NUTRITIONAL FACTS
(per serving, salad only)
Calories: 351
Carbohydrates: 433.1 g
Cholesterol: 79 mg
Fat: 2.5 g
Calories From Fat: 10.2%
Protein: 26 g
Sodium: 193 mg

1. Rinse the shrimp. Place enough water to cover the shrimp in a medium-sized saucepan, and bring to a boil over high heat. Add the shrimp and boil for 1 to 2 minutes, or until the shrimp turn pink. Drain well, and allow to come to room temperature.

2. Rinse the scallops. Place enough water to cover the scallops in the same saucepan, and bring to a boil over high heat. Add the scallops and boil for 2 to 3 minutes, or until the scallops are no longer translucent. Drain well, and allow to come to room temperature.

3. Cook the tortellini according to package instructions. Drain, rinse with cool water, and drain again. Allow the tortellini to come to room temperature.

4. Combine the shrimp, scallops, tortellini, red pepper, green pepper, onion, artichokes, and parsley in a salad bowl. Add the dressing, and toss gently to coat. Cover and refrigerate for several hours or overnight.

5. Remove the salad from the refrigerator 1 hour before serving, and toss gently to blend. Make a wreath of the radicchio leaves on each of 6 dinner plates, and spoon the seafood salad in the center of each wreath. Garnish with a sprig of parsley, if desired, and serve immediately.

A Scallop Story

Scallops are bivalve mollusks. Like the clam, which is also a bivalve mollusk, the scallop has a two-part hinged shell. When a scallop swims, it snaps its shell together. As a result of this constant motion, the muscle controlling the shell becomes very large. This muscle, called the "eye," is the delicious, white, plump part of the scallop that is eaten.

When buying scallops, look for seafood that is firm, sweet smelling, and free of cloudy liquid. Steer clear of any scallops that have an ammonia- or sulfur-like odor. To make sure that they are at their freshest, try to buy scallops the same day you intend to use them. Then store them in the coldest part of the refrigerator until you're ready to prepare your dish.

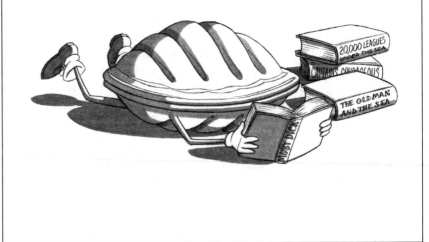

Seafood and Pasta Salad

This contemporary salad, made with fresh dill and curly pasta, is a refreshing way to enjoy seafood. Serve with low-fat blueberry muffins.

6 ounces rotini pasta
½ cup frozen peas, thawed
6 ounces medium shrimp, peeled and deveined
6 ounces sea scallops
¼ cup minced fresh parsley
2 scallions, thinly sliced
2 tablespoons minced fresh dill
4 cups butterhead lettuce leaves
4 sprigs fresh dill (optional)
1 mango, cut into 12 slices (optional)

1. Cook the pasta according to package directions. Drain, rinse with cool water, and drain again. Set aside.

2. Cook the peas according to package directions. Drain well, and allow to come to room temperature.

3. Rinse the shrimp. Place enough water to cover the shrimp in a medium-sized saucepan, and bring to a boil over high heat. Add the shrimp and boil for 1 to 2 minutes, or until the shrimp turn pink. Drain well, and allow to come to room temperature.

4. Rinse the scallops. Place enough water to cover the scallops in the same saucepan, and bring to a boil over high heat. Add the scallops and boil for 2 to 3 minutes, or until the scallops are no longer translucent. Drain well, and allow to come to room temperature.

5. Combine the pasta, peas, shrimp, scallops, parsley, scallions, and dill in a salad bowl. Add the dressing, and toss gently to coat. Cover and refrigerate for several hours or overnight.

6. Remove the salad from the refrigerator 1 hour before serving, and toss gently to blend. Make a wreath of the lettuce leaves on each of 4 dinner plates, and spoon the seafood salad in the center of each wreath. If desired, garnish the top of each salad with a sprig of dill, and place mango slices off to one side. Serve immediately.

YIELD: 4 SERVINGS

Suggested Dressings

★ 1 recipe Lemon and Dill Vinaigrette (page 224)

1 recipe Lemon Vinaigrette (page 225)

½ cup commercial fat-free or low-fat lemon Dijon dressing

Time-Saving Tip
❑ Substitute 6 ounces of precooked shrimp for the home-cooked shrimp.

NUTRITIONAL FACTS
(per serving, salad only)
Calories: 361
Carbohydrates: 60.6 g
Cholesterol: 79 mg
Fat: 1.8 g
Calories From Fat: 9%
Protein: 27.7 g
Sodium: 185 mg

YIELD: **4** SERVINGS

Seafood, Asparagus, and Mango Salad

Once you have tasted this absolutely delectable salad, you will want to make it again and again. Serve with low-fat mango muffins.

Suggested Dressings

★ 1 recipe Curry Vinaigrette (page 220)

½ cup commercial fat-free or low-fat raspberry vinaigrette

8 ounces medium shrimp, peeled and deveined
8 ounces sea scallops
24 asparagus spears (1 pound), tough ends removed, or 1 can (15 ounces) asparagus spears, drained
2 large mangos or papayas, peeled, pitted, and thinly sliced
2 scallions, thinly sliced
1 avocado, peeled, pitted, and sliced (optional)
6 cups mixed baby greens

Serving Suggestion

For a more artistic presentation, first combine the shrimp, scallops, mangos, and avocado, if desired, in a salad bowl. Divide the mixed baby greens among 4 dinner plates, and spoon the seafood salad on top. Tuck whole spears of asparagus under the seafood salad, and drizzle the vinaigrette over each serving. Garnish with the scallions or with scallion flowers (page 42).

1. Rinse the shrimp. Place enough water to cover the shrimp in a medium-sized saucepan, and bring to a boil over high heat. Add the shrimp and boil for 1 to 2 minutes, or until the shrimp turn pink. Drain well, and allow to come to room temperature.

2. Rinse the scallops. Place enough water to cover the scallops in the same saucepan, and bring to a boil over high heat. Add the scallops and boil for 2 to 3 minutes, or until the scallops are no longer translucent. Drain well, and allow to come to room temperature.

3. Cut the asparagus into 2-inch lengths. If using fresh asparagus, cook in a steamer for 2 to 3 minutes, or just until fork tender. Drain well, and allow to come to room temperature.

4. Combine the shrimp, scallops, asparagus, mango or papaya, scallions, and avocado, if desired, in a salad bowl. Add the vinaigrette, and toss gently to coat.

5. To serve, divide the mixed baby greens among 4 dinner plates. Spoon the seafood salad on top of each bed of greens, and serve immediately.

Time-Saving Tip
❑ Substitute 8 ounces of precooked shrimp for the home-cooked shrimp.

NUTRITIONAL FACTS
(per serving, salad only)
Calories: 163
Carbohydrates: 20.2 g
Cholesterol: 79 mg
Fat: 1.5 g
Calories From Fat: 7.9%
Protein: 19.5 g
Sodium: 155 mg

Roasted Pepper and Tuna Salad With Capers

Tuna, capers, and roasted peppers laced with a tangy vinaigrette complement one another perfectly in this delightful salad. Serve with low-fat lemon poppy seed muffins.

2 red bell peppers
1 tuna steak (12 ounces)
2 tablespoons cold water
4 Roma tomatoes, seeded and diced
4 anchovy fillets, drained
2 tablespoons capers, rinsed and drained
2 red or white Belgian endives, separated into individual leaves
12 strands fresh chives (optional)

1. To roast the peppers, place the peppers on a baking sheet that has been lined with aluminum foil. Broil under a preheated broiler, turning the peppers as the skins blacken, for 20 to 25 minutes, or until the skins are charred all over. Once roasted, place in a plastic bag, seal, and allow to steam for 15 minutes. When the peppers are cool enough to handle, peel away the skin and remove the tops and seeds. (Do not rinse the peppers.) Cut the peppers into $1/2$-inch squares, and set aside.

2. Rinse the tuna, and place the tuna and the water in a covered microwave-safe dish. Microwave on high power for 6 to 7 minutes, or until the tuna is no longer red inside. Allow the tuna to cool for 10 minutes before cutting into cubes.

3. Combine the roasted peppers, tuna, tomatoes, anchovies, capers, and dressing in a salad bowl, and toss gently to coat. Cover and refrigerate for several hours.

4. To serve, arrange the Belgian endive leaves in a spoke design on each of 4 dinner plates. Spoon the tuna salad in the center, and, if desired, garnish each serving with long strands of chives that point upward from the center of the salad. Serve immediately.

YIELD: 4 SERVINGS

Suggested Dressings

★ 1 recipe Lemon Vinaigrette (page 225)

1 recipe Greek Vinaigrette (page 222)

$1/2$ cup commercial fat-free or low-fat lemon Dijon dressing

Time-Saving Tip
❑ Substitute $1/2$ cup commercial sweet roasted bell peppers for the home-made roasted peppers.

NUTRITIONAL FACTS
(per serving, salad only)
Calories: 162
Carbohydrates: 12.6 g
Cholesterol: 42 mg
Fat: 2 g
Calories From Fat: 10.8%
Protein: 24.7 g
Sodium: 266 mg

YIELD: 4 SERVINGS

Escolar Salad
With Fruit Salsa

Escolar has a white, meaty flesh with a very mild flavor. Like many saltwater fish, it is also high in omega-3 fatty acids—the fats that are actually good for you. A balsamic vinegar and lime juice reduction accents the mild flavor of the escolar, and adds an interesting dimension to the combination of shiitake mushrooms and fruit salsa.

NUTRITIONAL FACTS
(per serving, salad only)

Calories: 235
Carbohydrates: 33.7 g
Cholesterol: 44 mg
Fat: 3.6 g
Calories From Fat: 12.8%
Protein: 21.7 g
Sodium: 111 mg

Orange and Pineapple Salsa

2 navel oranges, peeled and diced

1 cup diced fresh pineapple

½ cup minced red onion

¼ cup minced red bell pepper

2 tablespoons coarsely chopped fresh cilantro

1 tablespoon white wine vinegar

1 tablespoon granulated sugar

1 cup diced grapefruit (optional)

1 skinless escolar fillet, salmon fillet,
or tuna steak (12 ounces)

3 ounces fresh shiitake mushrooms

¼ cup balsamic vinegar

2 tablespoons fresh lime juice

6 cups prewashed baby spinach, stems removed

4 sprigs fresh cilantro (optional)

1. Rinse the fish, and pat it dry with paper towels. Cut the fillet into thin strips, and set aside.

2. To make the salsa, combine all of the salsa ingredients, and stir to blend. Cover and refrigerate until ready to serve.

3. Remove and discard the stems from the shiitake mushrooms. To slice several mushrooms at one time, slightly overlap 3 to 4 mushrooms and cut into thin slices. Repeat with the remaining mushrooms.

4. Coat a large nonstick skillet with olive oil cooking spray, and preheat over medium heat. Add the mushrooms and stir-fry for 1 to 2 minutes, or until fork tender. Transfer the mushrooms to a dish, and allow to come to room temperature.

5. Increase the heat to medium-high, and add the fish to the same skillet. Stir-fry for 2 to 3 minutes, or until no longer translucent. Transfer the escolar to a dish, and cover loosely with aluminum foil.

6. Add the balsamic vinegar and lime juice to the same skillet, and reduce the heat to medium. Simmer, stirring occasionally, for 3 to 4 minutes, or until the mixture becomes syrupy.

7. Return the escolar to the skillet, and turn to coat with the glaze. Remove the skillet from the heat.

8. To serve, divide the spinach among 4 dinner plates. Distribute the escolar and mushrooms over each bed of spinach, and spoon the salsa over each serving. Garnish with a sprig of cilantro, if desired, and serve immediately.

YIELD: **4** SERVINGS

Grilled Lemon-Marinated Tuna Salad

The flavor of the remarkable lemon marinade used in this salad is further enhanced when the tuna is grilled over hot coals. The tuna is then arranged on a bed of mixed baby greens and vegetables, and topped with a tart vinaigrette. Delicious!

Suggested Dressings

★ 1 recipe Lemon Vinaigrette (page 225)

1 recipe Lemon and Dill Vinaigrette (page 224)

½ cup commercial fat-free or low-fat lemon Dijon dressing

½ cup commercial fat-free or low-fat Greek vinaigrette

Lemon Marinade

2 tablespoons fresh lemon juice
2 cloves garlic, crushed
1 teaspoon sesame seeds
⅛ teaspoon salt
⅛ teaspoon freshly ground pepper

1 tuna steak (12 ounces)
1 pound new potatoes, halved
6 cups mixed baby greens
1 red bell pepper, cut into julienne strips
1 cup thin red onion rings
1 large tomato, cut into wedges
1½ cups commercial fat-free seasoned croutons
4 tomato roses (page 179) (optional)

1. Rinse the tuna, and pat it dry with paper towels.

2. To make the marinade, combine all of the marinade ingredients in a nonmetal dish, and stir to blend. Add the tuna and turn to coat. Cover and refrigerate for 30 minutes, turning the tuna at least once.

3. While the tuna is marinating, cook the potatoes in a large steamer for 20 to 25 minutes, or until fork tender. Drain well, and allow to come to room temperature.

4. Remove the tuna from the marinade, discarding the marinade, and place it over moderately hot coals on a grill coated with cooking spray. (If available, use a grilling grid coated with cooking spray.*) Cover the grill and cook for 5 minutes on each side, or until the tuna is no longer red inside. Alternatively, cook the tuna in the microwave oven by placing the tuna and 2 tablespoons of water in a covered microwave-safe dish. Microwave on high power for 6 to 7 minutes. Allow the tuna to cool for 10 minutes before cutting into thin slices.

5. Combine the potatoes, mixed baby greens, red pepper, onion rings, tomato, and croutons in a salad bowl. Add just enough dressing to lightly coat, and toss gently to mix.

6. To serve, divide the potato mixture among 4 dinner plates. Top each serving with slices of tuna, and drizzle with the remaining dressing. Garnish each salad with a tomato rose, if desired, and serve immediately.

* A grilling grid is a flat porcelain-enameled steel grate with multiple holes. When placed directly on the cooking grate of a grill, it is excellent for grilling vegetables, seafood, or other foods that are too small or fragile to cook over a conventional grate.

NUTRITIONAL FACTS
(per serving, salad only)

Calories: 200
Carbohydrates: 23.4 g
Cholesterol: 38 mg
Fat: 1.5 g
Calories From Fat: 6.8%
Protein: 23.8 g
Sodium: 104 mg

Tuna Talk

Tuna is a mild-flavored fish, with flesh that is firm, fatty, and deep-red in color. It is found in the Mediterranean Sea, as well as in the warm waters of the Pacific, Indian, and Atlantic Oceans. Among the familiar tuna, the best for eating are the yellowfin, bluefin, Atlantic bonito, blackfin, and bigeye.

When choosing tuna, look for steaks that are 1 inch thick and translucent red in color, with a moist sheen on the surface. If you buy prepackaged fresh tuna, make sure that there is no visible liquid in the container. Like all seafood, tuna should be refrigerated as soon as you get it home, and used as soon as possible.

YIELD: 4 SERVINGS

Mediterranean Grilled Tuna Salad

Grilling lends a subtle smoky flavor to the tuna and red pepper, transforming this salad into a memorable feast. Serve with pita bread.

Suggested Dressings

★ 1 recipe Lemon Vinaigrette (page 225)

1 recipe Greek Vinaigrette (page 222)

½ cup commercial fat-free or low-fat Greek vinaigrette

½ cup commercial fat-free or low-fat lemon Dijon dressing

Time-Saving Tip
❏ Substitute ½ cup of commercial sweet roasted bell peppers for the home-made roasted peppers.

Marinade

¼ cup plus 2 tablespoons fresh lemon juice

2 tablespoons minced fresh parsley

½ teaspoon freshly ground pepper

1 tuna steak (12 ounces)

2 red bell peppers

2 pounds new potatoes, halved

4 hard-boiled eggs, whites only, each cut into 8 wedges

4 Roma tomatoes, quartered

2 cups red leaf lettuce, torn into generous bite-sized pieces

2 cups escarole, torn into generous bite-sized pieces

2 tablespoons capers, rinsed and drained

1. Rinse the tuna, and pat it dry with paper towels.

2. To make the marinade, combine all of the marinade ingredients in a nonmetal dish. Add the tuna, and turn to coat. Cover and refrigerate for 30 minutes.

3. To grill the red peppers, place the peppers over hot coals on a grill coated with cooking spray. Cover the grill and cook for 14 to 20 minutes, or until the skin is charred all over, turning the peppers as the skins blacken. Alternatively, place the peppers under a pre-heated broiler, and broil for 20 to 25 minutes. Once the skin has blackened, place the peppers in a plastic bag, seal, and allow to steam for 15 minutes. When the peppers are cool enough to handle, peel away the skin and remove the tops and seeds. (Do not rinse the peppers.) Cut the peppers into strips and set aside.

4. Cook the potatoes in a large steamer for 20 to 25 minutes, or until fork tender. Drain well, and allow to come to room temperature.

5. Remove the tuna from the marinade, discarding the marinade, and place it over moderately hot coals on a grill coated with cooking spray. (If available, use a grilling grid coated with cooking spray.*) Cover the grill and cook for 5 minutes on each side, or until the tuna is no longer red inside. Alternatively, place the tuna under a preheated broiler, 4 inches from the heat source, and broil for 4 to 5 minutes on each side. Allow the tuna to cool for 10 minutes before cutting into $1/4$-inch-thick slices.

6. To serve, combine the tuna, roasted peppers, potatoes, eggs, tomatoes, lettuce, escarole, and capers in a salad bowl. Add the dressing, and toss gently to coat. Serve immediately.

* A grilling grid is a flat porcelain-enameled steel grate with multiple holes. When placed directly on the cooking grate of a grill, it is excellent for grilling vegetables, seafood, or other foods that are too small or fragile to cook over a conventional grate.

NUTRITIONAL FACTS
(per serving, salad only)

Calories: 401
Carbohydrates: 45.6 g
Cholesterol: 77 mg
Fat: 2.6 g
Calories From Fat: 5.7%
Protein: 50.3 g
Sodium: 202 mg

Serving Suggestion

For a more artistic presentation, first combine the red leaf lettuce and escarole, and divide among 4 dinner plates. Arrange the tuna slices in the center of the lettuce, and, in spoke fashion, surround the tuna with sections of tomatoes, potatoes, roasted pepper, and eggs. Distribute the capers over the top, and drizzle vinaigrette over each serving. Finally, garnish each salad with a tomato rose (page 179), if desired.

Salad Niçoise With Pasta and Grilled Tuna

YIELD: 4 SERVINGS

Suggested Dressings

★ 1 recipe Salad Niçoise Vinaigrette (page 233)

1 recipe Caper Vinaigrette (page 217)

½ cup commercial fat-free or low-fat lemon Dijon dressing

Looking for a new twist on the traditional Salad Niçoise? I've replaced the traditional potatoes with pasta, and the canned tuna with grilled fresh tuna. The result is a refreshingly new dish that still retains the character of the original salad.

Marinade

3 tablespoons fresh lemon juice

⅛ teaspoon salt

⅛ teaspoon freshly ground pepper

1 tuna steak (12 ounces)

6 ounces ziti pasta

8 ounces green beans, trimmed and halved

¼ cup minced fresh parsley

3 hard-boiled eggs, whites only, coarsely chopped

8 anchovy fillets, drained and separated

2 scallions, thinly sliced

12 pitted Niçoise olives (optional)*

3 Roma tomatoes, cut into wedges

6 cups mixed baby greens

12 strands fresh chives (optional)

* Grown in the Provence region of France, Niçoise olives are tiny, tender, and green or purple-black in color. Look for them in gourmet stores.

1. Rinse the tuna, and pat it dry with paper towels.

2. To make the marinade, combine all of the marinade ingredients in a nonmetal dish, and stir to blend. Add the tuna and turn to coat. Cover and refrigerate for 30 minutes, turning the tuna at least once.

3. Cook the pasta according to package directions. Drain, rinse with cool water, and drain again. Set aside.

4. Cook the green beans in a steamer for 7 minutes, or until fork tender. Drain well, and allow to come to room temperature.

5. Combine the pasta, greens beans, parsley, eggs, anchovies, scallions, and olives, if desired, in a salad bowl. Add just enough dressing to coat, and toss gently. Cover and set aside at room temperature for up to 1 hour, or refrigerate for several hours.

6. Remove the tuna from the marinade, discarding the marinade, and place it over moderately hot coals on a grill coated with cooking spray. (If available, use a grilling grid coated with cooking spray.*) Cover the grill and cook for 5 minutes on each side, or until the tuna is no longer red inside. Alternatively, place the tuna under a preheated broiler, 4 inches from the heat source, and broil for 5 to 6 minutes on each side. Allow the tuna to cool for 10 minutes before cutting into slices or cubes.

7. To serve, add the tomatoes to the salad, and toss to blend. Make a bed of the mixed baby greens in the center of each of 4 dinner plates. Spoon the pasta salad in the center of the greens, and slightly flatten the mixture. Arrange the tuna over the pasta, and drizzle the remaining dressing over each serving. Finally, if desired, garnish each serving with long strands of chives that point upward from the center the salad, and serve immediately.

* A grilling grid is a flat porcelain-enameled steel grate with multiple holes. When placed directly on the cooking grate of a grill, it is excellent for grilling vegetables, seafood, or other foods that are too small or fragile to cook over a conventional grate.

NUTRITIONAL FACTS
(per serving, salad only)

Calories: 358
Carbohydrates: 55.9 g
Cholesterol: 38 mg
Fat: 1.5 g
Calories From Fat: 7.7%
Protein: 32.5 g
Sodium: 182 mg

Salad Niçoise

YIELD: 4 SERVINGS

Suggested Dressings

★ 1 Recipe Salad Niçoise
Vinaigrette (page 233)

1 recipe Lemon Vinaigrette
(page 225)

½ cup commercial fat-free
or low-fat lemon Dijon
dressing

*This is probably one of the best known and widely featured entrée salads,
and for good reason. It is tasty and easy to prepare, and—with very
little alteration to the traditional ingredients—it is light
and healthy, too.*

1 pound new potatoes, sliced ½ inch thick
1 tablespoon dry white wine
2 scallions, thinly sliced
¼ cup minced fresh parsley
2 tablespoons finely chopped shallot
8 ounces green beans, trimmed
3 Roma tomatoes, cut into wedges
2 heads Boston lettuce, torn into generous bite-sized pieces (about 6 cups)
1 can (9 ounces) light tuna packed in water, drained and flaked
3 hard-boiled eggs, whites only, quartered
8 anchovy fillets, drained and separated
8 pitted Niçoise olives (optional)*
1 tablespoon capers, rinsed and drained
Chopped fresh chives (optional)

* Grown in the Provence region of France, Niçoise olives are tiny, tender, and
green or purple-black in color. Look for them in gourmet stores.

1. Cook the potatoes in a large steamer for 20 to 25 minutes, or
until fork tender. Drain well, and transfer to a medium-sized bowl.

2. While the potatoes are warm, add the wine, scallions, parsley,
and shallot to the bowl, along with 3 tablespoons of the dressing.
Toss gently to coat, cover, and set aside at room temperature for up
to 1 hour.

3. While the potatoes are marinating, cook the green beans in a
steamer for 7 minutes, or until fork tender. Drain well, and allow to
come to room temperature.

4. Combine the potato mixture, green beans, tomatoes, lettuce,
tuna, eggs, anchovies, and olives, if desired, in a salad bowl. Add
the remaining dressing, and toss gently to blend.

5. To serve, divide the salad among 4 dinner plates. Garnish each serving with the capers and chives, if desired, and serve immediately.

Serving Suggestion

For a more artistic presentation, first make the potato mixture as described above. Then combine the green beans and tomatoes in one bowl, and place the lettuce in another bowl. Add just enough dressing to each to make the vegetables and lettuce glisten, and toss to coat. Arrange the dressed lettuce in the center of each of 4 dinner plates, and spoon the potato salad in the center. Decoratively place the green bean and tomato mixture, tuna, egg whites, and anchovies around the potato salad, and garnish with the capers and, if desired, the olives and chives. Finally, drizzle the remaining dressing over each serving.

NUTRITIONAL FACTS
(per serving, salad only)

Calories: 252
Carbohydrates: 32.3 g
Cholesterol: 26 mg
Fat: 2.4 g
Calories From Fat: 8.2%
Protein: 28.7 g
Sodium: 603 mg

Southwestern Tuna Salad

YIELD: **4 SERVINGS**

A tomatillo is a Mexican green tomato that resembles a cherry tomato, but is firmer and more tart. When this unique vegetable is combined with traditional Southwestern ingredients, you have a wonderful dressing that beautifully complements tuna salad. Serve with corn muffins.

Suggested Dressing

★ 1 recipe Tomatillo Dressing (page 239)

1 tuna steak (12 ounces)
2 tablespoons cold water
6 cups prewashed fresh baby spinach, stems removed
2 Roma tomatoes, quartered
1 avocado, peeled, pitted, and thinly sliced
1 cup julienne strips jicama*
1 can (4.5 ounces) chopped green chilies, drained
2 ounces grated fat-free Monterey Jack cheese
½ cup halved black olives, drained (optional)
8 canned whole baby sweet corn, drained

NUTRITIONAL FACTS
(per serving, salad only)

Calories: 336
Carbohydrates: 26 g
Cholesterol: 35 mg
Fat: 10.3 g
Calories From Fat: 27.4%
Protein: 35.6 g
Sodium: 226 mg

* A root vegetable resembling a turnip, jicama can be found in the produce section of many supermarkets.

1. Rinse the tuna, and place the tuna and the water in a covered microwave-safe dish. Microwave on high power for 6 to 7 minutes, or until the tuna is no longer red inside. Allow the tuna to cool for 10 minutes before cutting into thin slices or cubes.

2. Combine the tuna, spinach, tomatoes, avocado, jicama, chilies, cheese, and olives, if desired, in a salad bowl. Add the dressing, and toss gently to coat.

3. To serve, divide the salad among 4 dinner plates. Garnish each serving with 2 ears of baby sweet corn, and serve immediately.

Serving Suggestion

For a more artistic presentation, first divide the spinach among 4 dinner plates. Fan slices of tuna over the spinach, and randomly distribute the tomatoes, avocado, jicama, chilies, cheese, and olives, if desired, over the salad. Finally, spoon the dressing over the salad, and garnish each serving with 2 ears of baby sweet corn.

Tuna, Avocado, and Spinach Salad

YIELD: 4 SERVINGS

The contrasting colors of the ingredients in this salad make the dish as attractive as it is flavorful. Serve with low-fat lemon muffins.

1 tuna steak (12 ounces)
2 tablespoons cold water
1 medium tomato
6 cups prewashed baby spinach, stems removed
1 avocado, peeled, pitted, and diced
1 cup alfalfa sprouts

1. Rinse the tuna, and place the tuna and the water in a covered microwave-safe dish. Microwave on high power for 5 to 7 minutes, or until the tuna is no longer red inside. Allow the tuna to cool for 10 minutes before cutting into slices or cubes.

2. Thinly slice the tomato. Then cut each slice in half.

3. To serve, combine the tuna, tomato, spinach, avocado, and sprouts in a salad bowl. Add the dressing, and toss gently to coat. Serve immediately.

Serving Suggestion

For a more artistic presentation, make a bed of the spinach on each of 4 dinner plates. Arrange slices of tuna to form a *V* down the middle of the greens. Then arrange slices of tomato in the center, starting at the top of the *V* and going down to the point. Arrange a row of the sprouts down the middle of the tomatoes, and randomly sprinkle the avocado over all. Finally, drizzle dressing over each salad and garnish with long shoots of chives, if desired.

Suggested Dressings

★ 1 recipe Lemon Vinaigrette (page 225)

1 recipe Southwestern Vinaigrette (page 235)

½ cup commercial fat-free or low-fat lemon Dijon dressing

½ cup commercial fat-free or low-fat peppercorn ranch dressing

NUTRITIONAL FACTS
(per serving, salad only)

Calories: 199
Carbohydrates: 5.6 g
Cholesterol: 32 mg
Fat: 10.1 g
Calories From Fat: 44.9%
Protein: 22.2 g
Sodium: 59 mg

Santa Fe Grilled Tuna Salad

This unforgettable salad has a subtle Southwestern flavor that will linger long after the first bite. Serve with quesadillas.

Suggested Dressings

★ 1 recipe Cilantro Vinaigrette (page 219)

1 recipe Mexican Vinaigrette (page 228)

½ cup commercial fat-free or low-fat Santa Fe blend dressing

Time-Saving Tip
❏ Substitute ¼ cup of your favorite commercial Southwestern marinade for the lemon marinade.

Lemon Marinade

¼ cup fresh lemon juice
2 tablespoons coarsely chopped fresh cilantro
¼ teaspoon salt
¼ teaspoon freshly ground pepper

1 tuna steak (12 ounces)
2 pounds new potatoes, sliced 1 inch thick
4 scallions, thinly sliced
1½ cups commercial fat-free seasoned croutons
3 Roma tomatoes, cut into wedges
1 avocado, peeled, pitted, and cubed
¾ cup julienne strips jicama*
6 cups prewashed baby spinach, stems removed
12 canned whole baby sweet corn, drained (optional)

* A root vegetable resembling a turnip, jicama can be found in the produce section of many supermarkets.

1. Rinse the tuna, and pat it dry with paper towels.

2. To make the marinade, combine all of the marinade ingredients in a nonmetal dish, and stir to blend well. Add the tuna and turn to coat. Cover and refrigerate for 30 minutes, turning the tuna once.

3. Remove the tuna from the marinade, discarding the marinade, and place over moderately hot coals on a grill coated with cooking spray. (If available, use a grilling grid coated with cooking spray.*) Cover the grill and cook for 5 minutes on each side, or until the tuna is no longer red inside. Alternatively, place the tuna under a preheated broiler, 4 inches from the heat source, and broil for 5 to 6 minutes on each side. Allow the tuna to cool for 10 minutes before cutting into large cubes.

4. Cook the potatoes in a large steamer for 20 to 25 minutes, or until fork tender. Drain well.

5. Transfer the warm potatoes to a salad bowl, and add the tuna and scallions. Add 3 to 4 tablespoons of the dressing, or just enough to lightly coat the tuna mixture, and toss gently. Cover and refrigerate for 30 minutes.

6. Add the croutons, tomatoes, avocado, jicama, and spinach to the tuna mixture, and toss gently. Add the remaining dressing, and toss gently to coat.

7. To serve, divide the salad among 6 dinner plates. Garnish each serving with 2 ears of baby sweet corn, if desired, and serve immediately.

* A grilling grid is a flat porcelain-enameled steel grate with multiple holes. When placed directly on the cooking grate of a grill, it is excellent for grilling vegetables, seafood, or other foods that are too small or fragile to cook over a conventional grate.

NUTRITIONAL FACTS
(per serving, salad only)

Calories: 253
Carbohydrates: 46.1 g
Cholesterol: 0 mg
Fat: 6.5 g
Calories From Fat: 21.3%
Protein: 7.7 g
Sodium: 120 mg

Tuna, Pasta, and Tomato Salad

The vibrant flavors of sun-dried tomatoes, basil, and balsamic vinegar elevate this simple tuna-and-pasta salad to new heights. Make extra, and invite friends over for a casual culinary experience. Serve with crusty Italian bread.

Serving Suggestion

For a more artistic presentation, first make a bed of arugula on each of 4 dinner plates. Spoon the tuna salad in the center of each bed, and garnish each serving with a tomato rose (page 179), if desired.

NUTRITIONAL FACTS
(per serving, salad only)

Calories: 378
Carbohydrates: 50.2 g
Cholesterol: 32 mg
Fat: 6.3 g
Calories From Fat: 37.4%
Protein: 29.9 g
Sodium: 290 mg

8 ounces tricolor radiatori pasta
1 tuna steak (12 ounces)
2 tablespoons cold water
½ cup sun-dried tomatoes
½ teaspoon extra virgin olive oil
4 cloves garlic, chopped
2 tablespoons balsamic vinegar
⅓ cup thinly sliced fresh basil
3 tablespoons chopped fresh Italian parsley
1 tablespoon capers, rinsed and drained
¼ teaspoon salt
¼ teaspoon freshly ground pepper

1. Cook the pasta according to package directions. Drain, rinse with cool water, and drain again. Set aside.

2. Rinse the tuna, and place the tuna and the water in a covered microwave-safe dish. Microwave on high power for 5 to 7 minutes, or until the tuna is no longer red inside. Allow the tuna to cool for 10 minutes before cutting into cubes.

3. Place the sun-dried tomatoes in a small heatproof bowl, and add enough boiling water to cover. Set aside for 5 to 15 minutes, or until the tomatoes are soft. Drain well, and cut into slivers. Set aside.

4. Coat a medium-sized nonstick skillet with olive oil cooking spray. Add the olive oil, and preheat over medium-high heat. Add the garlic and stir-fry for 1 minute. Add the tomatoes and stir-fry for an additional minute. Allow the tomatoes to come to room temperature.

5. Combine the balsamic vinegar, basil, parsley, capers, salt, and pepper in a salad bowl, and stir to blend. Add the pasta, tuna, and tomato mixture, and toss gently to blend. Cover and refrigerate for several hours or overnight.

6. Remove the salad from the refrigerator 1 hour before serving, and toss gently to blend. Serve immediately.

Tuna, Spinach, and Feta Salad

Enjoy this wonderful Mediterranean-inspired salad on your deck or patio. To complete the picture, add some warm pita bread and a bottle of your favorite wine.

6 cups prewashed baby spinach, stems removed
2 Roma tomatoes, quartered
1 cup thin red onion rings
1 can (9 ounces) light tuna packed in water, drained and flaked
1½ ounces feta cheese, crumbled
8 anchovy fillets, drained and separated
12 pitted Kalamata olives (optional)

1. Combine all of the salad ingredients except for the dressing in a salad bowl.

2. Add the vinaigrette to the salad, and toss gently to coat. Serve immediately.

Spinach Tips

Spinach adds a deep green color and a subtle but distinctive taste to salads. But because spinach is quite perishable—it stays fresh for only two or three days—you'll get the best results if you store it with care and use it as quickly as possible. If you buy loose (unpackaged) spinach, remove any blackened leaves and store the remaining spinach in a resealable plastic bag, as this will help it stay at its freshest. Do not wash the spinach until you are ready to use it. If you buy the prewashed variety, which comes packaged in plastic, open the bag and remove any blackened leaves before refrigerating your produce. Then reseal the bag and store it in your vegetable bin until you're ready to make your salad.

YIELD: 4 SERVINGS

Suggested Dressings

★ 1 recipe Caper Vinaigrette (page 217)

1 recipe Greek Vinaigrette (page 222)

½ cup commercial fat-free or low-fat Greek vinaigrette

½ cup commercial fat-free or low-fat lemon Dijon dressing

NUTRITIONAL FACTS (per serving, salad only)

Calories: 143
Carbohydrates: 8.3 g
Cholesterol: 29 mg
Fat: 3.3 g
Calories From Fat: 20.6%
Protein: 20.7 g
Sodium: 425 mg

YIELD: **4** SERVINGS

Tuna, Vegetable, and Green Rice Salad

This is a simple yet beautiful salad that you will want to prepare for family or guests. Although you can choose any number of different vegetables to adorn this salad, the dish will be most appealing if you select ingredients that complement one another in both taste and color.

Suggested Dressings

★ 1 recipe Italian Vinaigrette (page 224)

1 recipe Greek Vinaigrette (page 222)

½ cup commercial fat-free or low-fat Italian Parmesan cheese vinaigrette

½ cup commercial fat-free or low-fat classic herb vinaigrette

Green Rice

1 cup coarsely chopped Vidalia onion or other sweet onion
1 cup long-grain rice
1 can (14.5 ounces) fat-free chicken broth
¼ cup chopped fresh celery leaves
2 large cloves garlic, finely chopped
¼ teaspoon salt
¼ teaspoon freshly ground pepper
½ cup chopped fresh spinach
1 cup frozen peas, thawed
3 tablespoons chopped fresh parsley

2 cans (6 ounces each) solid white tuna packed in water, drained and flaked
1 pound beets, trimmed
2 cups broccoli florets
1 red bell pepper, cut into 1-inch squares
1 can (13 ounces) quartered artichoke hearts, drained
2 cups cherry tomatoes, stemmed
1 avocado, peeled, pitted, and cubed (optional)
½ cup pitted black olives (optional)

1. To make the green rice, coat a large nonstick saucepan with olive oil cooking spray, and preheat over medium heat. Add the onion and sauté for 3 minutes, stirring occasionally. Add the rice and sauté for 3 minutes, stirring occasionally. Add the chicken broth, celery leaves, garlic, salt, and pepper, and bring to a boil. Reduce the heat to low, cover, and simmer for 20 minutes.

2. Add the spinach, peas, and parsley to the rice, and stir gently to blend. Cover the saucepan and continue to cook for 5 additional minutes. Remove the saucepan from the heat and allow the rice to sit, covered, for 15 minutes, or until all of the liquid has been absorbed and the vegetables are cooked.

3. Coat a 6-cup bowl or mold with cooking spray, and spoon the tuna into the bottom of the bowl. Spread the green rice over the tuna, and use a spatula to press down on the rice, compacting it. Cover and refrigerate for several hours or overnight.

4. Place enough water to cover the beets in a large saucepan, and bring to a boil over high heat. Add the beets and simmer for 1 hour, or until fork tender. Drain well, and allow to cool to room temperature.

5. When the beets are cool, peel and remove the ends. Cut the beets into cubes, cover, and set aside until ready to serve.

6. Cook the broccoli in a steamer for 1 minute, or until bright green. Drain well, and allow to come to room temperature.

7. To serve, run a knife around the edge of the mold between the mold and the rice. Place a large platter over the mold, choosing one that will leave a 3-inch boarder around the rice. Invert the mold so that the rice is centered on the platter.

8. Arrange the beets, broccoli, red pepper, artichokes, cherry tomatoes, and avocado and olives, if desired, around the rice. Drizzle the vinaigrette over the entire salad, and serve immediately.

NUTRITIONAL FACTS
(per serving, salad only)

Calories: 442
Carbohydrates: 73 g
Cholesterol: 26 mg
Fat: 2.1 g
Calories From Fat: 4%
Protein: 39.5 g
Sodium: 807 mg

YIELD: **4 SERVINGS**

Tuscan Tuna and Bean Salad

This unusual entrée is a flavorful combination of colors, textures, and tastes. Serve with Italian bread.

Suggested Dressings

★ 1 recipe Italian Vinaigrette (page 224)

1 recipe Greek Vinaigrette (page 222)

½ cup commercial fat-free or low-fat Italian vinaigrette

½ cup commercial fat-free or low-fat Greek vinaigrette

Beans

1 cup dried great northern beans
¼ cup chopped onion
2 tablespoons diced red bell pepper
2 tablespoons diced carrot
2 tablespoons diced celery
1 tablespoon finely chopped garlic
1 tomato, chopped
2 cans (14.5 ounces each) fat-free chicken broth
½ teaspoon chopped fresh thyme
¼ teaspoon freshly ground pepper
⅛ teaspoon salt

8 ounces green beans, trimmed and cut into 2-inch lengths
1 can (13 ounces) quartered artichoke hearts, drained
1 red bell pepper, diced
1 jar (2 ounces) slivered pimientos, drained
1 can (9 ounces) solid white tuna in water, drained and flaked
3 ounces fat-free mozzarella cheese, cubed
8 pitted Kalamata olives (optional)
5 cups arugula, tough stems removed
2 tomatoes, thinly sliced

Time-Saving Tip

❑ Substitute 3 cups of canned great northern beans for the home-cooked beans. Drain the beans, and place in a medium-sized bowl. Add the thyme, pepper, and salt, and stir to blend well before proceeding with the recipe.

1. To make the beans, place the dried beans in a medium-sized bowl, and add enough cold water to bring the level 3 inches above the beans. Allow to sit uncovered overnight at room temperature.

2. Drain the soaked beans, and rinse with cold water.

3. Coat a large saucepan with olive oil cooking spray, and preheat over medium heat. Add the onion, red pepper, carrot, celery, and garlic, and stir-fry for 3 minutes. Add the beans, tomato, chicken broth, thyme, pepper, and salt, and bring to a boil over high heat. Reduce the heat to medium-low, and simmer for 40 minutes, or until the beans are tender. Remove the saucepan from the heat, cover, and allow the beans to come to room temperature.

4. While the beans are cooking, cook the green beans in a steamer for 7 minutes, or until fork tender. Drain well, and allow to come to room temperature.

5. Transfer the great northern beans and vegetables to a strainer, and drain off and discard the cooking liquid.

6. Place the bean and vegetable mixture, green beans, artichoke hearts, red pepper, pimientos, tuna, cheese, and olives, if desired, in a salad bowl. Add the vinaigrette, and toss gently to coat. Cover and refrigerate for several hours or overnight.

7. Remove the salad from the refrigerator 1 hour before serving, and toss gently to blend. Make a wreath of arugula on each of 4 dinner plates. Arrange the tomato slices on the inside of the wreath so that they overlap the arugula, and spoon the bean salad in the center. Serve immediately.

NUTRITIONAL FACTS
(per serving, salad only)

Calories: 380
Carbohydrates: 35.4 g
Cholesterol: 23 mg
Fat: 1.6 g
Calories From Fat: 4.5%
Protein: 43.2 g
Sodium: 697 mg

5

Tantalizing
Vegetarian Salads

Whether you have chosen a vegetarian lifestyle or are simply looking for an occasional culinary change of pace, you are in for a treat. In the following pages, over twenty-five recipes show just how appealing and satisfying vegetarian cuisine can be. Are you a pasta lover? If so, look for such offerings as Italian Pasta Salad, Orzo and Dried Tomato Salad, and Pasta Primavera Salad—dishes that unite a medley of fresh vegetables and seasonings with hearty pasta to make truly memorable entrées. Still other recipes pair the bounty of the garden with grains, legumes, and tofu. Sweet and savory dressings complete each creation, adding their own spark and interest. The result? Enticing yet wholesome main course salads that your whole family will love.

Greek Pasta Salad

An all-time favorite, traditional Greek salad is hard to improve upon, but here is my humble attempt. To create a rich contrast in colors and textures, I've added pasta to this salad, and have replaced the traditional mix of greens with spinach. Serve with warm pita breads.

8 ounces ziti pasta
6 cups prewashed baby spinach, stems removed
1 large ripe tomato, cut into 8 wedges
1 cup thin rings Vidalia onion or other sweet onion
1 green bell pepper, thinly sliced into rings
2 ounces feta cheese, crumbled
4 pepperoncini
4 hard-boiled eggs, whites only, quartered
8 pitted Kalamata olives (optional)
4 anchovy fillets, drained and separated (optional)

1. Cook the pasta according to package directions. Drain, rinse with cool water, and drain again. Allow the pasta to come to room temperature.

2. Combine the pasta, spinach, tomato, onion rings, green pepper rings, and feta cheese in a salad bowl. Add the vinaigrette, and toss gently to coat.

3. To serve, divide the salad among 4 dinner plates. Garnish each serving with a pepperoncini, 4 wedges of hard-boiled egg, and, if desired, 2 olives and 1 anchovy fillet. Serve immediately.

YIELD: 4 SERVINGS

Suggested Dressings

★ 1 recipe Greek Vinaigrette (page 222)

½ cup commercial fat-free or low-fat Greek vinaigrette

**NUTRITIONAL FACTS
(per serving, salad only)**

Calories: 218
Carbohydrates: 38.1 g
Cholesterol: 8 mg
Fat: 2.8 g
Calories From Fat: 11.4%
Protein: 11.2 g
Sodium: 199 mg

Artichoke and Pasta Salad

YIELD: **4** SERVINGS

Suggested Dressings

★ 1 recipe Tarragon Vinaigrette (page 238)

1 recipe Caper Vinaigrette (page 217)

½ cup commercial fat-free or low-fat Italian herb and cheese vinaigrette

½ cup commercial fat-free or low-fat lemon Dijon dressing

Time-Saving Tip

❑ Substitute ¾ cup of commercial sweet roasted bell peppers for the home-made roasted peppers.

After a friend described a fabulous vegetarian appetizer she had enjoyed, I devised this recipe to incorporate the same ingredients into an equally delectable salad. Serve this luxurious cornucopia of vegetables and pasta with a crusty loaf of French bread.

4 artichokes, stems and tough outer leaves removed, or 2 cans (14 ounces each) artichoke hearts or bottoms, drained and sliced
¼ cup fresh lemon juice
3 large red bell peppers
8 ounces ziti pasta
6 ounces fresh shiitake mushrooms
1 large red onion, thinly sliced and separated into rings
3 cups sliced prewashed baby spinach, stems removed
4 tomato roses (page 179) (optional)

1. If using fresh artichokes, place enough water to cover the artichokes in a large saucepan, and bring to a boil over medium-high heat. Reduce the heat to medium-low, and add the artichokes and lemon juice. Cover and cook for 45 minutes, or until fork tender. Remove from the heat, and allow to come to room temperature in the cooking liquid.

2. Drain the artichokes well. Remove and discard the artichoke leaves. Cut the heart of each artichoke into slices, and set aside.

3. To roast the peppers, place the peppers on a baking sheet that has been lined with aluminum foil. Broil under a preheated broiler, turning the peppers as the skins blacken, for 20 to 25 minutes, or until the skins are charred all over. Once roasted, place in a plastic bag, seal, and allow to steam for 15 minutes. When the peppers are cool enough to handle, peel away the skin and remove the tops and seeds. (Do not rinse the peppers.) Cut the peppers into wide strips, and set aside.

4. Cook the pasta according to package directions. Drain, rinse with cool water, and drain again. Set aside.

5. Remove and discard the stems from the shiitake mushrooms. To slice several mushrooms at one time, slightly overlap 3 to 4 mushrooms and cut into thin slices. Repeat with the remaining mushrooms. Set aside.

6. Coat a large nonstick skillet with olive oil cooking spray, and preheat over medium heat. Add the red onion, and sauté for 5 minutes, stirring occasionally. Add the mushrooms, and sauté for 5 additional minutes, or until the vegetables are fork tender. Allow the mixture to come to room temperature.

7. Combine the artichokes, roasted peppers, pasta, onions and mushrooms, and spinach in a salad bowl. Add the dressing, and toss gently to coat. Cover and refrigerate for several hours or overnight.

8. Remove the salad from the refrigerator 1 hour before serving, and toss gently to blend. Divide the salad among 4 dinner plates, and, if desired, garnish each serving with a tomato rose. Serve immediately.

NUTRITIONAL FACTS
(per serving, salad only)

Calories: 355
Carbohydrates: 83.1 g
Cholesterol: 0 mg
Fat: 0.7 g
Calories From Fat: 3.4%
Protein: 11.8 g
Sodium: 47 mg

Bella, Bella Bell Peppers

Bell peppers add crunch, a vivid color, and a sweet, fresh flavor to main course salads. And the proper selection and preparation of these peppers will help insure culinary success every time you use them.

When choosing a bell pepper, make sure that the skin has a glossy sheen rather than a wrinkled appearance. After the pepper is cut open, be sure to remove not just the seeds but also the thin white ridges found on the inner walls of the pepper. These ridges tend to be bitter in taste, especially when the peppers are eaten raw. Finally, enjoy your peppers as soon as possible after they are sliced or diced. This will prevent the edges from becoming dry, and the peppers from becoming limp and unappealing.

YIELD: **4** SERVINGS

Italian Pasta Salad

This savory creation is the Maserati of salads. Spread out a red and white checkered tablecloth, add a bottle of Chianti and a loaf of Italian bread, and you will be magically transported to an Italian villa.

Suggested Dressings

★ 1 recipe Italian Vinaigrette (page 224)

1 recipe Dijon Mustard Vinaigrette (page 221)

½ cup commercial fat-free or low-fat Italian vinaigrette

½ cup commercial fat-free or low-fat lemon Dijon dressing

8 ounces rotini or ziti pasta
1 cup small cauliflower florets
1 cup small broccoli florets
1 yellow bell pepper, diced
1 jar (4 ounces) sliced pimentos, drained
½ cup thinly sliced celery
½ cup diced red onion
5 cups prewashed baby spinach, stems removed
4 tomato roses (page 179) (optional)

**NUTRITIONAL FACTS
(per serving, salad only)**

Calories: 259
Carbohydrates: 52.1 g
Cholesterol: 0 mg
Fat: 1.3 g
Calories From Fat: 4.5%
Protein: 11.1 g
Sodium: 74 mg

1. Cook the pasta according to package directions. Drain, rinse with cool water, and drain again. Set aside.

2. Cook the cauliflower in a steamer for 3 minutes. Add the broccoli and cook for 2 additional minutes, or until the broccoli turns bright green. Rinse with cool water, and drain well.

3. Combine the pasta, cauliflower and broccoli, yellow pepper, pimientos, celery, and onion in a salad bowl. Add the dressing, and toss gently to coat. Cover and refrigerate for several hours or overnight.

4. Remove the salad from the refrigerator 1 hour before serving, and toss gently to blend. To serve, make a wreath of the spinach on each of 4 dinner plates. Spoon the pasta salad in the center of each wreath, and garnish each serving with a tomato rose, if desired. Serve immediately.

Making a Tomato Rose

For a special presentation, try placing a tomato rose beside each individual salad. This is an easy way to add a touch of both color and elegance to your dish.

To make a rose, start at the stalk end of a medium-sized tomato. Using a light sawing motion, cut a thin ½-inch-wide strip all around the tomato so that you end up with a long, continuous strip. (It's okay if a little of the flesh remains on the peel.) Just before you reach the last inch of the strip, cut a wider swath.

Lay the strip flat, with the skin side down. Starting at the wide end, begin rolling up the strip, just as you would a ribbon, so that the skin remains on the outside of the roll. When the strip is completely rolled, it should look like a rose. Store this garnish in a covered container in the refrigerator for up to one day before serving.

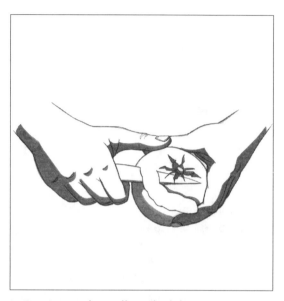

1. Starting at the stalk end of the tomato, cut a thin continuous ½-inch-wide strip of skin.

2. Lay the strip flat, skin side down, and begin rolling it up.

3. When the strip is completely rolled up, your tomato rose is ready.

YIELD: **4** SERVINGS

New Potato, Green Bean, and Pasta Salad

Hearty and satisfying, this salad is also highly versatile. For variety, try substituting asparagus for the green beans, or toss in additional condiments—such as Greek olives, pimiento strips, and parsley—for color and taste.

Suggested Dressings

★ 1 recipe Balsamic and Grainy Mustard Vinaigrette (page 214)

1 recipe Basil Dressing (page 216)

½ cup commercial fat-free or low-fat Italian Parmesan dressing

½ cup commercial fat-free or low-fat balsamic vinaigrette

6 ounces bow-tie or rotini pasta
1 pound new potatoes, sliced 1-inch thick
8 ounces green beans, trimmed and cut into 2-inch lengths
1 cup thin red onion rings
5 cups curly endive (frisée)
Chopped pimiento (optional)
4 sprigs parsley (optional)

1. Cook the pasta according to package directions. Drain, rinse with cool water, and drain again. Set aside.

2. Cook the potatoes in a large steamer for 20 to 25 minutes, or until fork tender. Transfer the potatoes to a strainer, and rinse with cold water. Drain well, and allow to come to room temperature.

3. Cook the green beans in a steamer for 8 minutes, or until fork tender. Transfer the beans to a strainer, and rinse with cold water. Drain well, and allow to come to room temperature.

4. Combine the pasta, potatoes, green beans, and onion rings in a salad bowl. Add the dressing, and toss gently to blend. Cover and refrigerate for several hours or overnight.

5. Remove the salad from the refrigerator 1 hour before serving, and toss gently. Make a wreath of the greens on each of 4 dinner plates, and mound the salad in the center of each wreath. Garnish each salad with chopped pimiento and a sprig of parsley, if desired, and serve immediately.

**NUTRITIONAL FACTS
(per serving, salad only)**

Calories: 308
Carbohydrates: 64.6 g
Cholesterol: 0 mg
Fat: 1.1 g
Calories From Fat: 3.3%
Protein: 10.5 g
Sodium: 114 mg

Pasta Primavera Salad

During the summer, when garden bounty is fresh and rich in taste, you will enjoy preparing this light salad. Serve with low-fat pineapple muffins.

8 ounces rotini or bow-tie pasta

¾ cup julienne strips carrots

24 fresh asparagus spears (1 pound), tough ends removed, or 1 can (15 ounces) asparagus spears, drained

2 leeks, cut into julienne strips

½ cup julienne strips yellow squash

3 tablespoons grated fat-free Parmesan cheese

Large basil leaves (optional)

Suggested Dressing

★ 1 recipe Basil Dressing (page 216)

1 recipe Pasta Vinaigrette (page 230)

½ cup commercial fat-free or low-fat Italian Parmesan dressing

½ cup commercial fat-free or low-fat peppercorn ranch dressing

1. Cook the pasta according to package directions. Drain, rinse with cool water, and drain again. Allow to come to room temperature.

2. Place enough water to cover the carrots in a large saucepan, and bring to a boil over high heat. Add the carrots and simmer for 6 minutes.

3. Cut the asparagus into 2-inch lengths. If using fresh asparagus, add the asparagus and the leeks to the carrots, and boil for 1 additional minute. (If using canned asparagus, add only the leeks to the saucepan.) Drain well, and allow the vegetables to come to room temperature.

4. Combine the pasta, carrots, asparagus, leeks, yellow squash, and Parmesan cheese in a salad bowl. Add the dressing, and toss gently to coat. Cover and refrigerate for several hours.

5. Remove the salad from the refrigerator 1 hour before serving, and toss gently. Divide the salad among 4 dinner plates. Garnish each serving with 2 to 3 large basil leaves, if desired, and serve immediately.

NUTRITIONAL FACTS
(per serving, salad only)

Calories: 236
Carbohydrates: 51.2 g
Cholesterol: 4 mg
Fat: 0.2 g
Calories From Fat: 3.4%
Protein: 9.1 g
Sodium: 68 mg

Orzo and Dried Tomato Salad

Dried tomatoes add a piquant flavor to this melange of diverse ingredients. Enjoy this dish as a light entrée or as picnic fare. Serve with pita crisps.

Time-Saving Tip
❏ Substitute ¼ cup of commercial sweet roasted bell peppers for the home-made roasted peppers.

8 ounces orzo pasta*
1 large red bell pepper
½ cup sun-dried tomatoes (packaged without oil)
½ cup diced red onion
1 clove garlic, finely chopped
1 teaspoon extra virgin olive oil
2 ½ tablespoons chopped fresh dill
1 tablespoon white wine vinegar
¼ teaspoon freshly ground pepper
⅛ teaspoon salt
2 ounces crumbled feta cheese (optional)
2 tablespoons toasted pine nuts (page 69) (optional)
2 Roma tomatoes, diced

* Orzo can be found in the pasta or rice section of most supermarkets.

1. Cook the orzo according to package directions. Drain, rinse with cool water, and drain again. Set aside.

2. To roast the pepper, place the pepper on a baking sheet that has been lined with aluminum foil. Broil the pepper under a preheated broiler, turning the pepper as the skin blackens, for 20 to 25 minutes, or until the skin is charred all over. Once roasted, place in a plastic bag, seal, and allow to steam for 15 minutes. When the pepper is cool enough to handle, peel away the skin and remove the top and seeds. (Do not rinse the pepper.) Cut the pepper into small squares and set aside.

3. Place the sun-dried tomatoes in a small heatproof bowl, and add enough boiling water to cover. Allow to sit for 5 to 15 minutes, or until the tomatoes are soft. Drain well, and cut into slivers.

4. Combine the orzo, roasted pepper, slivered tomatoes, onion, garlic, and olive oil in a medium-sized bowl, and toss gently to blend. Set aside for 10 minutes.

5. Add the dill, white wine vinegar, pepper, salt, and feta cheese and pine nuts, if desired, to the orzo mixture, and toss to blend. Cover and refrigerate for several hours.

6. Remove the salad from the refrigerator 1 hour before serving. Add the diced tomatoes, and toss gently to blend. Serve immediately.

Serving Suggestion

For a more artistic presentation, first make a wreath of arugula leaves on each of 4 dinner plates. Lightly coat four 1-cup molds with cooking spray, and pack the orzo salad into the molds. Then immediately unmold the salad in the center of each wreath of leaves. If desired, sprinkle each serving with crushed tomato topping (page 202).

NUTRITIONAL FACTS
(per serving)

Calories: 259
Carbohydrates: 53.1 g
Cholesterol: 0 mg
Fat: 1.4 g
Calories From Fat: 4.9%
Protein: 9.5 g
Sodium: 222 mg

YIELD: **4** SERVINGS

California Spinach, Alfalfa Sprouts, and Tofu Salad

Soy-based foods such as tofu are high in protein, and therefore make great meat substitutes. And while tofu is bland in taste, it readily absorbs other flavors, making it highly versatile. In this dish, tofu is combined with spinach, tomatoes, and other savory ingredients with delicious results. Serve with warm pita bread.

Suggested Dressings

★ 1 recipe Savory Vinaigrette (page 234)

1 recipe Cobb Salad Dressing (page 220)

½ cup commercial fat-free or low-fat roasted garlic dressing

½ cup commercial fat-free or low-fat peppercorn ranch dressing

---

1 package (12.3 ounces) low-fat extra-firm tofu

6 cups prewashed baby spinach, stems removed

3 Roma tomatoes, quartered

2 cups commercial fat-free seasoned croutons

1 cup alfalfa sprouts

1 small unpeeled cucumber, thinly sliced

¼ cup shredded fat-free Cheddar cheese

2 avocados, peeled, pitted, and cubed (optional)

NUTRITIONAL FACTS
(per serving, salad only)

Calories: 137
Carbohydrates: 32 g
Cholesterol: 0 mg
Fat: 0.8 g
Calories From Fat: 10.5%
Protein: 19.3 g
Sodium: 340 mg

1. To press the tofu, place the tofu between 2 flat plates. Then place two 2-pound cans on the upper plate. There should be just enough weight to cause the tofu to bulge slightly, but not enough to cause the tofu to split. Refrigerate for 1 hour.

2. Drain off any accumulated liquid from the tofu. Slice the tofu in half horizontally, and lightly coat it with some of the vinaigrette. Cover and refrigerate for 1 hour.

3. Transfer the tofu to a baking sheet, and place it under a preheated broiler, 3 inches from the heat source. Broil for 3 to 4 minutes on each side, or until golden brown. Cut the tofu into cubes, and allow to come to room temperature.

4. Combine the spinach, tomatoes, croutons, sprouts, cucumber, cheese, and avocados, if desired, in a salad bowl. Add the dressing, and toss to coat. Add the tofu, toss once more, and serve immediately.

Orange-Infused Grain Salad

This salad is similar to tabbouleh, but has the added allure of wild rice, dried fruit, and a tangy infusion of orange. Although it is an excellent vegetarian entrée, it can be complemented nicely by cubes of chicken, pork, or lamb.

Suggested Dressing

★ 1 recipe Tangy Orange Dressing (page 237)

1 cup bulghur wheat

½ cup wild rice, rinsed with cold water

¾ cup chopped mixed dried fruit, such as raisins, apricots, and dates

¼ cup plus 2 tablespoons minced scallions

¼ cup minced fresh mint

¼ cup minced fresh parsley

4 cups packed arugula leaves, stems removed

4 oranges, peeled, halved, and thinly sliced

**NUTRITIONAL FACTS
(per serving, salad only)**
Calories: 291
Carbohydrates: 64.9g
Cholesterol: 0 mg
Fat: 1.3 g
Calories From Fat: 3.7%
Protein: 10.5 g
Sodium: 38 mg

1. To cook the bulghur wheat, place the bulghur in a medium-sized heatproof bowl. Add 1½ cups of boiling water, cover with plastic wrap, and allow to sit for 20 minutes.

2. While the bulghur is sitting, place 2 cups of water in a medium-sized saucepan, and bring to a boil over high heat. Reduce the heat to low, and add the wild rice. Cover and simmer for 45 minutes or until tender. Drain well.

3. Pour the bulghur into a strainer lined with a double thickness of cheesecloth. Twist the cheesecloth around the bulghur, and squeeze out as much water as possible. Transfer the bulghur to a large bowl.

4. Add the wild rice, dried fruit, scallions, mint, parsley, and dressing to the bulghur, and toss gently to blend. Cover and refrigerate for several hours or overnight.

5. Remove the salad from the refrigerator 1 hour before serving, and toss gently to blend. To serve, make a wreath of the arugula leaves on each of 4 dinner plates. Arrange the orange slices so that they overlap the arugula, and spoon the grain salad in the center of each wreath. Serve immediately.

YIELD: **4** SERVINGS

Suggested Dressings

★ 1 recipe Spicy
Vinaigrette (page 236)

1 recipe Caribbean
Dressing (page 217)

½ cup commercial fat-free
or low-fat Oriental
dressing

Mixed Baby Greens
With Marinated Tofu

*This salad is a real showstopper. Serve with thin slices
of low-fat papaya bread.*

Marinade

2 tablespoons low-sodium soy sauce
2 tablespoons fat-free vegetable broth
1 tablespoon dark brown sugar
1 clove garlic, finely chopped
½-inch piece fresh ginger, peeled
¼ teaspoon Asian hot sauce or favorite hot pepper sauce

1 package (1 pound) low-fat extra-firm tofu
6 cups mixed baby greens
2 mangos, peeled, pitted, and thinly sliced
1 red bell pepper, cut into julienne strips
2 scallions, thinly sliced
2 carrots, peeled and shredded

1. To press the tofu, place the tofu between 2 flat plates. Then place two 2-pound cans on the upper plate. There should be just enough weight to cause the tofu to bulge slightly, but not enough to cause the tofu to split. Refrigerate for 1 hour.

2. Drain off any accumulated water from the tofu. Slice the block of tofu in half horizontally, and set aside.

3. To make the marinade, combine all of the marinade ingredients in a nonmetal dish, and stir to mix. Add the tofu and turn to coat. Cover and refrigerate for 1 to 2 hours, turning the tofu at least once.

4. Remove the tofu from the marinade, discarding the marinade, and transfer the tofu to a baking pan. Place under a preheated broiler, 4 inches from the heat source, and broil for 4 to 5 minutes on each side, or until golden brown. Cut each piece of tofu in half to make 4 servings.

5. Combine the mixed baby greens, mangos, and red pepper in a salad bowl. Add just enough dressing to coat, and toss gently.

6. To serve, divide the salad among 4 dinner plates, and top each with a serving of tofu. Garnish with the scallions and carrots, and serve immediately.

NUTRITIONAL FACTS
(per serving, salad only)
Calories: 180
Carbohydrates: 32.6 g
Cholesterol: 0 mg
Fat: 2.1 g
Calories From Fat: 11.5%
Protein: 12.7 g
Sodium: 442.6 mg

Serving Suggestion

For a more artistic presentation, first divide the mixed baby greens among 4 dinner plates. Place a serving of tofu in the center of the greens, and fan slices of mango on each side of the tofu. Randomly distribute the red pepper and carrots over the tofu, and spoon the dressing over the salad. Garnish with the scallions or with a scallion flower (page 42)

Indian Potato and Chickpea Salad

YIELD: 6 SERVINGS

This salad is an irresistible medley of new potatoes and chickpeas cloaked in an intensely spiced Indian dressing. The first time you enjoy it, try to imagine yourself sitting in a roadside restaurant within sight of the Taj Mahal. Serve with naan, an Indian flatbread, and light beer.

Suggested Dressings

★ 1 recipe Indian-Spiced Dressing (page 223)

2 pounds new potatoes
2 cans (15 ounces each) chickpeas, rinsed and drained
8 scallions, thinly sliced
1 tablespoon plus 1 teaspoon chopped fresh cilantro
6 sprigs fresh cilantro (optional)

NUTRITIONAL FACTS
(per serving, salad only)
Calories: 340
Carbohydrates: 68.2 g
Cholesterol: 0 mg
Fat: 2.1 g
Calories From Fat: 9.2%
Protein: 13.7 g
Sodium: 617 mg

1. Place enough water to cover the potatoes in a large saucepan, and bring to a boil over high heat. Add the potatoes and simmer for 25 minutes, or until fork tender. Drain, and allow to come to room temperature before cutting into cubes.

2. Combine the potatoes, chickpeas, scallions, and chopped cilantro in a salad bowl. Add the dressing, and toss gently to coat. Cover and set aside at room temperature for 1 hour to allow the flavors to blend.

3. To serve, stir the salad and divide among 6 dinner plates. Garnish each serving with a sprig of cilantro, if desired, and serve immediately.

Thai Tofu and Vegetable Salad

This rich, aromatic salad is a marvelous fusion of stir-fried vegetables and tofu arranged on a bed of bean threads, and laced with an Oriental style dressing. Serve with melon slices.

Suggested Dressings

★ 1 recipe Oriental Dressing (page 229)

1 recipe Spicy Vinaigrette (page 236)

½ cup commercial fat-free or low-fat Oriental dressing

½ cup commercial fat-free or low-fat sweet and sour dressing

NUTRITIONAL FACTS
(per serving, salad only)
Calories: 266
Carbohydrates: 48.3 g
Cholesterol: 0 mg
Fat: 1.7 g
Calories From Fat: 9.6%
Protein: 15.2 g
Sodium: 185 mg

---

6 ounces bean thread vermicelli (cellophane noodles), broken into 4-inch strands

1 package (12.3 ounces) low-fat extra-firm tofu

½ teaspoon Oriental sesame oil

4 cloves garlic, finely chopped

1 teaspoon finely chopped fresh ginger

1 teaspoon crushed red pepper

2 carrots, peeled and cut into julienne strips

1 red bell pepper, cut into julienne strips

6 ounces bok choy, sliced

1 can (7 ounces) whole baby sweet corn, drained

1½ cups broccoli florets

4 ounces fresh snow peas, strings removed

¼ cup chopped peanuts (optional)

4 scallion flowers (page 42) (optional)

1. Cook the vermicelli according to package directions. Drain, rinse with cool water, and drain again. Set aside.

2. To press the tofu, place the tofu between 2 flat plates. Then place two 2-pound cans on the upper plate. There should be just enough weight to cause the tofu to bulge slightly, but not enough to cause the tofu to split. Refrigerate for 1 hour.

3. Drain off any accumulated liquid from the tofu. Cut the tofu into cubes, and set aside.

4. Coat a large nonstick skillet with cooking spray. Add the sesame oil, and preheat over medium-high heat. Add the garlic, ginger, and crushed red pepper, and stir-fry for 1 minute. Add the carrots, red pepper, and bok choy, and stir-fry for 2 minutes. Add the corn, broccoli, and snow peas, and stir-fry for 2 minutes. Finally, add the tofu, and stir-fry for 2 additional minutes. Transfer the mixture to a large bowl, and allow to come to room temperature.

5. Add the dressing to the vegetable mixture, and toss gently to coat.

6. To serve, divide the pasta among 4 dinner plates, separating any strands that may be clinging to one another. Top each serving with the stir-fry mixture, and, if desired, garnish with a sprinkling of peanuts and a scallion flower. Serve immediately.

Red Pepper, Dried Tomato, and Feta Salad

This Mediterranean-inspired salad is perfect fare for an evening spent on your patio or deck. All you need is a warm breeze, a loaf of crusty bread, and a bottle of your favorite wine.

½ cup sun-dried tomatoes (packaged without oil)

6 cups prewashed baby spinach, stems removed

1 red bell pepper, cut into julienne strips

1 cup thin red onion rings

2 ounces feta cheese, crumbled

8 pitted Kalamata olives (optional)

4 tomato roses (page 179) (optional)

1. Place the sun-dried tomatoes in a small heatproof bowl, and add enough boiling water to cover. Allow to sit for 5 to 15 minutes, or until the tomatoes are soft. Drain well, and slice into slivers.

2. Combine the slivered tomatoes, spinach, red pepper, onion rings, feta cheese, and olives, if desired, in a salad bowl. Add the dressing, and toss gently to coat.

3. To serve, divide the salad among 4 dinner plates. Garnish each serving with a tomato rose, if desired, and serve immediately.

YIELD: 4 SERVINGS

Suggested Dressings

★ 1 recipe Red Wine Vinaigrette (page 232)

1 recipe Greek Vinaigrette (page 222)

½ cup commercial fat-free or low-fat red wine vinaigrette

½ cup commercial fat-free or low-fat lemon Dijon dressing

NUTRITIONAL FACTS
(per serving, salad only)

Calories: 87
Carbohydrates: 10.8 g
Cholesterol: 13 mg
Fat: 3.5 g
Calories From Fat: 33.1%
Protein: 5.3 g
Sodium: 349 mg

YIELD: **6** SERVINGS

Couscous Salad With Roasted Vegetables

NUTRITIONAL FACTS
(per serving)
Calories: 372
Carbohydrates: 71.4 g
Cholesterol: 0 mg
Fat: 4.8 g
Calories From Fat: 11.6%
Protein: 11.7 g
Sodium: 152 mg

Vegetables that have been herb-infused before roasting make any dish special. If you prefer to grill your vegetables, you will further enhance them with a distinctive smoky taste. Any leftover salad can be stuffed into pita bread and garnished with lettuce, tomato, red pepper, and red onion slices.

Roasted Vegetables

3 large red bell peppers

2 medium zucchini

3 medium carrots

1 large red onion

10 large cloves garlic

1 tablespoon extra virgin olive oil

1½ teaspoons dried oregano

1½ teaspoons dried thyme

1½ teaspoons dried rosemary

1 box (10 ounces) couscous

¼ cup plus 2 tablespoons fresh lemon juice

2 tablespoons capers, rinsed and drained

½ teaspoon extra virgin olive oil

¼ teaspoon salt

¼ teaspoon freshly ground pepper

3 tablespoons thinly sliced fresh basil (optional)

4 tomato roses (page 179) (optional)

1. To prepare the vegetables for roasting, first halve the red peppers lengthwise, and cut each half into 1-inch strips. Cut each zucchini in half crosswise, and cut each half into 4 wedges. Peel each carrot, cut in half crosswise, and cut each half into 4 wedges. Peel the onion, and cut into 8 wedges. Peel the garlic, leaving the cloves whole.

2. Combine the olive oil, oregano, thyme, and rosemary in a large bowl. Add the prepared vegetables, and toss well to mix.

3. Lightly coat a large nonstick baking sheet with 1-inch sides with olive oil cooking spray. Using a rubber spatula, turn the vegetables out onto the pan, spreading them into a single layer. Bake in a pre-heated 450°F oven, turning the vegetables every 15 minutes, for 45 to 50 minutes, or until the vegetables are fork tender and the edges are brown. Allow the vegetables to cool before cutting into cubes.

4. Prepare the couscous according to package directions. Transfer the cooked couscous to a large bowl, and fluff with a fork.

5. Add the roasted vegetable mixture and the lemon juice, capers, olive oil, salt, pepper, and basil, if desired, to the couscous, and toss gently to mix. Cover and refrigerate for several hours.

6. Remove the salad from the refrigerator 1 hour before serving, and toss gently to mix. Divide the salad among 4 dinner plates or bowls, and garnish each serving with a tomato rose, if desired. Serve immediately.

Quinoa Salad With Roasted Vegetable Salsa

YIELD: 4 SERVINGS

NUTRITIONAL FACTS
(per serving)
Calories: 293
Carbohydrates: 51.7 g
Cholesterol: 0 mg
Fat: 6.9 g
Calories From Fat: 19.8%
Protein: 11.2 g
Sodium: 243 mg

Quinoa (pronounced KEEN-wa) is a South American grain that is an excellent source of protein. In fact, it is higher in protein than any other grain. Fusing this Mediterranean-inspired salad with a roasted Southwestern salsa results in a wonderful taste experience. The zesty salsa can also be used to enhance a variety of other main course salads, including Chicken, Black Bean, and Corn Salad (page 40) and Red Pepper Fettuccine and Chicken Salad (page 54).

Roasted Vegetable Salsa

1 small eggplant (8 ounces), peeled and cut into ½-inch cubes

2 large red bell peppers, cut into ½-inch squares

1 zucchini, cut into ½-inch cubes

1 large carrot, peeled and cut into ½-inch cubes

1 red onion, cut into ½-inch cubes

2 teaspoons extra virgin olive oil

¼ teaspoon salt

¼ teaspoon freshly ground pepper

½ cup chopped fresh cilantro

¼ cup fresh lime juice

1 jalapeño chili, minced

2 cups cold water

1 cup quinoa, rinsed

¼ cup fresh lemon juice

1 teaspoon extra virgin olive oil

1 cup packed chopped fresh parsley

½ cup chopped scallions

¼ cup plus 2 tablespoons chopped fresh mint

1 teaspoon finely chopped garlic

¼ teaspoon salt

¼ teaspoon freshly ground pepper

2 tomatoes, seeded and chopped

4 sprigs fresh cilantro (optional)

1. To make the roasted vegetable salsa, combine the eggplant, red pepper, zucchini, carrot, onion, olive oil, salt, and pepper in a large bowl, and toss to mix well.

2. Coat a large nonstick baking pan with 1-inch sides with olive oil cooking spray, and transfer the vegetables to the pan, spreading them into a single layer. Bake in a preheated 450°F oven, turning every 15 minutes, for 45 to 50 minutes, or until the vegetables are fork tender and the edges are brown. Allow the vegetables to come to room temperature.

3. Transfer the roasted vegetables to a medium-sized bowl, and stir in the cilantro, lime juice, and jalapeño. Cover and refrigerate for several hours or overnight.

4. To make the quinoa salad, place the 2 cups of water in a medium-sized saucepan, and bring to a boil over high heat. Reduce the heat to low and add the quinoa. Cover the saucepan and simmer for 15 to 20 minutes, or until all of the water has been absorbed. Fluff the quinoa with 2 chopsticks or forks to release the steam, and allow to come to room temperature.

5. Combine the lemon juice and olive oil in a small jar with a tight-fitting lid, and shake to blend well. Add this mixture to the quinoa, and stir to mix. Add the parsley, scallions, mint, garlic, salt, and pepper, and toss gently to blend. Cover and refrigerate for several hours or overnight.

6. Remove the salad from the refrigerator 1 hour before serving. Add the tomatoes, and toss gently to blend.

7. To serve, divide the salad among 4 dinner plates, and top each serving with 1 or 2 large spoonfuls of roasted vegetable salsa. Garnish each serving with a sprig of cilantro, if desired, and serve immediately.

Cooking With Salsa

Salsa is the Spanish word for a sauce that, traditionally, consists of a mixture of diced chili peppers, tomatoes, cilantro, garlic, and salt. Typically, but not always, these ingredients are cooked.

Nowadays, creative cooks have developed a wide range of delicious salsas, some of which are made with vegetables, like the Roasted Vegetable Salsa found on page 192, and some of which are made with fruit, like the Orange and Pineapple Salsa found on page 152. Try using the salsa ideas presented in these pages as a springboard for your own salsa inventions. You're sure to "cook up" sauces that will enliven not only your main course salads, but a variety of other dishes as well.

Saffron Rice Salad With Roasted Peppers

YIELD: **4** SERVINGS

Suggested Dressings

★ 1 recipe Cilantro and Jalapeño Dressing (page 218)

1 recipe Southwestern Vinaigrette (page 235)

½ cup commercial fat-free or low-fat Southwestern dressing

NUTRITIONAL FACTS
(per serving, salad only)

Calories: 219
Carbohydrates: 46.6 g
Cholesterol: 0 mg
Fat: 1.4 g
Calories From Fat: 5.7%
Protein: 5.1 g
Sodium: 161 mg

This colorful salad provides an opportunity to experience the delights of fusion cooking—the melding of different cuisines in one glorious dish. Saffron rice and roasted peppers are reminiscent of the Mediterranean, while any of the suggested dressings will add a Southwestern touch. Grilled polenta would nicely complement this salad.

3 large red bell peppers
3 large yellow bell peppers
1 Vidalia onion or other sweet onion, coarsely chopped
2 cloves garlic, finely chopped
1 teaspoon extra virgin olive oil
1 cup arborio rice*
2 tablespoons fat-free vegetable broth
½ teaspoon saffron threads
4 tomato roses (page 179) (optional)

* A starchy short-grain rice often used to make risotto, arborio rice can be found in the rice section of many supermarkets and specialty stores.

1. To roast the peppers, place the peppers on a baking sheet that has been lined with aluminum foil. Broil under a preheated broiler, turning the peppers as the skins blacken, for 20 to 25 minutes, or until the skins are charred all over. Once roasted, place in a plastic bag, seal, and allow to steam for 15 minutes. When the peppers are cool enough to handle, peel away the skin and remove the tops and seeds. (Do not rinse the peppers.) Cut the peppers into ½-inch squares and set aside.

2. Coat a large nonstick saucepan with olive oil cooking spray, and preheat over medium-low heat. Add the onion, garlic, and olive oil, and cook, stirring occasionally, for 25 to 30 minutes, or until the vegetables are golden and tender. Allow to come to room temperature.

3. While the onion and garlic are cooking, cook the rice according to package directions. Transfer the cooked rice to a fine-sieved strainer, and rinse with cold water. Drain well, and transfer the rice to a salad bowl. Allow to come to room temperature.

4. Place the vegetable broth in a small saucepan, and cook over medium heat until warm. Place the broth and the saffron in a small dish, and allow to sit for 15 minutes to bring out the flavor and color of the saffron.

5. Add the roasted peppers, onion and garlic mixture, saffron mixture, and dressing to the rice, and toss gently to blend. Serve immediately, or cover and refrigerate for several hours, removing the salad from the refrigerator 1 hour before serving. Garnish each serving with a tomato rose, if desired.

Mediterranean Vegetable Salad

This salad combines roasted red and yellow peppers with a vinaigrette. The result not only has eye appeal, but also creates a marvelous intermingling of flavors. Serve with pita bread.

3 red bell peppers
3 yellow bell peppers
4 cups prewashed baby spinach, stems removed
4 firm ripe tomatoes, thinly sliced
8 pitted Kalamata olives, halved (optional)
2 ounces feta cheese, crumbled
Coarsely chopped fresh basil leaves (optional)

1. To roast the peppers, place the peppers on a baking sheet that has been lined with aluminum foil. Broil under a preheated broiler, turning the peppers as the skins blacken, for 20 to 25 minutes, or until the skins are charred all over. Once roasted, place in a plastic bag, seal, and allow to steam for 15 minutes. When the peppers are cool enough to handle, peel away the skin and remove the tops and seeds. (Do not rinse the peppers.) Cut the peppers into strips.

2. To serve, line the rim of a platter with the spinach leaves. Arrange the tomato slices in a ring that slightly overlaps the spinach. Then arrange the roasted peppers and, if desired, the olives in the center of the platter. Distribute the feta cheese over the peppers, and drizzle the vinaigrette over the entire salad. Garnish with fresh basil, if desired, and serve immediately.

YIELD: 4 SERVINGS

Suggested Dressings

★ 1 recipe Balsamic Vinaigrette (page 215)

1 recipe Greek Vinaigrette (page 222)

½ cup commercial fat-free or low-fat balsamic vinaigrette

½ cup commercial fat-free or low-fat Greek vinaigrette

NUTRITIONAL FACTS
(per serving, salad only)

Calories: 114
Carbohydrates: 18.1 g
Cholesterol: 13 mg
Fat: 3.6 g
Calories From Fat: 25.6%
Protein: 5.6 g
Sodium: 213 mg

Santa Fe Barley Salad

Barley and beans are an excellent high-protein, low-fat alternative to beef or poultry. And when combined with flavorful vegetables and a spicy vinaigrette, they become irresistible. Accompany this salad with tortillas.

Suggested Dressings

★ 1 recipe Southwestern Vinaigrette (page 235)

1 recipe Cilantro and Jalapeño Dressing (page 218)

½ cup commercial fat-free or low-fat Southwestern vinaigrette

½ cup commercial fat-free or low-fat roasted garlic dressing

3 cups water or vegetable broth
¾ cup pearl barley
2 red bell peppers
1 cup cooked or canned corn kernels
1 can (1 pound) black beans, rinsed and drained
¼ cup minced fresh cilantro
2 scallions, thinly sliced
18 baked tortilla strips (page 35) (optional)

Time-Saving Tip

❑ Substitute ½ cup commercial sweet roasted bell peppers for the home-made roasted peppers.

NUTRITIONAL FACTS (per serving, salad only)

Calories: 292
Carbohydrates: 60.8 g
Cholesterol: 0 mg
Fat: 1.1 g
Calories From Fat: 3%
Protein: 17.8 g
Sodium: 277 mg

1. Place the water or broth in a medium-sized saucepan, and bring to a boil over high heat. Reduce the heat to low and stir in the barley. Cover and simmer for 45 minutes, or until all of the liquid has been absorbed. Transfer the barley to a strainer, and rinse with cold water. Drain well, and allow to come to room temperature.

2. To roast the peppers, place the peppers on a baking sheet that has been lined with aluminum foil. Broil under a preheated broiler, turning the peppers as the skins blacken, for 20 to 25 minutes, or until the skins are charred all over. Once roasted, place in a plastic bag, seal, and allow to steam for 15 minutes. When the peppers are cool enough to handle, peel away the skin and remove the tops and seeds. (Do not rinse the peppers.) Cut the peppers into ½-inch squares.

3. Combine the cooked barley, roasted peppers, corn, black beans, cilantro, and scallions in a salad bowl. Add the dressing, and toss gently to coat. Cover and refrigerate for several hours or overnight.

4. Remove the salad from the refrigerator 1 hour before serving, and toss gently. To serve, divide the salad among 6 dinner plates or bowls. If desired, garnish each serving with baked tortilla strips by placing several strips in the center of the salad so that they point upwards. Serve immediately.

Southwestern Wild Rice and Bean Salad

In this salad, wild rice and beans are combined with a variety of ingredients, creating a satisfying medley of flavors and textures. Serve with squares of grilled polenta.

| 1 cup wild rice |
| 4 cups water or vegetable broth |
| 1 can (15 ounces) light red kidney beans, rinsed and drained |
| 1 cup packed prewashed baby spinach, stems removed, torn into bite-sized pieces |
| 1 cup diced jicama* |
| 1 cup cooked or canned corn kernels |
| ¼ cup shredded fat-free Monterey Jack cheese |
| 1 cup diced red onion |
| 1 cup diced tomato |

* A root vegetable resembling a turnip, jicama can be found in the produce section of many supermarkets.

1. Place the rice in a fine-sieved strainer, and rinse with cold water.

2. Combine the rice and the water or broth in a medium-sized saucepan, and bring to a boil over medium-high heat. Reduce the heat to medium-low and simmer uncovered for 30 minutes, or until the rice is tender and the grains just begin to open. Drain well, and allow to come to room temperature.

3. Combine the rice, kidney beans, spinach, jicama, corn, and cheese in a salad bowl. Add the dressing, and toss gently to coat.

4. To serve, divide the salad among 4 dinner plates. Garnish the top of each salad with the onion and tomato, and serve immediately.

YIELD: 4 SERVINGS

Suggested Dressings

★ 1 recipe Southwestern Vinaigrette (page 235)

1 recipe Cilantro and Jalapeño Dressing (page 218)

½ cup commercial fat-free or low-fat Southwestern Caesar dressing

---

NUTRITIONAL FACTS (per serving, salad only)

Calories: 602
Carbohydrates: 109.1 g
Cholesterol: 5 mg
Fat: 1.9 g
Calories From Fat: 2.7%
Protein: 42.4 g
Sodium: 247 mg

Tabbouleh

YIELD: 4 SERVINGS

A bulghur wheat salad, tabbouleh is very popular throughout the Middle East, and has rapidly gained in popularity in North America, as well. This versatile salad is delicious when piled on a plate and surrounded by wedges of warm pita bread, scallions, cherry tomatoes, chunks of feta cheese, and Kalamata olives. For variety, try topping the salad with grilled vegetable kebabs.

NUTRITIONAL FACTS
(per serving)
Calories: 218
Carbohydrates: 42.4 g
Cholesterol: 0 mg
Fat: 3.7 g
Calories From Fat: 14%
Protein: 9.5 g
Sodium: 352 mg

1 cup bulghur wheat
¼ cup fresh lemon juice
2 teaspoons extra virgin olive oil
2 large tomatoes, seeded and chopped
1 cup packed chopped fresh parsley
½ cup chopped scallions
¼ cup plus 2 tablespoons chopped fresh mint
1 teaspoon finely chopped garlic
½ teaspoon salt
¼ teaspoon freshly ground pepper

1. To cook the bulghur wheat, place the bulghur in a medium-sized heatproof bowl. Add 1½ cups of boiling water, cover with plastic wrap, and allow to sit for 20 minutes.

2. Pour the bulghur into a strainer lined with a double thickness of cheesecloth. Twist the cheesecloth around the bulghur, and squeeze out as much water as possible. Transfer the bulghur to a large bowl.

3. Combine the lemon juice and olive oil in a small jar with a tight-fitting lid, and shake to blend well. Add the lemon juice mixture and all of the remaining ingredients to the bulghur, and toss gently to blend. Cover and refrigerate for several hours or overnight.

4. Remove the salad from the refrigerator 1 hour before serving. Toss gently, and serve immediately.

Black Bean, Corn, and Veggie Burger Salad

This quick-and-easy salad is both delicious and attractive. It is also a savory treat when made with grilled chicken. Serve with grilled polenta.

1 tablespoon plus 1 teaspoon Cajun spices

4 frozen meatless burgers

1 can (15 ounces) black beans, rinsed and drained

2 cups cooked or canned corn kernels

4 cups prewashed baby spinach, stems removed

½ cup diced red onion

1 avocado, peeled, pitted, and cubed (optional)

1. Spread the Cajun spices over a dinner plate and turn the burgers in the spices, lightly coating both sides.

2. Cook the meatless burgers according to package directions. Cut each burger into 2 pieces, and set aside.

3. Combine the black beans and corn in a medium-sized bowl.

4. To serve, divide the spinach among 4 dinner plates. Spoon a layer of black beans and corn over the spinach. Then arrange 2 burger halves in the center of each salad, slightly overlapping the halves. Distribute the onion and, if desired, the avocado over the top, and drizzle the dressing over each serving. Serve immediately.

YIELD: 4 SERVINGS

Suggested Dressings

★ 1 recipe Southwestern Vinaigrette (page 235)

1 recipe Mexican Vinaigrette (page 228)

½ cup commercial fat-free or low-fat Southwestern vinaigrette

½ cup commercial fat-free or low-fat roasted garlic dressing

NUTRITIONAL FACTS
(per serving, salad only)
Calories: 537
Carbohydrates: 95.9 g
Cholesterol: 0 mg
Fat: 1.8 g
Calories From Fat: 3.4%
Protein: 38.9 g
Sodium: 363 mg

Getting the Most From Corn

Although canned and frozen corn are great time-savers whenever you're in a rush, nothing has the sweet taste and pleasing texture of fresh corn. The following steps will give you the best results whenever you want to use fresh corn kernels in a salad.

1. Remove the husk and silk from an ear of corn.

2. Cut off the stem end to provide an even base on which to stand the cob.

3. Dip the ear of corn in boiling water for 1 to 2 minutes; then rinse with cold water. (This will prevent the milk from bursting out of the kernels when you scrape them off the ear.)

4. Hold the corn upright, cut end down, on a plate. Then use a sharp knife to slice downward, removing a few rows of kernels at a time. One ear of corn will yield approximately ½ cup of kernels.

5. Use the kernels as is, or boil or steam them briefly if your recipe calls for cooked corn.

Hummus

One of the highlights of a trip to Israel was a lunch served at a kibbutz overlooking the sea of Galilee. There, I enjoyed a wonderful hummus salad surrounded by freshly baked pita bread. Fortunately, it's easy to prepare and enjoy this Mideastern delight at home.

Time-Saving Tip

❑ Substitute a 1-pound can (1½ cups) of chickpeas for the home-cooked chickpeas.

1 cup dried chickpeas
4 large cloves garlic, peeled
1 scallion, cut into 1-inch lengths
½ cup fresh lemon juice
¼ cup tahini paste*
2 tablespoons chopped fresh parsley
2 teaspoons low-sodium soy sauce
1 teaspoon chopped fresh cilantro
1 teaspoon ground cumin
1 teaspoon extra virgin olive oil
¼ teaspoon salt
¼ teaspoon freshly ground pepper
1 tablespoon plus 1 teaspoon extra virgin olive oil (optional)
⅛ teaspoon paprika (optional)
Chopped fresh parsley (optional)

* Tahini paste, a condiment made from hulled sesame seeds, is a popular ingredient in Middle Eastern cuisine. Look for it in health food and specialty stores.

1. Place the chickpeas in a large nonmetal bowl, and add enough water to cover. Cover and allow to sit overnight at room temperature.

2. Transfer the soaked chickpeas to a colander, and rinse with cold water.

3. Place 2 cups of cold water in a medium-sized saucepan, and bring to a boil over medium-high heat. Add the chickpeas, cover, and cook for 10 minutes. Reduce the heat to medium-low, cover, and simmer for 90 minutes, or until the chickpeas are soft, adding more water as necessary.

4. Transfer the chickpeas to a colander placed over a large bowl, and drain well, reserving the cooking liquid. Set aside 8 to 12 chickpeas for a garnish.

5. Place the garlic and scallion in a food processor, and process the mixture until chopped. Add the chickpeas and 1/4 cup of the reserved cooking liquid, and purée, stopping the machine occasionally to scrape the sides of the work bowl with a rubber spatula.

6. Gradually add the lemon juice to the chickpea mixture, and process until the mixture is smooth. Add the tahini paste, parsley, soy sauce, cilantro, cumin, olive oil, salt, and pepper, and process until smooth, adding additional reserved cooking liquid, 1 tablespoon at a time, until the hummus has a spreadable consistency but is still somewhat stiff.

7. Transfer the hummus to a covered bowl, and refrigerate for several hours or overnight.

8. To serve, divide the hummus among 4 dinner plates. If desired, mix the olive oil and paprika together, and drizzle the mixture over the hummus. Finally, garnish with the parsley, if desired, and serve immediately. Accompany the salad with warm pita bread.

NUTRITIONAL FACTS
(per serving)

Calories: 208
Carbohydrates: 34.6 g
Cholesterol: 0 mg
Fat: 4.2 g
Calories From Fat: 17.4%
Protein: 10.3 g
Sodium: 204 mg

Chickpea and Artichoke Salad

YIELD: 4 SERVINGS

This salad is ideal to take along on a picnic or a walk through the woods. Just tuck it into a basket along with a French baguette, some wedges of cheese, a bunch or two of grapes, and a bottle of red wine.

Suggested Dressings

★ 1 recipe Italian Vinaigrette (page 224)

1 recipe Greek Vinaigrette (page 222)

½ cup commercial fat-free or low-fat Italian vinaigrette

½ cup commercial fat-free or low-fat Italian Parmesan dressing

¼ cup sun-dried tomatoes (packaged without oil)
1 can (15 ounces) chickpeas, rinsed and drained
1 can (13 ounces) quartered artichoke hearts, drained
1 cup thinly sliced prewashed baby spinach, stems removed
½ cup ½-inch squares red bell pepper
½ cup thinly sliced celery
¼ cup thin red onion rings
1 jar (2 ounces) sliced pimientos, drained
1 cup cherry tomatoes, stemmed and halved
½ cup pitted black olives, drained (optional)

Serving Suggestion

For a more artistic presentation, first divide 6 cups of spinach leaves among 4 dinner plates. Spoon the chickpea salad in the center of the spinach, and randomly distribute the cherry tomatoes and, if desired, the olives over the salad. If desired, sprinkle each serving with crushed tomato topping (page 202).

1. Place the sun-dried tomatoes in a small heatproof bowl, and add enough boiling water to cover. Allow to sit for 5 to 15 minutes, or until the tomatoes are soft. Drain well, and cut into slivers.

2. Combine the slivered tomatoes, chickpeas, artichoke hearts, spinach, red pepper, celery, onion rings, and pimientos in a salad bowl. Add the dressing, and toss gently to coat. Cover and refrigerate for several hours or overnight.

3. To serve, add the cherry tomatoes and, if desired, the olives to the chickpea salad, and toss gently to blend. Serve immediately.

NUTRITIONAL FACTS (per serving, salad only)

Calories: 220
Carbohydrates: 44 g
Cholesterol: 0 mg
Fat: 1.9 g
Calories From Fat: 7.2%
Protein: 11.8 g
Sodium: 488 mg

Making Crushed Tomato Topping

A sprinkling of crushed tomato topping can quickly add both color and flavor to your salads. And this garnish is so easy to make! Simply place ¼ cup of coarsely chopped dried tomatoes—packaged without oil, of course—in a food processor, and process the tomatoes until they're finely chopped. Use the topping immediately, or store in an airtight container for up to two days.

Portabella, Red Pepper, and Eggplant Salad

YIELD: 4 SERVINGS

Portabella mushrooms are giant cultivated mushrooms that are dark brown in color and have a rich taste and meaty texture. When coated with a tangy vinaigrette before roasting, these mushrooms become a memorable addition to this special salad.

8 large Portabella mushrooms, quartered

2 large red bell peppers, each cut into 8 wedges

1 large red onion, peeled and quartered

2 Japanese eggplants (8 ounces each), sliced into ¼-inch-thick rounds

1½ tablespoons extra virgin olive oil

½ cup sun-dried tomatoes (packaged without oil)

6 cups prewashed baby spinach, stems removed

Suggested Dressings

★ 1 recipe Lemon Vinaigrette (page 225)

1 recipe Caper Vinaigrette (page 217)

½ cup commercial fat-free or low-fat Italian vinaigrette

½ cup commercial fat-free or low-fat herb dressing

NUTRITIONAL FACTS
(per serving, salad only)

Calories: 126
Carbohydrates: 17 g
Cholesterol: 0 mg
Fat: 5.9 g
Calories From Fat: 37.5%
Protein: 5.1 g
Sodium: 56 mg

1. Combine the mushrooms, red peppers, onion, and eggplant in a large bowl. Add the olive oil and 5 tablespoons of the dressing, and toss gently to coat.

2. Coat a large nonstick baking pan with 1-inch sides with olive oil cooking spray, and transfer the vegetables to the pan, spreading them into a single layer. Bake in a preheated 450°F oven, turning every 15 minutes, for 1 hour, or until the vegetables are fork tender and the edges are brown. Allow the vegetables to come to room temperature.

3. While the vegetables are roasting, place the sun-dried tomatoes in a small heatproof bowl, and add enough boiling water to cover. Allow to sit for 5 to 15 minutes, or until the tomatoes are soft. Drain well, and slice into slivers.

4. When the roasted vegetables are cool, add the tomato slivers, and stir to mix.

5. To serve, divide the spinach among 4 dinner plates. Spoon the roasted vegetables in the center of each bed of spinach, and drizzle the remaining dressing over each serving. Serve immediately.

YIELD: 4 SERVINGS

Turkish Eggplant Salad
(Patlican Salatasi)

*The recipe for this tempting salad came from a
university professor who had lived in Turkey.
Serve with warm pita bread.*

NUTRITIONAL FACTS
(per serving)
Calories: 90
Carbohydrates: 16.3 g
Cholesterol: 0 mg
Fat: 2.9 g
Calories From Fat: 25.3%
Protein: 2.7 g
Sodium: 147 mg

1 eggplant (2 pounds), sliced horizontally into $\frac{1}{2}$-inch thick slices
Salt
Olive oil cooking spray
2 cloves garlic
2 tablespoons fresh lemon juice
2 teaspoons extra virgin olive oil
$\frac{1}{2}$ teaspoon freshly ground pepper
$\frac{1}{4}$ teaspoon salt
$\frac{1}{4}$ cup chopped fresh parsley
3 Roma tomatoes, cut into wedges
4 lemon wedges
12 pitted Kalamata olives (optional)

1. Lightly sprinkle both sides of each eggplant slice with salt, and place the slices in a colander. Allow the eggplant to sit for 30 minutes or more. (This process will eliminate any bitterness.)

2. Rinse the eggplant with cool water, drain, and pat dry with paper towels. Lightly coat both sides with the olive oil cooking spray.

3. Place the eggplant slices over moderately hot coals on a grill coated with cooking spray. Cover the grill and cook for 5 minutes on each side, or until golden brown and fork tender. Allow the eggplant to come to room temperature before removing the skin. Alternatively, place the eggplant slices on a baking sheet that has been coated with olive oil cooking spray and broil under a preheated broiler, 3 inches from the heat source, for 4 to 5 minutes on each side.

4. Place the garlic in a food processor, and process until chopped. Add the eggplant, and process until smooth. Add the lemon juice, olive oil, pepper, and salt, and process just until well mixed. This salad can be served at room temperature, or it can be refrigerated in a covered container for several hours.

5. To serve, divide the salad among 4 dinner plates, and garnish with the chopped parsley. Surround each serving with wedges of tomatoes and lemon, and, if desired, with the olives. Serve immediately.

The Surprising Eggplant

What a surprise it was to learn that eggplants are either male or female! This difference in gender is especially important because, although the seeds of all eggplants are bitter, those of the male tend to be less bitter than those of the female.

How can you tell the difference between male and female eggplants? Look at the blossom end. The male usually has a rounder, smoother blossom end, while the female's blossom end is more oval in shape with a deep indentation.

Vegetarian Teriyaki Citrus Delight

This entrée features an assortment of steamed vegetables crowned with a special citrus dipping sauce. Accompany this unusual hot salad with spicy brown rice or black beans, if desired.

NUTRITIONAL FACTS
(per serving)
Calories: 323
Carbohydrates: 72.2 g
Cholesterol: 0 mg
Fat: 2.2 g
Calories From Fat: 5.5%
Protein: 11.2 g
Sodium: 847 mg

Teriyaki Citrus Sauce

1 potato (3 ounces), peeled and quartered

3 large cloves garlic

2 teaspoons chopped fresh ginger

½ cup fresh orange juice

¼ cup low-sodium teriyaki marinade

½ cup honey

2 tablespoons fresh lemon juice

1 tablespoon canola oil

¼ teaspoon salt

¼ teaspoon freshly ground pepper

2 ½ pounds new potatoes, halved

1¾ pounds cauliflower florets

1¾ pounds baby carrots

1¾ pounds fresh asparagus spears, tough ends removed

1¾ pounds broccoli florets

1. To make the teriyaki citrus sauce, place enough water to cover the new potato in a small saucepan, and bring to a simmer over medium-high heat. Add the potato and simmer for 25 minutes, or until fork tender. Drain well.

2. Place the garlic and ginger in a food processor, and process until finely chopped. Add the potato and process until smooth. (The mixture may form a ball.) Add all of the remaining sauce ingredients, and process until smooth. Transfer the sauce to a covered container and refrigerate until ready to serve. Serve at room temperature.

3. Place enough water to cover the new potatoes in a large saucepan, and bring to a boil over medium-high heat. Add the potatoes and simmer for 20 to 25 minutes, or until fork tender. Drain well.

4. While the potatoes are cooking, cook the cauliflower and carrots in a large steamer for 5 minutes. Add the asparagus, and cook for another 4 minutes. Add the broccoli, and cook for 2 additional minutes. Drain well.

5. To serve, spoon the sauce into four $1/2$-cup serving dishes. Arrange a dish in the center of each of 6 dinner plates, and surround it with the hot vegetables, arranging the vegetables either in sections or as a melange. Serve immediately.

Fruit Salad With Strawberry Sorbet

YIELD: **4** SERVINGS

Fruit salads are a delicious means of including health-promoting antioxidants in your diet. This salad is not only good for you, but looks beautiful, as well. Serve with low-fat mango bread. For variety, substitute your favorite fruits for those suggested below.

**NUTRITIONAL FACTS
(per serving)**
Calories: 275
Carbohydrates: 68.1 g
Cholesterol: 0 mg
Fat: 1.2 g
Calories From Fat: 6.2%
Protein: 2.4 g
Sodium: 12 mg

1 pint commercial strawberry sorbet,
or 1 recipe Strawberry Sorbet (page 210)

$1\frac{1}{2}$ cups diced papaya

$1\frac{1}{2}$ cups diced kiwi fruit

$1\frac{1}{2}$ cups raspberries

$1\frac{1}{2}$ cups blueberries

$1\frac{1}{2}$ cups diced pineapple

$1\frac{1}{2}$ cups diced cantaloupe

1. Either place a scoop of sorbet in each of 4 sherbet dishes, and place a dish in the center of each of 4 dinner plates; or directly mound the sorbet in the center of each plate.

2. Surround the sorbet with segments of diced papaya, kiwi fruit, raspberries, blueberries, pineapple, and cantaloupe, and serve immediately.

Pear, Stilton, and Endive Salad

This salad unites pears and Stilton cheese for a light yet richly rewarding main course. A quality American blue cheese such as Maytag blue would also add distinction to this salad.

Suggested Dressings

★ 1 recipe Pear Dressing (page 231)

½ cup commercial fat-free or low-fat raspberry vinaigrette

1 tablespoon fresh lemon juice
6 ripe red pears, cored and cut into ¼-inch-thick wedges
1 bunch red leaf lettuce
24 leaves Belgian endive (about 3 heads)
2 ounces Stilton cheese, crumbled
Edible flowers (optional)

**NUTRITIONAL FACTS
(per serving, salad only)**
Calories: 316
Carbohydrates: 64.3 g
Cholesterol: 11 mg
Fat: 6.3 g
Calories From Fat: 16.1%
Protein: 9.6 g
Sodium: 278 mg

1. Place the lemon juice and pear wedges in a plastic resealable bag. Seal the bag, and turn to coat the pears with the juice.

2. To serve, divide the red leaf lettuce among 4 dinner plates. Over each bed of lettuce, arrange 6 endive leaves like the spokes of a wheel, with the tips pointing toward the rim of the plate. Then arrange the pear wedges in spoke fashion so that they slightly overlap the endive leaves. Place some of the Stilton cheese in the center of each salad, and drizzle the dressing over each serving. Garnish with edible flowers, if desired, and serve immediately.

A Pear Primer

Did you know that store-bought pears are often too firm to eat right away because they have not been tree-ripened? Although your pears will ripen eventually if placed in the refrigerator, they will do so very slowly. To ripen them more quickly, store them at room temperature. To further speed ripening, place the pears in a closed brown paper bag. You'll know that the pears are ready to eat when they yield to pressure when gently pressed on the neck.

Although a wide variety of pears are grown, you're likely to find only a few at your local market. The following are the most commonly available varieties.

Top Left and Center Left: Shrimp
and Saffron Rice Salad (page 138)

Center Right: Salmon, Avocado,
Feta, and Onion Salad (page 127)

Bottom: Mediterranean Grilled Tuna
Salad (page 156)

Top: Tuna, Vegetable, and Green Rice Salad (page 168)

Center: Shrimp Salad With Fruit Salsa (page 143)

Bottom: Caesar Salad With Grilled Salmon (page 124)

Melon and Berry Salad With Yogurt

During the hot summer months, I frequently serve a fruit salad for dinner. The combination of melon slices, yogurt, and granola is appropriately light for the season, yet satisfying. Serve with low-fat pineapple muffins.

2 honeydew melons, peeled and cut into thin wedges

2 cantaloupes, peeled and cut into thin wedges

4 cups fat-free blueberry yogurt

1 pint raspberries or strawberries

1 cup commercial low-fat granola (optional)

**NUTRITIONAL FACTS
(per serving)**
Calories: 230
Carbohydrates: 45.4 g
Cholesterol: 0 mg
Fat: 1 g
Calories From Fat: 4.4%
Protein: 3.1 g
Sodium: 42 mg

1. Arrange the slices of honeydew and cantaloupe melon around the rim of each of 4 dinner plates, alternating slices of the 2 melons and leaving a space in the center of the plate. Set aside.

2. Either place 1 cup of the yogurt in each of four 1-cup serving dishes, and place a dish in the center of each plate of melon; or directly spoon 1 cup of yogurt onto the center of each plate.

3. Distribute the raspberries over the melon slices. If desired, sprinkle 1/4 cup of granola over each serving of yogurt. Serve immediately.

Anjou. Large and yellow-green in color, Anjou pears tend to be very sweet, and are delicious eaten fresh or cooked. They are available from October through May.

Bartlett (Williams). These aromatic pears can be found in both yellow and red varieties. They are available from July through December.

Bosc. With its long neck and light rusted skin, the Bosc is best when cooked, although it can be eaten fresh. This variety is available from September through May.

Comice. This large, plump pear has a pale yellow-green skin. Comice pears are very soft, and delicious eaten fresh. They are especially good served with cheese, nuts, and a fine sweet wine. These pears are available from October through January.

Making Strawberry Sorbet

When the weather is warm, a salad that features luscious summer fruit provides a welcome change of pace from the usual green salad. And what better addition to your fruit salad than a cooling scoop of fruit sorbet? Certainly, many high-quality commercial sorbets are now available, but when you find yourself with a bit more time, you may want to follow the recipe below to make your own flavorful confection. This sorbet can be used in such creations as Fruit Salad With Strawberry Sorbet (page 207), or can be served alone as a simple yet impressive dessert.

Strawberry Sorbet

YIELD: **4** SERVINGS

1 cup cold water

1 cup granulated sugar

1 quart strawberries, hulled

1 tablespoon fresh lemon juice

1. To make a basic syrup, combine the water and sugar in a small saucepan. Bring the mixture to a boil over medium heat, stirring occasionally. Allow the mixture to simmer for 1 minute. Transfer the syrup to a small bowl, cover, and refrigerate for several hours or overnight.

2. Place the strawberries in the work bowl of a food processor, and process until puréed. Add the lemon juice and $2/3$ cup of the basic syrup, and blend well to mix.

3. Transfer the strawberry mixture to an ice cream maker, and prepare according to manufacturer's instructions. Serve the sorbet immediately, or store in the freezer for up to 1 week. If frozen, allow the sorbet to soften at room temperature for 15 to 20 minutes before serving.

6

The Finishing Touch—
Flavorful Salad Dressings

For many people, a salad isn't complete without the addition of a great dressing. Certainly, the right dressing can enhance a salad by intensifying and complementing the flavors of its main ingredients, transforming even an ordinary dish into special-occasion fare.

This chapter provides over fifty ways to make your next salad special. Are you longing for a taste of the islands? Try tangy Caribbean Dressing. Prefer a Southwestern experience? Top your next salad with chili-spiced Cilantro Vinaigrette. Or add the intrigue of the Orient with Mandarin Dressing. Whatever your choice, you'll be delighted to know that your dressing is as low in fat as it is high in flavor. What a healthy and delicious way to make the "best dressed" list!

Anchovy and Mustard Vinaigrette

This assertive vinaigrette is creamy in texture and rich in flavor—a great choice for a main course meat salad.

YIELD: 4 SERVINGS

1 new potato (1½–2 ounces), peeled and quartered, or ⅓ cup prepared instant mashed potatoes (see at right)

2 cloves garlic, peeled

1 shallot, peeled

3 anchovy fillets, drained

¼ cup plus 2 tablespoons fat-free chicken broth, vegetable broth, or water

2 tablespoons red wine vinegar

2 tablespoons Dijon mustard

2 teaspoons extra virgin olive oil

1 teaspoon dried basil

½ teaspoon freshly ground pepper

¼ teaspoon salt

1. Place enough water to cover the potato in a small saucepan, and bring to a simmer over medium-high heat. Add the potato and simmer uncovered for 25 minutes, or until fork tender. Allow the potato to come to room temperature.

2. Place the garlic and shallot in a food processor fitted with a metal blade, or in a blender, and process until finely chopped. Add the anchovies and potato, and process until smooth. (The mixture may form a ball.) Add all of the remaining ingredients, and process until blended. Alternatively, place the potato in a jar with a tight-fitting lid, and mash with a fork. Finely chop the garlic, shallot, and anchovies, and add them to the jar along with the remaining ingredients. Shake until well blended.

3. Use the dressing immediately, or place in a covered container and refrigerate until ready to use.

NUTRITIONAL FACTS (per serving)
Calories: 42   Carbs: 2.9 g   Cholesterol: 3 mg   Fat: 2.9 g
Calories From Fat: 54.7%   Protein: 2.6 g   Sodium: 387 mg

Instant Potatoes to the Rescue!

Many of the dressings in this chapter are creamy, yet contain little or no fat. What's the secret? In most cases, you'll find that the ingredients list includes one small new potato. When peeled, cooked, and puréed, this simple ingredient adds body to the dressing without a large dose of oil.

Of course, the cooking and puréeing of a potato is a somewhat time-consuming process. But by keeping a box of instant mashed potatoes in your pantry, you'll be able to quickly make a great substitute for this handy purée.

Simply follow the package directions for making ⅓ cup of mashed potatoes—an amount that is usually considered to be one serving. To keep the fat and sodium counts down, you'll want to substitute water for the suggested milk, and omit the butter and salt. To make ⅓ cup of potatoes using most brands, you must first bring 8½ tablespoons of water to a boil in a small pot. Remove the pot from the heat, and stir in 6 tablespoons of the potato flakes. Let the mixture stand until the flakes are moist, and whip them lightly with a fork. Then substitute the resulting product for the puréed potato, using a whisk, blender, or food processor to mix it with the dressing's other ingredients. The result? Low-fat, full-bodied dressings in a flash!

Apple Cider Vinaigrette

This light and piquant vinaigrette is well suited to the vibrant flavors of a Southwestern salad.

YIELD: 4 SERVINGS

3 tablespoons apple cider vinegar

3 tablespoons fat-free chicken broth or water

2 tablespoons Dijon mustard

2 tablespoons light corn syrup

2 tablespoons finely chopped Vidalia onion or other sweet onion

½ teaspoon celery seed

¼ teaspoon salt

¼ teaspoon freshly ground pepper

1. Place all of the ingredients in a jar with a tight-fitting lid, and shake until well blended.

2. Use the dressing immediately, or refrigerate until ready to use.

NUTRITIONAL FACTS (per serving)

Calories: 40   Carbs: 9.6 g   Cholesterol: 0 mg   Fat: 0.4 g
Calories From Fat: 7.9%   Protein: 1 g   Sodium: 220 mg

Balsamic and Grainy Mustard Vinaigrette

The sweet-and-piquant taste of balsamic vinegar and the tangy flavor of grainy mustard is a perfect complement to a variety of meat and vegetarian salads.

YIELD: 4 SERVINGS

¼ cup plus 2 tablespoons fat-free chicken broth, vegetable broth, or water

2 ½ tablespoons balsamic vinegar

1 tablespoon grainy mustard

2 teaspoons extra virgin olive oil

1 large clove garlic, crushed

¼ teaspoon salt

¼ teaspoon freshly ground pepper

Dash Worcestershire sauce

Dash hot pepper sauce

1. Place all of the ingredients in a jar with a tight-fitting lid, and shake until well blended.

2. Use the dressing immediately, or refrigerate until ready to use.

NUTRITIONAL FACTS (per serving)

Calories: 27   Carbs: 1.3 g   Cholesterol: 0 mg   Fat: 2.4 g
Calories From Fat: 67.9%   Protein: 1.3 g   Sodium: 186 mg

Balsamic and Walnut Oil Vinaigrette

The zesty taste of balsamic vinegar and the nutty flavor of walnut oil harmonize perfectly in this delicate vinaigrette.

YIELD: 4 SERVINGS

1 new potato (1½–2 ounces), peeled and quartered, or ⅓ cup prepared instant mashed potatoes (page 213)

1 clove garlic, peeled

¼ cup fat-free chicken broth, vegetable broth, or water

3 tablespoons balsamic vinegar

2 tablespoons dry white wine

1½ teaspoons walnut oil

1 teaspoon low-sodium soy sauce

¼ teaspoon freshly ground pepper

⅛ teaspoon salt

1. Place enough water to cover the potato in a small saucepan, and bring to a simmer over medium-high heat. Add the potato and simmer uncovered for 25 minutes, or until fork tender. Allow the potato to come to room temperature.

2. Place the garlic in a food processor fitted with a metal blade, or in a blender, and process until finely chopped. Add the potato, and process until smooth. (The mixture may form a ball.) Add all of the remaining ingredients, and process until well blended. Alternatively, place the potato in a jar with a tight-fitting lid, and mash with a fork. Finely chop the garlic, and add it to the jar along with the remaining ingredients. Shake until well blended.

3. Use the dressing immediately, or place in a covered container and refrigerate until ready to use.

NUTRITIONAL FACTS (per serving)
Calories: 31   Carbs: 2.8 g   Cholesterol: 0 mg   Fat: 1.7 g
Calories From Fat: 50.6%   Protein: 1 g   Sodium: 150 mg

Balsamic Vinaigrette

The piquant flavor of balsamic vinegar, which also has an unmistakable touch of sweetness, can embolden a simple main course salad or balance a hearty one.

YIELD: 4 SERVINGS

1 new potato (1½–2 ounces), peeled and quartered, or ⅓ cup prepared instant mashed potatoes (page 213)

1 shallot, peeled

¼ cup plus 2 tablespoons fat-free chicken broth, vegetable broth, or water

2 tablespoons balsamic vinegar

1 tablespoon sherry vinegar

2 teaspoons extra virgin olive oil

⅛ teaspoon salt

⅛ teaspoon freshly ground pepper

1. Place enough water to cover the potato in a small saucepan, and bring to a simmer over medium-high heat. Add the potato and simmer uncovered for 25 minutes, or until fork tender. Allow the potato to come to room temperature.

2. Place the shallot in a food processor fitted with a metal blade, or in a blender, and process until finely chopped. Add the potato, and process until smooth. (The mixture may form a ball.) Add all of the remaining ingredients, and process until well blended. Alternatively, place the potato in a jar with a tight-fitting lid, and mash with a fork. Finely chop the shallot, and add it to the jar along with the remaining ingredients. Shake until well blended.

3. Use the dressing immediately, or place in a covered container and refrigerate until ready to use.

NUTRITIONAL FACTS (per serving)
Calories: 34   Carbs: 3.3 g   Cholesterol: 0 mg   Fat: 2.3 g
Calories From Fat: 52.4%   Protein: 1.3 g   Sodium: 94 mg

Basil Dressing

Basil has been called the "royal herb," and for good reason. Use it to impart a delightfully pungent flavor and luscious green color to your dressings.

YIELD: **4** SERVINGS

1 new potato (1½–2 ounces), peeled and quartered, or ⅓ cup prepared instant mashed potatoes (page 213)

2 cloves garlic

3 tablespoons finely chopped fresh basil

¼ cup plus 2 tablespoons fat-free chicken broth, vegetable broth, or water

2 tablespoons fresh lemon juice

2 tablespoons Dijon mustard

1 tablespoon sherry vinegar

2 teaspoons extra virgin olive oil

¼ teaspoon salt

¼ teaspoon freshly ground pepper

1. Place enough water to cover the potato in a small saucepan, and bring to a simmer over medium-high heat. Add the potato and simmer uncovered for 25 minutes, or until fork tender. Allow the potato to come to room temperature.

2. Place the garlic in a food processor fitted with a metal blade, or in a blender, and process until finely chopped. Add the potato and basil, and process until smooth. (The mixture may form a ball.) Add all of the remaining ingredients, and process until blended. Alternatively, place the potato in a jar with a tight-fitting lid, and mash with a fork. Finely chop the garlic and basil, and add them to the jar along with the remaining ingredients. Shake until well blended.

3. Use the dressing immediately, or place in a covered container and refrigerate until ready to use.

NUTRITIONAL FACTS (per serving)
Calories: 37   Carbs: 3 g   Cholesterol: 0 mg   Fat: 2.6 g
Calories From Fat: 55.1%   Protein: 1.8 g   Sodium: 185 mg

Caesar Dressing

This zesty yet creamy dressing is the traditional topping for the salad that bears its name. It also makes a great dip for fresh vegetables.

YIELD: **4** SERVINGS

1 new potato (1½–2 ounces), peeled and quartered, or ⅓ cup prepared instant mashed potatoes (page 213)

1 large clove garlic, peeled

2 anchovy fillets, drained

¼ cup plus 3 tablespoons fat-free chicken broth, vegetable broth, or water

2 tablespoons fresh lemon juice

2 teaspoons extra virgin olive oil

1 teaspoon Dijon mustard

½ teaspoon Worcestershire sauce

¼ teaspoon salt

¼ teaspoon freshly ground pepper

1. Place enough water to cover the potato in a small saucepan, and bring to a simmer over medium-high heat. Add the potato and simmer uncovered for 25 minutes, or until fork tender. Allow the potato to come to room temperature.

2. Place the garlic in a food processor fitted with a metal blade, or in a blender, and process until finely chopped. Add the potato and anchovies, and process until smooth. (The mixture may form a ball.) Add all of the remaining ingredients, and process until blended. Alternatively, place the potato in a jar with a tight-fitting lid, and mash with a fork. Finely chop the garlic and anchovies, and add them to the jar along with the remaining ingredients. Shake until well blended.

3. Use the dressing immediately, or place in a covered container and refrigerate until ready to use.

NUTRITIONAL FACTS (per serving)
Calories: 37   Carbs: 2.7 g   Cholesterol: 2 mg   Fat: 2.5 g
Calories From Fat: 53.9%   Protein: 2.1 g   Sodium: 241 mg

Caper Vinaigrette

A tangy dressing accented by the intense saltiness of capers, this vinaigrette nicely complements most seafood salads.

YIELD: 4 SERVINGS

1 new potato (1½–2 ounces), peeled and quartered, or ⅓ cup prepared instant mashed potatoes (page 213)

¼ cup plus 2 tablespoons fat-free chicken broth, vegetable broth, or water

2 tablespoons tarragon wine vinegar

1 tablespoon Dijon mustard

2 teaspoons extra virgin olive oil

½ teaspoon Worcestershire sauce

¼ teaspoon freshly ground pepper

⅛ teaspoon salt

1½ tablespoons capers, rinsed and drained

1. Place enough water to cover the potato in a small saucepan, and bring to a simmer over medium-high heat. Add the potato and simmer uncovered for 25 minutes, or until fork tender. Allow the potato to come to room temperature.

2. Place the potato in a food processor fitted with a metal blade, or in a blender, and process until smooth. (It may form a ball.) Add all of the remaining ingredients except for the capers, and process until blended. Add the capers, and lightly blend to mix. Alternatively, place the potato in a jar with a tight-fitting lid, and mash with a fork. Add the remaining ingredients, and shake until well blended.

3. Use the dressing immediately, or place in a covered container and refrigerate until ready to use.

NUTRITIONAL FACTS (per serving)

Calories: 33 Carbs: 2.5 g Cholesterol: 0 mg Fat: 2.4 g
Calories From Fat: 58.4% Protein: 1.4 g Sodium: 198 mg

Caribbean Dressing

This spicy dressing is the perfect accent for a seafood salad.

YIELD: 4 SERVINGS

1 new potato (1½–2 ounces), peeled and quartered, or ⅓ cup prepared instant mashed potatoes (page 213)

2 cloves garlic, peeled

2 tablespoons finely chopped fresh mint

2 tablespoons finely chopped fresh basil

2 tablespoons finely chopped fresh cilantro

¼ cup fat-free chicken broth, vegetable broth, or water

3 tablespoons fresh lime juice

2 tablespoons dark brown sugar

2 teaspoons canola oil

1 teaspoon Asian hot sauce or favorite hot pepper sauce

1. Place enough water to cover the potato in a small saucepan, and bring to a simmer over medium-high heat. Add the potato and simmer uncovered for 25 minutes, or until fork tender. Allow the potato to come to room temperature.

2. Place the garlic in a food processor fitted with a metal blade, or in a blender, and process until finely chopped. Add the potato, and process until smooth. (The mixture may form a ball.) Add all of the remaining ingredients, and process until blended. Alternatively, place the potato in a jar with a tight-fitting lid, and mash with a fork. Finely chop the garlic, and add it to the jar along with the remaining ingredients. Shake until well blended.

3. Use the dressing immediately, or place in a covered container and refrigerate until ready to use.

NUTRITIONAL FACTS (per serving)

Calories: 66 Carbs: 10.8 g Cholesterol: 0 mg Fat: 2.5 g
Calories From Fat: 30.7% Protein: 1.6 g Sodium: 39 mg

Champagne Vinaigrette

This richly flavored, creamy vinaigrette would add a dazzling sparkle to nearly any main course beef salad.

YIELD: 4 SERVINGS

1 new potato (1½–2 ounces), peeled and quartered, or ⅓ cup prepared instant mashed potatoes (page 213)
2 shallots, peeled
¼ cup plus 2 tablespoons fat-free chicken broth, vegetable broth, or water
¼ cup champagne vinegar
1 tablespoon Dijon mustard
1 tablespoon granulated sugar
2 teaspoons extra virgin olive oil
¼ teaspoon salt
¼ teaspoon freshly ground pepper

1. Place enough water to cover the potato in a small saucepan, and bring to a simmer over medium-high heat. Add the potato and simmer uncovered for 25 minutes, or until fork tender. Allow the potato to come to room temperature.

2. Place the shallots in a food processor fitted with a metal blade, or in a blender, and process until finely chopped. Add the potato, and process until smooth. (The mixture may form a ball.) Add all of the remaining ingredients, and process until well blended. Alternatively, place the potato in a jar with a tight-fitting lid, and mash with a fork. Finely chop the shallots, and add them to the jar along with the remaining ingredients. Shake until well blended.

3. Use the dressing immediately, or place in a covered container and refrigerate until ready to use.

NUTRITIONAL FACTS (per serving)

Calories: 53   Carbs: 7.8 g   Cholesterol: 0 mg   Fat: 2.4 g
Calories From Fat: 36.7%   Protein: 1.7 g   Sodium: 186 mg

Cilantro and Jalapeño Dressing

Spicy-hot, and boasting both the distinctive fragrance of cilantro and the bite of jalapeños, this dressing would add zest to any Southwestern salad.

YIELD: 4 SERVINGS

1 new potato (1½–2 ounces), peeled and quartered, or ⅓ cup prepared instant mashed potatoes (page 213)
2 jalapeño chilies, seeded
¼ cup fat-free chicken broth, vegetable broth, or water
3 tablespoons fresh lemon juice
2 tablespoons honey
2 teaspoons extra virgin olive oil
¼ teaspoon salt
¼ teaspoon freshly ground pepper
¼ cup chopped fresh cilantro

1. Place enough water to cover the potato in a small saucepan, and bring to a simmer over medium-high heat. Add the potato and simmer uncovered for 25 minutes, or until fork tender. Allow the potato to come to room temperature.

2. Place the jalapeño chilies in a food processor fitted with a metal blade, or in a blender, and process until finely chopped. Add the potato, and process until smooth. (The mixture may form a ball.) Add all of the remaining ingredients except for the cilantro, and process until blended. Add the cilantro, and blend with on/off pulses until well mixed. Alternatively, place the potato in a jar with a tight-fitting lid, and mash with a fork. Finely chop the chilies and cilantro, and add them to the jar along with the remaining ingredients. Shake until well blended.

3. Use the dressing immediately, or place in a covered container and refrigerate until ready to use.

NUTRITIONAL FACTS (per serving)

Calories: 75   Carbs: 13.5 g   Cholesterol: 0 mg   Fat: 2.5 g
Calories From Fat: 27.2%   Protein: 1.7 g   Sodium: 195 mg

Cilantro Vinaigrette

Cilantro rules! This creamy vinaigrette, marked by the distinctive flavor of this aromatic herb, is the perfect dressing for a Southwestern-style pasta or seafood salad.

YIELD: **4** SERVINGS

1 new potato (1½–2 ounces), peeled and quartered, or ⅓ cup prepared instant mashed potatoes (page 213)

1 large clove garlic, peeled

1 serrano chili, seeded*

¼ cup plus 2 tablespoons fat-free chicken broth, vegetable broth, or water

3 tablespoons fresh lime juice

1 tablespoon red wine vinegar

1 tablespoon honey

1 tablespoon Dijon mustard

2 teaspoons extra virgin olive oil

¼ teaspoon salt

¼ teaspoon hot pepper sauce

⅓ cup packed coarsely chopped fresh cilantro

* To protect your hands from the seeds of the chili, be sure to use rubber or latex gloves when working with the pepper, and to wash the knife and cutting board immediately after use.

1. Place enough water to cover the potato in a small saucepan, and bring to a simmer over medium-high heat. Add the potato and simmer uncovered for 25 minutes, or until fork tender. Allow the potato to come to room temperature.

2. Place the garlic and chili in a food processor fitted with a metal blade, or in a blender, and process until finely chopped. Add the potato, and process until smooth. (The mixture may form a ball.) Add all of the remaining ingredients except for the cilantro, and process until blended. Add the cilantro, and blend with on/off pulses until well mixed. Alternatively, place the potato in a jar with a tight-fitting lid, and mash with a fork. Finely chop the garlic, chili, and cilantro, and add them to the jar along with the remaining ingredients. Shake until well blended.

3. Use the dressing immediately, or place in a covered container and refrigerate until ready to use.

NUTRITIONAL FACTS (per serving)
Calories: 61   Carbs: 9.6 g   Cholesterol: 0 mg   Fat: 2.6 g
Calories From Fat: 33%   Protein: 2.1 g   Sodium: 234 mg

Citrus Vinaigrette

This sweet and tangy vinaigrette can instantly enliven an Oriental-style salad, as well as a seafood or poultry salad.

YIELD: **4** SERVINGS

¼ cup fresh orange juice

1 tablespoon fresh lime juice

¼ cup rice vinegar

2 tablespoons fat-free chicken broth or water

2 teaspoons canola oil

½ tablespoon light corn syrup

½ teaspoon low-sodium soy sauce

¼ teaspoon salt

¼ teaspoon freshly ground pepper

1. Place all of the ingredients in a jar with a tight-fitting lid, and shake until well blended.

2. Use the dressing immediately, or refrigerate until ready to use.

NUTRITIONAL FACTS (per serving)
Calories: 38   Carbs: 5 g   Cholesterol: 0 mg   Fat: 2.3 g
Calories From Fat: 48.7%   Protein: 0.5 g   Sodium: 133 mg

Cobb Salad Dressing

This is the ultimate topping for the salad made famous by Bob Cobb's Brown Derby restaurant in Los Angeles, California.

YIELD: 4 SERVINGS

1 new potato (1½–2 ounces), peeled and quartered, or ⅓ cup prepared instant mashed potatoes (page 213)

1 clove garlic, peeled

¼ cup plus 2 tablespoons fat-free chicken broth, vegetable broth, or water

2 tablespoons red wine vinegar

½ tablespoon honey

½ tablespoon fresh lemon juice

2 teaspoons olive oil

1 teaspoon Worcestershire sauce

½ teaspoon granulated sugar

½ teaspoon dry mustard

½ teaspoon freshly ground pepper

¼ teaspoon salt

1. Place enough water to cover the potato in a small saucepan, and bring to a simmer over medium-high heat. Add the potato and simmer uncovered for 25 minutes, or until fork tender. Allow the potato to come to room temperature.

2. Place the garlic in a food processor fitted with a metal blade, or in a blender, and process until finely chopped. Add the potato, and process until smooth. (The mixture may form a ball.) Add all of the remaining ingredients, and process until well blended. Alternatively, place the potato in a jar with a tight-fitting lid, and mash with a fork. Finely chop the garlic, and add it to the jar along with the remaining ingredients. Shake until well blended.

3. Use the dressing immediately, or place in a covered container and refrigerate until ready to use.

NUTRITIONAL FACTS (per serving)
Calories: 54 Carbs: 8.4 g Cholesterol: 0 mg Fat: 2.3 g
Calories From Fat: 34.5% Protein: 1.6 g Sodium: 196 mg

Curry Vinaigrette

Aromatic with ginger and curry, this Indian-style dressing is wonderful on a variety of meat, poultry, and seafood salads.

YIELD: 4 SERVINGS

1 new potato (1½–2 ounces), peeled and quartered, or ⅓ cup prepared instant mashed potatoes (page 213)

½ teaspoon chopped fresh ginger

1 clove garlic, peeled

¼ cup plus 2 tablespoons fat-free chicken broth or water

2 tablespoons fresh lime juice

2 tablespoons rice vinegar

1 tablespoon honey

2 teaspoons canola oil

½ teaspoon curry powder

¼ teaspoon Asian hot sauce or other hot pepper sauce

⅛ teaspoon salt

1. Place enough water to cover the potato in a small saucepan, and bring to a simmer over medium-high heat. Add the potato and simmer uncovered for 25 minutes, or until fork tender. Allow the potato to come to room temperature.

2. Place the ginger and garlic in a food processor fitted with a metal blade, or in a blender, and process until finely chopped. Add the potato, and process until smooth. (The mixture may form a ball.) Add all of the remaining ingredients, and process until well blended. Alternatively, place the potato in a jar with a tight-fitting lid, and mash with a fork. Finely chop the ginger and garlic, and add them to the jar along with the remaining ingredients. Shake until well blended.

3. Use the dressing immediately, or place in a covered container and refrigerate until ready to use.

NUTRITIONAL FACTS (per serving)
Calories: 50 Carbs: 7.7 g Cholesterol: 0 mg Fat: 2.3 g
Calories From Fat: 36.9% Protein: 1.4 g Sodium: 142 mg

Dijon Mustard Vinaigrette

This robust vinaigrette can provide the dominant flavor for many beef and vegetarian salads.

YIELD: **4** SERVINGS

1 new potato (1½–2 ounces), peeled and quartered, or ⅓ cup prepared instant mashed potatoes (page 213)

1 shallot, peeled

2 tablespoons coarsely chopped fresh parsley

¼ cup plus 3 tablespoon fat-free chicken broth, vegetable broth, or water

2 tablespoons red wine vinegar

2 ½ teaspoons Dijon mustard

2 teaspoons extra virgin olive oil

⅛ teaspoon salt

⅛ teaspoon freshly ground pepper

1. Place enough water to cover the potato in a small saucepan, and bring to a simmer over medium-high heat. Add the potato and simmer uncovered for 25 minutes, or until fork tender. Allow the potato to come to room temperature.

2. Place the shallot in a food processor fitted with a metal blade, or in a blender, and process until finely chopped. Add the parsley, and process until finely chopped. Add the potato, and process until smooth. (The mixture may form a ball.) Add all of the remaining ingredients, and process until well blended. Alternatively, place the potato in a jar with a tight-fitting lid, and mash with a fork. Finely chop the shallot and parsley, and add them to the jar along with the remaining ingredients. Shake until well blended.

3. Use the dressing immediately, or place in a covered container and refrigerate until ready to use.

NUTRITIONAL FACTS (per serving)
Calories: 30 Carbs: 4.2 g Cholesterol: 0 mg Fat: 1.3 g
Calories From Fat: 33.2% Protein: 2.1 g Sodium: 142 mg

Epicurean Vinaigret

A powerful combination of spices offset by a touch of honey results in a versatile dressing that would enhance almost any salad.

YIELD: **4** SERVINGS

1 new potato (1½–2 ounces), peeled and quartered, or ⅓ cup prepared instant mashed potatoes (page 213)

½ cup finely chopped fresh cilantro

¾ cup apple cider vinegar

¼ cup honey

1 teaspoon Oriental sesame oil

1 teaspoon curry powder

¼ teaspoon salt

¼ teaspoon freshly ground pepper

⅛ teaspoon ground ginger

1. Place enough water to cover the potato in a small saucepan, and bring to a simmer over medium-high heat. Add the potato and simmer uncovered for 25 minutes, or until fork tender. Allow the potato to come to room temperature.

2. Place the potato in a food processor fitted with a metal blade, or in a blender, and process until smooth. (It may form a ball.) Add all of the remaining ingredients, and process until well blended. Alternatively, place the potato in a jar with a tight-fitting lid, and mash with a fork. Add the remaining ingredients, and shake until well blended.

3. Use the dressing immediately, or place in a covered container and refrigerate until ready to use.

NUTRITIONAL FACTS (per serving)
Calories: 35 Carbs: 6.3 g Cholesterol: 0 mg Fat: 1.4 g
Calories From Fat: 30% Protein: 1 g Sodium: 98 mg

German Potato Salad Vinaigrette

This creamy vinaigrette was designed to intensify the flavors of a traditional German potato salad.

YIELD: 4 SERVINGS

2 shallots, finely chopped

⅓ cup white wine vinegar

3 tablespoons fat-free chicken broth, vegetable broth, or water

2 tablespoons Dijon mustard

1 teaspoon extra virgin olive oil

½ teaspoon freshly ground pepper

¼ teaspoon salt

1. Place the shallots, white wine vinegar, and broth or water in a medium-sized saucepan. Bring to a simmer over medium heat, stirring occasionally. Remove the saucepan from the heat, and stir in all of the remaining ingredients. Allow the vinaigrette to come to room temperature.

2. Use the vinaigrette immediately, or cover and refrigerate until ready to use.

NUTRITIONAL FACTS (per serving)

Calories: 28 Carbs: 3.8 g Cholesterol: 0 mg Fat: 1.5 g
Calories From Fat: 39.9% Protein: 1.2 g Sodium: 253 mg

Greek Vinaigrette

Designed to complement a classic Greek salad, this zesty vinaigrette would enhance other salads, as well.

YIELD: 4 SERVINGS

1 new potato (1½–2 ounces), peeled and quartered, or ⅓ cup prepared instant mashed potatoes (page 213)

1 large clove garlic, peeled

¼ cup plus 2 tablespoons fat-free chicken broth, vegetable broth, or water

2 tablespoons red wine vinegar

2 teaspoons extra virgin olive oil

1½ teaspoons dried oregano

½ teaspoon dry mustard

½ teaspoon granulated sugar

½ teaspoon dried basil

¼ teaspoon fresh lemon juice

⅛ teaspoon salt

⅛ teaspoon freshly ground pepper

1. Place enough water to cover the potato in a small saucepan, and bring to a simmer over medium-high heat. Add the potato and simmer uncovered for 25 minutes, or until fork tender. Allow the potato to come to room temperature.

2. Place the garlic in a food processor fitted with a metal blade, or in a blender, and process until finely chopped. Add the potato, and process until smooth. (The mixture may form a ball.) Add all of the remaining ingredients, and process until well blended. Alternatively, place the potato in a jar with a tight-fitting lid, and mash with a fork. Finely chop the garlic, and add it to the jar along with the remaining ingredients. Shake until well blended.

3. Use the dressing immediately, or place in a covered container and refrigerate until ready to use.

NUTRITIONAL FACTS (per serving)

Calories: 35 Carbs: 3.3 g Cholesterol: 0 mg Fat: 2.4 g
Calories From Fat: 53.1% Protein: 1.4 g Sodium: 94 mg

Honey Dijon Vinaigrette

The tangy flavor of Dijon mustard is nicely complemented by the sweetness of honey in this versatile vinaigrette.

YIELD: 4 SERVINGS

1 new potato (1½–2 ounces), peeled and quartered, or ⅓ cup prepared instant mashed potatoes (page 213)

¼ cup plus 2 tablespoons fat-free chicken broth, vegetable broth, or water

2 tablespoons honey

2 tablespoons granulated sugar

2 tablespoons white wine vinegar

1 tablespoon Dijon mustard

2 teaspoons canola oil

½ teaspoon celery seed

½ teaspoon paprika

⅛ teaspoon salt

1. Place enough water to cover the potato in a small saucepan, and bring to a simmer over medium-high heat. Add the potato and simmer uncovered for 25 minutes, or until fork tender. Allow the potato to come to room temperature.

2. Place the potato in a food processor fitted with a metal blade, or in a blender, and process until smooth. (It may form a ball.) Add all of the remaining ingredients, and process until well blended. Alternatively, place the potato in a jar with a tight-fitting lid, and mash with a fork. Add the remaining ingredients, and shake until well blended.

3. Use the dressing immediately, or place in a covered container and refrigerate until ready to use.

NUTRITIONAL FACTS (per serving)
Calories: 90   Carbs: 17.6 g   Cholesterol: 0 mg   Fat: 2.6 g
Calories From Fat: 23.1%   Protein: 1.5 g   Sodium: 164 mg

Indian-Spiced Dressing

This fragrant dressing adds just the right amount of spice to an exotic Indian salad.

YIELD: 4 SERVINGS

¼ cup fresh lime juice

¼ cup fat-free chicken broth, vegetable broth, or water

2 teaspoons extra virgin olive oil

2 teaspoons low-sodium soy sauce

1 teaspoon crushed red pepper

1 teaspoon ground cumin

¼ teaspoon salt

1. Place all of the ingredients in a jar with a tight-fitting lid, and shake until well blended.

2. Use the dressing immediately, or refrigerate until ready to use.

NUTRITIONAL FACTS (per serving)
Calories: 30   Carbs: 2 g   Cholesterol: 0 mg   Fat: 2.4 g
Calories From Fat: 63.9%   Protein: 1 g   Sodium: 267 mg

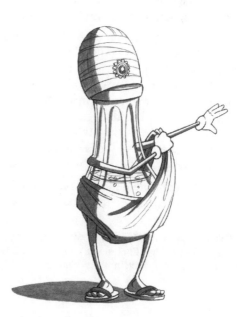

Italian Vinaigrette

This version of the classic Italian vinaigrette boasts a blend of savory spices and just the right amount of olive oil and vinegar.

YIELD: 4 SERVINGS

1 new potato (1½–2 ounces), peeled and quartered, or ⅓ cup prepared instant mashed potatoes (page 213)

3 cloves garlic, peeled

¼ cup plus 2 tablespoons fat-free chicken broth, vegetable broth, or water

2 tablespoons red wine vinegar

2 teaspoons extra virgin olive oil

1 teaspoon granulated sugar

¼ teaspoon dried oregano

¼ teaspoon salt

⅛ teaspoon crushed red pepper

1. Place enough water to cover the potato in a small saucepan, and bring to a simmer over medium-high heat. Add the potato and simmer uncovered for 25 minutes, or until fork tender. Allow the potato to come to room temperature.

2. Place the garlic in a food processor fitted with a metal blade, or in a blender, and process until finely chopped. Add the potato, and process until smooth. (The mixture may form a ball.) Add all of the remaining ingredients, and process until well blended. Alternatively, place the potato in a jar with a tight-fitting lid, and mash with a fork. Finely chop the garlic, and add it to the jar along with the remaining ingredients. Shake until well blended.

3. Use the dressing immediately, or place in a covered container and refrigerate until ready to use.

NUTRITIONAL FACTS (per serving)
Calories: 32   Carbs: 2.8 g   Cholesterol: 0 mg   Fat: 2.3 g
Calories From Fat: 55.5%   Protein: 1.3 g   Sodium: 183 mg

Lemon and Dill Vinaigrette

This creamy vinaigrette—with just the right balance of lemon and dill—is an excellent dressing for seafood salads.

YIELD: 4 SERVINGS

1 new potato (1½–2 ounces), peeled and quartered, or ⅓ cup prepared instant mashed potatoes (page 213)

3 cloves garlic, peeled

¼ cup plus 2 tablespoons fat-free chicken broth, vegetable broth, or water

3 tablespoons fresh lemon juice

1 tablespoon finely chopped fresh dill, or 1¼ teaspoons dried dill

2 teaspoons extra virgin olive oil

½ teaspoon freshly ground pepper

¼ teaspoon salt

1½ tablespoons capers, rinsed and drained

1. Place enough water to cover the potato in a small saucepan, and bring to a simmer over medium-high heat. Add the potato and simmer uncovered for 25 minutes, or until fork tender. Allow the potato to come to room temperature.

2. Place the garlic in a food processor fitted with a metal blade, or in a blender, and process until finely chopped. Add the potato, and process until smooth. (The mixture may form a ball.) Add all of the remaining ingredients except for the capers, and process until well blended. Add the capers, and, using on/off pulses, blend lightly. Alternatively, place the potato in a jar with a tight-fitting lid, and mash with a fork. Finely chop the garlic, and add it to the jar along with the remaining ingredients. Shake until well blended.

3. Use the dressing immediately, or place in a covered container and refrigerate until ready to use.

NUTRITIONAL FACTS (per serving)
Calories: 37   Carbs: 3.8 g   Cholesterol: 0 mg   Fat: 2.3 g
Calories From Fat: 49%   Protein: 1.6 g   Sodium: 214 mg

Lemon and Honey Vinaigrette

A marriage of sweet and tart flavors, this vinaigrette would enhance most seafood and poultry salads.

YIELD: **4** SERVINGS

¼ cup fresh lemon juice

2 tablespoons fat-free chicken broth or water

1 tablespoon honey

1 teaspoon extra virgin olive oil

⅛ teaspoon salt

⅛ teaspoon freshly ground pepper

1. Place all of the ingredients in a jar with a tight-fitting lid, and shake until well blended.

2. Use the dressing immediately, or refrigerate until ready to use.

NUTRITIONAL FACTS (per serving)
Calories: 30   Carbs: 5.8 g   Cholesterol: 0 mg   Fat: 1.1 g
Calories From Fat: 29.1%   Protein: 0.4 g   Sodium: 61 mg

Lemon Vinaigrette

Wonderfully versatile, this tangy vinaigrette is especially delicious on seafood and grain salads.

YIELD: **4** SERVINGS

1 new potato (1½–2 ounces), peeled and quartered, or ⅓ cup prepared instant mashed potatoes (page 213)

¼ cup fresh lemon juice

¼ cup fat-free chicken broth or water

1 tablespoon Dijon mustard

1 tablespoon white wine vinegar

2 teaspoons extra virgin olive oil

½ teaspoon freshly ground pepper

½ teaspoon dried oregano

¼ teaspoon salt

1. Place enough water to cover the potato in a small saucepan, and bring to a simmer over medium-high heat. Add the potato and simmer uncovered for 25 minutes, or until fork tender. Allow the potato to come to room temperature.

2. Place the potato in a food processor fitted with a metal blade, or in a blender, and process until smooth. (It may form a ball.) Add all of the remaining ingredients, and process until well blended. Alternatively, place the potato in a jar with a tight-fitting lid, and mash with a fork. Add the remaining ingredients, and shake until well blended.

3. Use the dressing immediately, or place in a covered container and refrigerate until ready to use.

NUTRITIONAL FACTS (per serving)
Calories: 36   Carbs: 3.6 g   Cholesterol: 0 mg   Fat: 2.5 g
Calories From Fat: 53.7%   Protein: 1.1 g   Sodium: 213 mg

Lime Vinaigrette

This tangy vinaigrette, sparked with just the right amount of chili powder, deliciously imparts Southwestern flair to any main course salad.

YIELD: 4 SERVINGS

1 new potato (1½–2 ounces), peeled and quartered, or ⅓ cup prepared instant mashed potatoes (page 213)

1 clove garlic, peeled

¼ cup plus 2 tablespoons fat-free chicken broth, vegetable broth, or water

3 tablespoons fresh lime juice

1 tablespoon red wine vinegar

2 teaspoons extra virgin olive oil

1 teaspoon Dijon mustard

½ teaspoon chili powder

⅛ teaspoon salt

⅛ teaspoon freshly ground pepper

1. Place enough water to cover the potato in a small saucepan, and bring to a simmer over medium-high heat. Add the potato and simmer uncovered for 25 minutes, or until fork tender. Allow the potato to come to room temperature.

2. Place the garlic in a food processor fitted with a metal blade, or in a blender, and process until chopped. Add the potato, and process until smooth. (The mixture may form a ball.) Add all of the remaining ingredients, and process until well blended. Alternatively, place the potato in a jar with a tight-fitting lid, and mash with a fork. Finely chop the garlic, and add it to the jar along with the remaining ingredients. Shake until well blended.

3. Use the dressing immediately, or place in a covered container and refrigerate until ready to use.

NUTRITIONAL FACTS (per serving)
Calories: 34   Carbs: 3.3 g   Cholesterol: 0 mg   Fat: 2.4 g
Calories From Fat: 53%   Protein: 1.4 g   Sodium: 113 mg

Mandarin Dressing

A poultry or seafood salad is the perfect destination for this sweet Oriental dressing.

YIELD: 4 SERVINGS

¼ cup plus ½ tablespoon cold water, divided

¾ teaspoon cornstarch

⅓ cup rice vinegar

2 tablespoons granulated sugar

2 tablespoons low-sodium ketchup

2 teaspoons low-sodium soy sauce

1. Place 1½ tablespoons of the water and all of the cornstarch in a small heavy saucepan, and stir to blend well. Add the remaining water and all of the remaining ingredients, and stir to blend well.

2. Place the saucepan over medium heat, and cook, stirring frequently, for 18 to 20 minutes, or until the dressing thickens. Remove the saucepan from the heat, and set aside to cool.

3. Use the dressing immediately, or cover and allow to remain at room temperature for up to several hours.

NUTRITIONAL FACTS (per serving)
Calories: 38   Carbs: 10.2 g   Cholesterol: 0 mg   Fat: 0 g
Calories From Fat: 0.6%   Protein: 0.3 g   Sodium: 102 mg

Mango Chutney Vinaigrette

This spicy vinaigrette is excellent on grain, poultry, and seafood salads.

YIELD: 4 SERVINGS

¼ cup mango chutney

¼ cup fat-free chicken broth or water

2 tablespoons rice vinegar

2 teaspoons canola oil

1 teaspoon Dijon mustard

1 teaspoon honey

¼ teaspoon salt

¼ teaspoon Asian hot sauce or favorite hot pepper sauce

1. Place all of the ingredients in a food processor fitted with a metal blade, or in a blender, and process until smooth.

2. Use the dressing immediately, or place in a covered container and refrigerate until ready to use.

NUTRITIONAL FACTS (per serving)

Calories: 68   Carbs: 11.9 g   Cholesterol: 0 mg   Fat: 2.4 g
Calories From Fat: 29.8%   Protein: 0.8 g   Sodium: 185 mg

Maytag Blue Cheese and Balsamic Vinaigrette

The combination of richly flavored blue cheese and piquant yet sweet balsamic vinegar yields an intense taste that lingers long after the first bite.

YIELD: 4 SERVINGS

1 new potato (1½–2 ounces), peeled and quartered, or ⅓ cup prepared instant mashed potatoes (page 213)

¼ ounce Maytag Blue cheese or other blue cheese

¼ cup plus 2 tablespoons fat-free chicken broth, vegetable broth, or water

2 tablespoons balsamic vinegar

2 teaspoons extra virgin olive oil

¼ teaspoon salt

¼ teaspoon freshly ground pepper

1. Place enough water to cover the potato in a small saucepan, and bring to a simmer over medium-high heat. Add the potato and simmer uncovered for 25 minutes, or until fork tender. Allow the potato to come to room temperature.

2. Place the potato and blue cheese in a food processor fitted with a metal blade, or in a blender, and process until smooth. (The mixture may form a ball.) Add all of the remaining ingredients, and process until well blended. Alternatively, place the potato and cheese in a jar with a tight-fitting lid, and mash with a fork. Add the remaining ingredients, and shake until well blended.

3. Use the dressing immediately, or place in a covered container and refrigerate until ready to use.

NUTRITIONAL FACTS (per serving)

Calories: 35   Carbs: 2.2 g   Cholesterol: 1 mg   Fat: 2.8 g
Calories From Fat: 62.4%   Protein: 1.6 g   Sodium: 163 mg

Mexican Vinaigrette

This dressing is spicy enough to add a real kick to any Mexican or Southwestern salad.

YIELD: 4 SERVINGS

1 new potato (1½–2 ounces), peeled and quartered, or ⅓ cup prepared instant mashed potatoes (page 213)

¼ cup plus 2 tablespoons fat-free chicken broth, vegetable broth, or water

3 tablespoons apple cider vinegar

2 teaspoons low-sodium soy sauce

2 teaspoons extra virgin olive oil

¾ teaspoon dried tarragon

¾ teaspoon dried oregano

⅛ teaspoon salt

⅛ teaspoon freshly ground pepper

1. Place enough water to cover the potato in a small saucepan, and bring to a simmer over medium-high heat. Add the potato and simmer uncovered for 25 minutes, or until fork tender. Allow the potato to come to room temperature.

2. Place the potato in a food processor fitted with a metal blade, or in a blender, and process until smooth. (It may form a ball.) Add all of the remaining ingredients, and process until well blended. Alternatively, place the potato in a jar with a tight-fitting lid, and mash with a fork. Add the remaining ingredients, and shake until well blended.

3. Use the dressing immediately, or place in a covered container and refrigerate until ready to use.

NUTRITIONAL FACTS (per serving)

Calories: 33   Carbs: 2.9 g   Cholesterol: 0 mg   Fat: 2.3 g
Calories From Fat: 54.6%   Protein: 1.5 g   Sodium: 194 mg

Orange Vinaigrette

This tangy vinaigrette is certain to enliven any Asian-style salad.

YIELD: 4 SERVINGS

¼ cup fresh orange juice

2 tablespoons rice vinegar

½ tablespoon light corn syrup

1 tablespoon Dijon mustard

1 tablespoon low-sodium soy sauce

2 teaspoons finely chopped fresh ginger

2 teaspoons canola oil

⅛ teaspoon salt

⅛ teaspoon Asian hot sauce or favorite hot pepper sauce

1. Place all of the ingredients in a jar with a tight-fitting lid, and shake until well blended.

2. Use the dressing immediately, or refrigerate until ready to use.

NUTRITIONAL FACTS (per serving)

Calories: 41   Carbs: 4.8 g   Cholesterol: 0 mg   Fat: 2.5 g
Calories From Fat: 51.1%   Protein: 0.5 g   Sodium: 267 mg

Oriental Chicken Salad Vinaigrette

This sweet and sour vinaigrette can transform any chicken salad into an Oriental delight.

YIELD: 4 SERVINGS

2 tablespoons apple cider vinegar

2 tablespoons fat-free chicken broth or water

1 tablespoon granulated sugar

½ tablespoon light corn syrup

1 teaspoon canola oil

¼ teaspoon salt

¼ teaspoon freshly ground pepper

1. Place all of the ingredients in a jar with a tight-fitting lid, and shake until well blended.

2. Use the dressing immediately, or refrigerate until ready to use.

NUTRITIONAL FACTS (per serving)
Calories: 31   Carbs: 5.6 g   Cholesterol: 0 mg   Fat: 1.1 g
Calories From Fat: 30%   Protein: 0.3 g   Sodium: 108 mg

Oriental Dressing

A wonderfully sweet and sour dressing, this brings the essence of Asian cuisine to your salad bowl.

YIELD: 4 SERVINGS

1 new potato (1½–2 ounces), peeled and quartered, or ⅓ cup prepared instant mashed potatoes (page 213)

1 teaspoon chopped fresh ginger

1 clove garlic, peeled

¼ cup fat-free chicken broth or water

2 tablespoons rice vinegar

2 tablespoons honey

1 tablespoon rice wine

2 teaspoons canola oil

½ teaspoon low-sodium soy sauce

½ teaspoon Oriental sesame oil

⅛ teaspoon salt

⅛ teaspoon Asian hot sauce or other hot pepper sauce

1. Place enough water to cover the potato in a small saucepan, and bring to a simmer over medium-high heat. Add the potato and simmer uncovered for 25 minutes, or until fork tender. Allow the potato to come to room temperature.

2. Place the ginger and garlic in a food processor fitted with a metal blade, or in a blender, and process until finely chopped. Add the potato, and process until smooth. (The mixture may form a ball.) Add all of the remaining ingredients, and process until well blended. Alternatively, place the potato in a jar with a tight-fitting lid, and mash with a fork. Finely chop the ginger and garlic, and add them to the jar along with the remaining ingredients. Shake until well blended.

3. Use the dressing immediately, or place in a covered container and refrigerate until ready to use.

NUTRITIONAL FACTS (per serving)
Calories: 67   Carbs: 11.1 g   Cholesterol: 0 mg   Fat: 2.9 g
Calories From Fat: 34.7%   Protein: 1 g   Sodium: 125 mg

Oriental Plum Dressing

This creamy and intensely sweet dressing adds a unique flavor to a wide range of Oriental-style seafood and poultry salads.

YIELD: 4 SERVINGS

1 tablespoon dry mustard

2 tablespoons hot water

½ cup plum sauce*

3 tablespoons rice vinegar

1 tablespoon granulated sugar

1 tablespoon low-sodium soy sauce

1 teaspoon Oriental sesame oil

¼ teaspoon salt

* A sweet Chinese condiment, plum sauce can be found in the Asian section of most supermarkets.

1. Place the dry mustard and hot water in a medium-sized bowl, and stir until smooth. Add all of the remaining ingredients, and stir until well blended.

2. Use the dressing immediately, or cover and refrigerate until ready to use.

NUTRITIONAL FACTS (per serving)
Calories: 111   Carbs: 23.4 g   Cholesterol: 0 mg   Fat: 1.5 g
Calories From Fat: 39.9%   Protein: 0.6 g   Sodium: 703 mg

Pasta Vinaigrette

This creamy vinaigrette intensifies the flavors of salad ingredients, and is an especially delicious addition to pasta salads.

YIELD: 4 SERVINGS

1 new potato (1½–2 ounces), peeled and quartered, or ⅓ cup prepared instant mashed potatoes (page 213)

1 clove garlic, peeled

¼ cup plus 2 tablespoons fat-free chicken broth, vegetable broth, or water

¼ cup white wine vinegar

2 tablespoons fresh lime juice

2 teaspoons extra virgin olive oil

½ teaspoon dry mustard

¼ teaspoon salt

¼ teaspoon freshly ground pepper

⅛ teaspoon paprika

1. Place enough water to cover the potato in a small saucepan, and bring to a simmer over medium-high heat. Add the potato and simmer uncovered for 25 minutes, or until fork tender. Allow the potato to come to room temperature.

2. Place the garlic in a food processor fitted with a metal blade, or in a blender, and process until finely chopped. Add the potato, and process until smooth. (The mixture may form a ball.) Add all of the remaining ingredients, and process until well blended. Alternatively, place the potato in a jar with a tight-fitting lid, and mash with a fork. Finely chop the garlic, and add it to the jar along with the remaining ingredients. Shake until well blended.

3. Use the dressing immediately, or place in a covered container and refrigerate until ready to use.

NUTRITIONAL FACTS (per serving)
Calories: 34   Carbs: 3.3 g   Cholesterol: 0 mg   Fat: 2.3 g
Calories From Fat: 53.1%   Protein: 1.3 g   Sodium: 238 mg

Pear Dressing

This sweet and creamy dressing will enhance any fruit salad.

YIELD: **4** SERVINGS

1 ripe red pear, peeled, cored, and coarsely chopped

½ cup rice vinegar

¼ cup fat-free chicken broth or water

1 tablespoon honey

½ teaspoon walnut oil

⅛ teaspoon salt

⅛ teaspoon freshly ground pepper

1. Place the pear and rice vinegar in a medium-sized saucepan, and bring to a boil over medium-high heat. Cook, stirring occasionally, for 6 to 8 minutes, or until the liquid is reduced by half. Allow the mixture to come to room temperature.

2. Place the pear mixture in a food processor fitted with a metal blade, or in a blender, and process until finely chopped. Add all of the remaining ingredients, and process until well blended.

3. Use the dressing immediately, or place in a covered container and refrigerate until ready to use.

NUTRITIONAL FACTS (per serving)

Calories: 59   Carbs: 14.5 g   Cholesterol: 0 mg   Fat: 0.8 g
Calories From Fat: 10.3%   Protein: 0.9 g   Sodium: 77 mg

Potato Salad Vinaigrette

With its distinctive tangy taste, this vinaigrette helps elevate potato salad to main course status.

YIELD: **4** SERVINGS

2 shallots, peeled

3 tablespoons tarragon white wine vinegar

3 tablespoons fat-free chicken broth, vegetable broth, or water

3 tablespoons Dijon mustard

½ teaspoon freshly ground pepper

¼ teaspoon salt

1. Place the shallots in a food processor fitted with a metal blade, or in a blender, and process until finely chopped. Add all of the remaining ingredients, and process until well blended. Alternatively, finely chop the shallots, and place the shallots and the remaining ingredients in a jar with a tight-fitting lid. Shake until well blended.

2. Use the dressing immediately, or place in a covered container and refrigerate until ready to use.

NUTRITIONAL FACTS (per serving)

Calories: 20   Carbs: 3.5 g   Cholesterol: 0 mg   Fat: 0.5 g
Calories From Fat: 19.1%   Protein: 1.4 g   Sodium: 300 mg

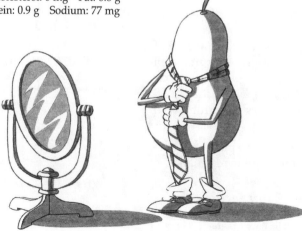

Raspberry Vinaigrette

A creamy vinaigrette with the intense flavor of raspberries, this is delicious on a poultry, seafood, or pork salad.

YIELD: 6 SERVINGS

1 new potato (1½–2 ounces), peeled and quartered, or ⅓ cup prepared instant mashed potatoes (page 213)

½ teaspoon finely chopped fresh ginger

½ teaspoon finely chopped garlic

½ teaspoon finely chopped shallot

¼ cup plus 2 tablespoons fat-free chicken broth or water

¼ cup raspberry vinegar

2 tablespoons granulated sugar

2 teaspoons canola oil

1 teaspoon Dijon mustard

⅛ teaspoon salt

⅛ teaspoon freshly ground pepper

1 tablespoon poppy seeds (optional)

1. Place enough water to cover the potato in a small saucepan, and bring to a simmer over medium-high heat. Add the potato and simmer uncovered for 25 minutes, or until fork tender. Allow the potato to come to room temperature.

2. Place the potato in a food processor fitted with a metal blade, or in a blender, and process until smooth. (The mixture may form a ball.) Add all of the remaining ingredients, and process until well blended. Alternatively, place the potato in a jar with a tight-fitting lid, and mash with a fork. Add the remaining ingredients, and shake until well blended.

3. Use the dressing immediately, or place in a covered container and refrigerate until ready to use.

NUTRITIONAL FACTS (per serving)
Calories: 38   Carbs: 6.2 g   Cholesterol: 0 mg   Fat: 1.6 g
Calories From Fat: 33.4%   Protein: 0.9 g   Sodium: 73 mg

Red Wine Vinaigrette

This classic vinaigrette—boldly flavored and creamy in consistency—can be used to dress most main course salads.

YIELD: 4 SERVINGS

1 new potato (1½–2 ounces), peeled and quartered, or ⅓ cup prepared instant mashed potatoes (page 213)

¼ cup plus 1 tablespoon fat-free chicken broth, vegetable broth, or water

3 tablespoons red wine vinegar

2 teaspoons extra virgin olive oil

½ teaspoon freshly ground pepper

¼ teaspoon salt

1. Place enough water to cover the potato in a small saucepan, and bring to a simmer over medium-high heat. Add the potato and simmer uncovered for 25 minutes, or until fork tender. Allow the potato to come to room temperature.

2. Place the potato in a food processor fitted with a metal blade or in a blender, and process until smooth. (It may form a ball.) Add all of the remaining ingredients, and process until well blended. Alternatively, place the potato in a jar with a tight-fitting lid, and mash with a fork. Add the remaining ingredients, and shake until well blended.

3. Use the dressing immediately, or place in a covered container and refrigerate until ready to use.

NUTRITIONAL FACTS (per serving)
Calories: 29   Carbs: 2.4 g   Cholesterol: 0 mg   Fat: 2.3 g
Calories From Fat: 60.6%   Protein: 1 g   Sodium: 130 mg

Top: Couscous Salad With
Roasted Vegetables (page 190)

Center: Melon and Berry Salad
With Yogurt (page 209)

Bottom: Mixed Baby Greens
With Marinated Tofu (page 186)

Top: Santa Fe Barley Salad
(page 196)

Center: Pear, Stilton, and Endive
Salad (page 208)

Bottom: New Potato, Green Bean,
and Pasta Salad (page 180)

Roasted Red Pepper Dressing

This spicy dressing is so rich in flavor that it can become addictive. Serve it on a Southwestern salad or as a baked potato topping.

YIELD: 4 SERVINGS

2 large red bell peppers, or ½ cup commercial sweet roasted bell peppers

2 large cloves garlic, peeled

¼ cup plus 2 tablespoons fat-free chicken broth, vegetable broth, or water

2 tablespoons coarsely chopped fresh cilantro

2 tablespoons red wine vinegar

½ tablespoon Dijon mustard

2 teaspoons extra virgin olive oil

1 teaspoon granulated sugar

½ teaspoon Worcestershire sauce

⅛ teaspoon salt

⅛ teaspoon hot pepper sauce

1. To roast the peppers, place the peppers on a baking sheet that has been lined with aluminum foil. Broil the peppers under a preheated broiler, turning the peppers as the skins blacken, for 20 to 25 minutes, or until the skins are charred all over. Once roasted, place in a plastic bag, seal, and allow to steam for 15 minutes. When the peppers are cool enough to handle, peel away the skin and remove the tops and seeds. (Do not rinse the peppers.)

2. Place the garlic in a food processor fitted with a metal blade, or in a blender, and process until finely chopped. Add the roasted peppers, and process to purée. Add all of the remaining ingredients, and process until well blended.

3. Use the dressing immediately, or place in a covered container and refrigerate until ready to use.

NUTRITIONAL FACTS (per serving)
Calories: 43   Carbs: 5 g   Cholesterol: 0 mg   Fat: 2.5 g
Calories From Fat: 45.4%   Protein: 1.9 g   Sodium: 146 mg

Salad Niçoise Vinaigrette

This classic creamy vinaigrette is the ultimate way to dress the traditional Salad Niçoise.

YIELD: 4 SERVINGS

1 new potato (1½–2 ounces), peeled and quartered, or ⅓ cup prepared instant mashed potatoes (page 213)

1 shallot, peeled

¼ cup plus 2 tablespoons fat-free chicken broth, vegetable broth, or water

3 tablespoons white wine vinegar

1 tablespoon fresh lemon juice

2 teaspoons extra virgin olive oil

½ teaspoon dry mustard

½ teaspoon freshly ground pepper

¼ teaspoon salt

¼ teaspoon dried basil

⅛ teaspoon dried tarragon

1. Place enough water to cover the potato in a small saucepan, and bring to a simmer over medium-high heat. Add the potato and simmer uncovered for 25 minutes, or until fork tender. Allow to come to room temperature.

2. Place the shallot in a food processor fitted with a metal blade, or in a blender, and process until finely chopped. Add the potato, and process until smooth. (The mixture may form a ball.) Add all of the remaining ingredients, and process until well blended. Alternatively, place the potato in a jar with a tight-fitting lid, and mash with a fork. Finely chop the shallot, and add it to the jar with the remaining ingredients. Shake until well blended.

3. Use the dressing immediately, or place in a covered container and refrigerate until ready to use.

NUTRITIONAL FACTS (per serving)
Calories: 36   Carbs: 3.8 g   Cholesterol: 0 mg   Fat: 2.3 g
Calories From Fat: 49.8%   Protein: 1.5 g   Sodium: 183 mg

Salsa Dressing

This spicy dressing, made with traditional salsa ingredients, is the perfect way to add zest to a Southwestern salad.

YIELD: 4 SERVINGS

2 medium tomatoes, seeded and diced (about 2 cups)

3 tablespoons fresh lime juice

2 tablespoons white wine vinegar

2 tablespoons chopped fresh cilantro

2 teaspoons extra virgin olive oil

2 jalapeño chilies, seeded and finely chopped,* or 2 tablespoons canned chopped green chilies, drained

1/2 teaspoon granulated sugar

1/2 teaspoon freshly ground pepper

1/4 teaspoon salt

* To protect your hands from the seeds of the jalapeños, be sure to wear rubber or latex gloves when working with the peppers, and to wash the knife and cutting board immediately after use.

1. Place all of the ingredients in a medium-sized bowl, and stir until well blended.

2. Use the dressing immediately, or cover and refrigerate until ready to use.

NUTRITIONAL FACTS (per serving)

Calories: 35   Carbs: 4.1 g   Cholesterol: 0 mg   Fat: 2.3 g
Calories From Fat: 52.9%   Protein: 0.6 g   Sodium: 270 mg

Savory Vinaigrette

This creamy vinaigrette adds a delicious touch to both spinach and pasta salads.

YIELD: 4 SERVINGS

1 new potato (1 1/2–2 ounces), peeled and quartered, or 1/3 cup prepared instant mashed potatoes (page 213)

1 clove garlic, peeled

1/4 cup plus 2 tablespoons fat-free chicken broth, vegetable broth, or water

2 tablespoons white wine vinegar

1 tablespoon Dijon mustard

2 teaspoons extra virgin olive oil

1/2 teaspoon dried basil

1/2 teaspoon freshly ground pepper

1/4 teaspoon salt

1/4 teaspoon dried thyme

1. Place enough water to cover the potato in a small saucepan, and bring to a simmer over medium-high heat. Add the potato and simmer uncovered for 25 minutes, or until fork tender. Allow the potato to come to room temperature.

2. Place the garlic in a food processor fitted with a metal blade, or in a blender, and process until finely chopped. Add the potato and process until smooth. (The mixture may form a ball.) Add the remaining ingredients, and process until well blended. Alternatively, place the potato in a jar with a tight-fitting lid, and mash with a fork. Finely chop the garlic, and add it to the jar along with the remaining ingredients. Shake until well blended.

3. Use the dressing immediately, or place in a covered container and refrigerate until ready to use.

NUTRITIONAL FACTS (per serving)

Calories: 34   Carbs: 2.8 g   Cholesterol: 0 mg   Fat: 2.4 g
Calories From Fat: 56%   Protein: 1.5 g   Sodium: 230 mg

Southwestern Vinaigrette

Bursting with the flavors of Southwestern cuisine, this spicy vinaigrette will nicely accent most poultry, grain, and beef salads.

YIELD: **4** SERVINGS

1 new potato (1½–2 ounces), peeled and quartered, or ⅓ cup prepared instant mashed potatoes (page 213)

1 clove garlic, peeled

¼ cup plus 2 tablespoons fat-free chicken broth, vegetable broth, or water

3 tablespoons white wine vinegar

1 tablespoon Dijon mustard

2 teaspoons extra virgin olive oil

1 teaspoon ground cumin

½ teaspoon freshly ground pepper

⅛ teaspoon salt

⅛ teaspoon chili powder

⅛ teaspoon cayenne pepper (optional)

1. Place enough water to cover the potato in a small saucepan, and bring to a simmer over medium-high heat. Add the potato and simmer uncovered for 25 minutes, or until fork tender. Allow the potato to come to room temperature.

2. Place the garlic in a food processor fitted with a metal blade, or in a blender, and process until finely chopped. Add the potato, and process until smooth. (The mixture may form a ball.) Add all of the remaining ingredients, and process until well blended. Alternatively, place the potato in a jar with a tight-fitting lid, and mash with a fork. Finely chop the garlic, and add it to the jar along with the remaining ingredients. Shake until well blended.

3. Use the dressing immediately, or place in a covered container and refrigerate until ready to use.

NUTRITIONAL FACTS (per serving)

Calories: 37   Carbs: 3.2 g   Cholesterol: 0 mg   Fat: 2.6 g
Calories From Fat: 54.8%   Protein: 1.6 g   Sodium: 165 mg

Soy Sauce Dressing

Unlike most Oriental dressings, this creation has a surprisingly creamy consistency that deliciously smothers a chicken salad.

YIELD: **4** SERVINGS

½ cup fat-free or low-fat mayonnaise

¼ cup mango chutney, chopped

3 tablespoons low-sodium soy sauce

¼ teaspoon ground ginger

⅛ teaspoon Asian hot sauce or favorite hot pepper sauce

Dash salt

1. Place all of the ingredients in a small bowl, and blend gently with a whisk until well mixed.

2. Use the dressing immediately, or cover and refrigerate until ready to use.

NUTRITIONAL FACTS (per serving)

Calories: 71   Carbs: 17 g   Cholesterol: 0 mg   Fat: 0.1 g
Calories From Fat: 1%   Protein: 0.7 g   Sodium: 834 mg

Soy Sauce Vinaigrette

This sweet and sour vinaigrette was created especially for Kitch's Chicken and Pasta Salad (page 45).

YIELD: 6 SERVINGS

⅓ cup low-sodium soy sauce

⅓ cup white wine vinegar

3 tablespoons granulated sugar

2 tablespoons fat-free chicken broth or water

½ tablespoon canola oil

¼ teaspoon freshly ground pepper

1. Place all of the ingredients in a jar with a tight-fitting lid, and shake until well blended.

2. Use the dressing immediately, or refrigerate until ready to use.

NUTRITIONAL FACTS (per serving)
Calories: 45   Carbs: 8.5 g   Cholesterol: 0 mg   Fat: 1.2 g
Calories From Fat: 21.3%   Protein: 1.1 g   Sodium: 544 mg

Spicy Vinaigrette

This highly spiced vinaigrette features a combination of Oriental flavors.

YIELD: 4 SERVINGS

1 new potato (1½–2 ounces), peeled and quartered, or ⅓ cup prepared instant mashed potatoes (page 213)

1 scallion, cut into 1-inch lengths

3 tablespoons fat-free chicken broth or water

2 tablespoons low-sodium soy sauce

2 tablespoons rice wine

2 tablespoons honey

2 tablespoons rice vinegar

2 teaspoons canola oil

½ teaspoon Asian hot sauce or other hot pepper sauce

⅛ teaspoon salt

⅛ teaspoon Oriental sesame oil

1. Place enough water to cover the potato in a small saucepan, and bring to a simmer over medium-high heat. Add the potato and simmer uncovered for 25 minutes, or until fork tender. Allow the potato to come to room temperature.

2. Place the scallion in a food processor fitted with a metal blade, or in a blender, and process until chopped. Add the potato, and process until smooth. (The mixture may form a ball.) Add all of the remaining ingredients, and process until well blended. Alternatively, place the potato in a jar with a tight-fitting lid, and mash with a fork. Finely chop the scallion, and add it to the jar along with the remaining ingredients. Shake until well blended.

3. Use the dressing immediately, or place in a covered container and refrigerate until ready to use.

NUTRITIONAL FACTS (per serving)
Calories: 89   Carbs: 14.7 g   Cholesterol: 0 mg   Fat: 2.5 g
Calories From Fat: 25.2%   Protein: 2 g   Sodium: 473 mg

Tangerine Vinaigrette

The intense citrus flavor of this vinaigrette adds a pleasing piquancy to poultry and beef salads.

YIELD: 4 SERVINGS
---

1 new potato (1½–2 ounces), peeled and quartered, or ⅓ cup prepared instant mashed potatoes (page 213)

1 shallot, peeled

¼ cup fresh tangerine juice

3 tablespoons hot honey mustard or Dijon mustard

2 tablespoons fat-free chicken broth or water

2 tablespoons rice vinegar

2 teaspoons canola oil

½ teaspoon freshly ground pepper

¼ teaspoon salt

1. Place enough water to cover the potato in a small saucepan, and bring to a simmer over medium-high heat. Add the potato and simmer uncovered for 25 minutes, or until fork tender. Allow the potato to come to room temperature.

2. Place the shallot in a food processor fitted with a metal blade, or in a blender, and process until finely chopped. Add the potato, and process until smooth. (The mixture may form a ball.) Add all of the remaining ingredients, and process until well blended. Alternatively, place the potato in a jar with a tight-fitting lid, and mash with a fork. Finely chop the shallot, and add it to the jar along with the remaining ingredients. Shake until well blended.

3. Use the dressing immediately, or place in a covered container and refrigerate until ready to use.

NUTRITIONAL FACTS (per serving)
Calories: 45   Carbs: 5.1 g   Cholesterol: 0 mg   Fat: 2.7 g
Calories From Fat: 49%   Protein: 1.1 g   Sodium: 245 mg

Tangy Orange Dressing

This citrus vinaigrette was designed to add a bite to grain-based creations such as Orange-Infused Grain Salad (page 185).

YIELD: 4 SERVINGS

¼ cup fresh orange juice

2 tablespoons fresh lemon juice

2 tablespoons sherry vinegar

1 tablespoon Dijon mustard

1 tablespoon light corn syrup

1 teaspoon extra virgin olive oil

½ teaspoon finely grated orange peel

½ teaspoon freshly ground pepper

⅛ teaspoon salt

1. Place all of the ingredients in a jar with a tight-fitting lid, and shake until well blended.

2. Use the dressing immediately, or refrigerate until ready to use.

NUTRITIONAL FACTS (per serving)
Calories: 24   Carbs: 3.2 g   Cholesterol: 0 mg   Fat: 1.3 g
Calories From Fat: 45.8%   Protein: 0.3 g   Sodium: 181 mg

Tarragon Vinaigrette

A creamy vinaigrette accented by the distinctive flavor of tarragon, this dressing adds a delicate taste to most poultry and vegetarian salads.

YIELD: 4 SERVINGS

1 new potato (1½–2 ounces), peeled and quartered, or ⅓ cup prepared instant mashed potatoes (page 213)

1 clove garlic, peeled and finely chopped

1 shallot, peeled and finely chopped

2 tablespoons finely chopped fresh tarragon, or 2 teaspoons dried tarragon

¼ cup plus 2 tablespoons fat-free chicken broth, vegetable broth, or water

2 tablespoons sherry vinegar

1 tablespoon Dijon mustard

½ teaspoon extra virgin olive oil

⅛ teaspoon salt

⅛ teaspoon freshly ground pepper

1. Place enough water to cover the potato in a small saucepan, and bring to a simmer over medium-high heat. Add the potato and simmer uncovered for 25 minutes, or until fork tender. Allow the potato to come to room temperature.

2. Place the garlic, shallot, and tarragon in a food processor fitted with a metal blade, or in a blender, and process until blended. Add the potato, and process until smooth. (The mixture may form a ball.) Add all of the remaining ingredients, and process until well blended. Alternatively, place the potato in a jar with a tight-fitting lid, and mash with a fork. Finely chop the garlic and shallot, and add them to the jar along with the remaining ingredients. Shake until well blended.

3. Use the dressing immediately, or place in a covered container and refrigerate until ready to use.

NUTRITIONAL FACTS (per serving)
Calories: 44   Carbs: 4.7 g   Cholesterol: 0 mg   Fat: 2.6 g
Calories From Fat: 46.4%   Protein: 2.1 g   Sodium: 143 mg

Teriyaki Vinaigrette

This sweet vinaigrette is a delight when combined with a poultry or seafood salad.

YIELD: 4 SERVINGS

1 new potato (1½–2 ounces), peeled and quartered, or ⅓ cup prepared instant mashed potatoes (page 213)

3 tablespoons rice vinegar

2 tablespoons low-sodium soy sauce

1 tablespoon light corn syrup

2 teaspoons canola oil

¼ teaspoon finely chopped fresh ginger

¼ teaspoon freshly ground pepper

⅛ teaspoon salt

1. Place enough water to cover the potato in a small saucepan, and bring to a simmer over medium-high heat. Add the potato and simmer uncovered for 25 minutes, or until fork tender. Allow the potato to come to room temperature.

2. Place the potato in a food processor fitted with a metal blade, or in a blender, and process until smooth. (It may form a ball.) Add all of the remaining ingredients, and process until well blended. Alternatively, place the potato in a jar with a tight-fitting lid, and mash with a fork. Add all of the remaining ingredients, and shake to blend well.

3. Use the dressing immediately, or place in a covered container and refrigerate until ready to use.

NUTRITIONAL FACTS (per serving)
Calories: 48   Carbs: 6.9 g   Cholesterol: 0 mg   Fat: 2.3 g
Calories From Fat: 40.6%   Protein: 0.6 g   Sodium: 373 mg

Tomatillo Dressing

Cloaked in this creamy, tart dressing, even the simplest of poultry or seafood salads becomes a memorable Southwestern feast.

NUTRITIONAL FACTS (per serving)
Calories: 71   Carbs: 11.5 g   Cholesterol: 3 mg   Fat: 1.5 g
Calories From Fat: 17.1%   Protein: 4.6 g   Sodium: 183 mg

YIELD: **4** SERVINGS

4 tomatillos

2 large cloves garlic, peeled

2 jalapeño chilies, seeded*

½ cup coarsely chopped fresh cilantro

¼ cup fresh lime juice

¾ teaspoon freshly ground pepper

¼ teaspoon salt

1 cup plain low-fat yogurt

* To protect your hands from the seeds of the jalapeños, be sure to wear rubber or latex gloves when working with the peppers, and to wash the knife and cutting board immediately after use.

1. Peel off and discard the husks and stems of the tomatillos, and wash to remove the sticky resinous material that covers them. Thinly slice the tomatillos.

2. Coat a medium-sized nonstick skillet with cooking spray, and preheat over medium-high heat. Add the tomatillos and stir-fry for 4 minutes, or until fork-tender. Set aside.

3. Place the garlic and jalapeños in a food processor fitted with a metal blade, or in a blender, and process until finely chopped. Add the tomatillos and cilantro, and process until chopped. Add the lime juice, pepper, and salt, and process to blend well. Add the yogurt, and, using on/off pulses, blend gently. Alternatively, finely chop the tomatillos, garlic, jalapeños, and cilantro, and place in a small bowl with all of the remaining ingredients. Stir to blend well.

4. Use the dressing immediately, or place in a covered container and refrigerate until ready to use.

Seeding Chilies

An easy way to remove the seeds from jalapeño or serrano chilies is to cut the chilies in half and use a narrow grapefruit spoon to scoop out the seeds. In addition to being quick and effective, this is far safer than scooping out the seeds with your fingertips—a practice that can be quite painful because of the irritating oils of the chilies. In fact, even when using a spoon to remove the seeds, it is best to wear plastic or latex gloves for protection.

Tomato Vinaigrette

With its robust flavor and chunky texture, this vinaigrette is the perfect partner for a beef or vegetarian main course salad.

YIELD: 4 SERVINGS

1 shallot, peeled and finely chopped

1 large clove garlic, peeled and finely chopped

8 ounces ripe tomatoes, seeded and chopped

1 tablespoon chopped fresh parsley

1 tablespoon dry white wine

½ tablespoon tomato paste

½ teaspoon freshly ground pepper

¼ teaspoon dried oregano

¼ teaspoon salt

⅛ teaspoon dried basil

¼ cup fat-free chicken broth, vegetable broth, or water

2 ½ tablespoons red wine vinegar

1. Coat a medium-sized nonstick skillet with cooking spray, and preheat over medium heat. Add the shallot and garlic, and cook for 2 minutes, stirring frequently. Add the tomatoes, parsley, wine, tomato paste, pepper, oregano, salt, and basil, and cook, stirring occasionally, for 5 additional minutes or until thick. Allow the mixture to come to room temperature.

2. Transfer the tomato mixture to a food processor fitted with a metal blade, or to a blender, and process until smooth. Add the broth or water and the vinegar, and blend well.

3. Use the dressing immediately, or place in a covered container and refrigerate until ready to use.

NUTRITIONAL FACTS (per serving)
Calories: 15   Carbs: 3 g   Cholesterol: 0 mg   Fat: 0.1 g
Calories From Fat: 4.5%   Protein: 1.2 g   Sodium: 187 mg

Vietnamese Vinaigrette

This unique vinaigrette beautifully complements Vietnamese Beef Salad (page 103).

YIELD: 4 SERVINGS

⅔ cup rice vinegar

½ cup cold water

1 tablespoon granulated sugar

¼ teaspoon salt

¼ teaspoon freshly ground pepper

1. Place all of the ingredients in a jar with a tight-fitting lid, and shake until well blended.

2. Use the dressing immediately, or refrigerate until ready to use.

NUTRITIONAL FACTS (per serving)
Calories: 18   Carbs: 5.5 g   Cholesterol: 0 mg   Fat: 0 g
Calories From Fat: 0.1%   Protein: 0 g   Sodium: 89 mg

White Wine Vinaigrette

With its creamy texture and tangy flavor, this vinaigrette can be used to dress a variety of salads.

YIELD: 4 SERVINGS

1 new potato (1½–2 ounces), peeled and quartered, or ⅓ cup prepared instant mashed potatoes (page 213)
3 cloves garlic, peeled
¼ cup plus 2 tablespoons fat-free chicken broth, vegetable broth, or water
¼ cup white wine vinegar
2 tablespoons Dijon mustard
1 teaspoon extra virgin olive oil
⅛ teaspoon hot pepper sauce
⅛ teaspoon salt

1. Place enough water to cover the potato in a small saucepan, and bring to a simmer over medium-high heat. Add the potato and simmer uncovered for 25 minutes, or until fork tender. Allow the potato to come to room temperature.

2. Place the garlic in a food processor fitted with a metal blade, or in a blender, and process until finely chopped. Add the potato, and process until smooth. (The mixture may form a ball.) Add all of the remaining ingredients, and process until well blended. Alternatively, place the potato in a jar with a tight-fitting lid, and mash with a fork. Finely chop the garlic, and add it to the jar along with the remaining ingredients. Shake until well blended.

3. Use the dressing immediately, or place in a covered container and refrigerate until ready to use.

NUTRITIONAL FACTS (per serving)
Calories: 20   Carbs: 3.6 g   Cholesterol: 0 mg   Fat: 0.5 g
Calories From Fat: 17.1%   Protein: 1.7 g   Sodium: 210 mg

Yogurt and Cucumber Dressing

A combination of soothing yogurt, crisp cucumbers, and other flavorful ingredients, this dressing adds a cool and exotic touch to Indian salads. You can also serve it as a condiment with Indian meals.

YIELD: 4 SERVINGS

1½ cups plain low-fat yogurt
2 cucumbers, thinly sliced
½ cup low-fat sour cream
2 tomatoes, seeded and cubed
1 small onion, chopped
2 tablespoons finely chopped fresh cilantro
½ teaspoon ground cumin
½ teaspoon freshly ground pepper
¼ teaspoon salt
⅛ teaspoon cayenne pepper

1. Place a fine-sieved strainer over a large bowl, and spoon the yogurt into the strainer. Place another fine-sieved strainer over a different bowl, and place the sliced cucumbers in the strainer. Allow both the yogurt and the cucumbers to sit at room temperature for 1 hour.

2. Remove the cucumbers and yogurt from the strainers, and transfer them to a large bowl, discarding any accumulated liquid. Add all of the remaining ingredients, and stir gently to blend.

3. Use the dressing immediately, or cover and refrigerate until ready to use.

NUTRITIONAL FACTS (per serving)
Calories: 147   Carbs: 21.6 g   Cholesterol: 11 mg   Fat: 3.3 g
Calories From Fat: 19.5%   Protein: 8.8 g   Sodium: 237 mg

Metric Conversion Tables

Common Liquid Conversions

Measurement	=	Milliliters
$1/4$ teaspoon	=	1.25 milliliters
$1/2$ teaspoon	=	2.50 milliliters
$3/4$ teaspoon	=	3.75 milliliters
1 teaspoon	=	5.00 milliliters
$1\,1/4$ teaspoons	=	6.25 milliliters
$1\,1/2$ teaspoons	=	7.50 milliliters
$1\,3/4$ teaspoons	=	8.75 milliliters
2 teaspoons	=	10.0 milliliters
1 tablespoon	=	15.0 milliliters
2 tablespoons	=	30.0 milliliters

Measurement	=	Liters
$1/4$ cup	=	0.06 liters
$1/2$ cup	=	0.12 liters
$3/4$ cup	=	0.18 liters
1 cup	=	0.24 liters
$1\,1/4$ cups	=	0.30 liters
$1\,1/2$ cups	=	0.36 liters
2 cups	=	0.48 liters
$2\,1/2$ cups	=	0.60 liters
3 cups	=	0.72 liters
$3\,1/2$ cups	=	0.84 liters
4 cups	=	0.96 liters
$4\,1/2$ cups	=	1.08 liters
5 cups	=	1.20 liters
$5\,1/2$ cups	=	1.32 liters

Converting Fahrenheit to Celsius

Fahrenheit	=	Celsius
200–205	=	95
220–225	=	105
245–250	=	120
275	=	135
300–305	=	150
325–330	=	165
345–350	=	175
370–375	=	190
400–405	=	205
425–430	=	220
445–450	=	230
470–475	=	245
500	=	260

Conversion Formulas

LIQUID When You Know	Multiply By	To Determine
teaspoons	5.0	milliliters
tablespoons	15.0	milliliters
fluid ounces	30.0	milliliters
cups	0.24	liters
pints	0.47	liters
quarts	0.95	liters

WEIGHT When You Know	Multiply By	To Determine
ounces	28.0	grams
pounds	0.45	kilograms

Index